THE GREAT
FOOD PROCESSOR
COOKBOOK

Yvonne Young Tarr

THE GREAT FOOD PROCESSOR COOKBOOK

Random House
New York

Library of Congress Cataloging in Publication Data

Tarr, Yvonne Young.
  The great food processor cookbook.

  Includes index.
  1. Cookery. 2. Kitchen utensils. I. Title.
II. Title: Food processor cookbook.
TX652.T36   641.5'89   76-14159
ISBN 0-394-40523-4
ISBN 0-394-73284-7 pbk.

Manufactured in the United States of America

98

Food for jacket photograph designed and prepared by Yvonne Young Tarr.
Illustrated with line drawings by Pat Stewart.

Acknowledgments

The following machines were used in conjunction with the preparation of the book, and Yvonne Young Tarr wishes to thank the manufacturers and distributors that gave assistance:

The Cuisinart Food Processor (Cuisinart is a trademark of Cuisinarts, Inc., of Greenwich, Connecticut).

The KitchenAid K5A Food Preparer (KitchenAid is a registered trademark of Hobart Corporation, Troy, Ohio).

The Starmix MX 4 (Starmix is a registered trademark of ELECTROSTAR Schoettle KG, West Germany and is imported and distributed by Consolidated Distributors, Inc., Arlington, Virginia).

CONTENTS

· v ·

THE GREAT
FOOD PROCESSOR
COOKBOOK

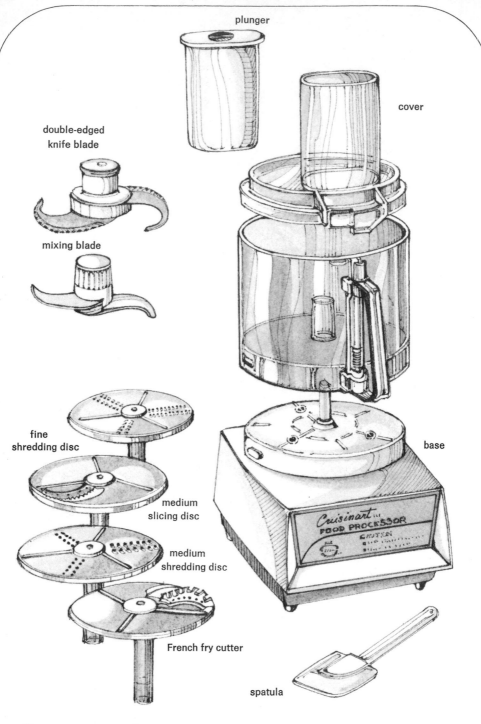

plunger

cover

double-edged
knife blade

mixing blade

fine
shredding disc

medium
slicing disc

medium
shredding disc

French fry cutter

base

spatula

CUISINART FOOD PROCESSOR

THE GREAT FOOD PROCESSORS

Behold the Great Food Processors . . . those dream machines that exemplify our speed-and-luxury-oriented way of life. Delivered from the twelve-hour day our ancestors endured, bequeathed the four-day week, we toil not, neither do we hand-chop, mince, or purée. Our bread doughs are almost magically kneaded into submission. Our duxelles practically hash themselves. Our *génoises* bubble into being within the sturdy tracery of our mechanized wire whisks. The legend of the great food processors typifies this unique time when speed-machines (witness the pocket calculator) infiltrate our family lives as never before. No incongruity exists between this and our trend toward a more natural and self-sufficient way of life. Our machines make it practical for the first time for us to bypass processed-supermarket and freezer-packaged restaurant foods. We can munch fresh home-baked, preservative-free breads, machine-grind our own grains into flour, eat the highest-quality gourmet foods at home, and do so with a minimum (after the initial outlay) of expense. For strange as it may seem, gourmet cooking and savings do go hand in pocket.

The Cuisinart processor (and the Robot Coupe*) was born in France, that thrifty but elegant *grand'mére* of the culinary arts. The machine has style, it has speed, it has good looks, it does what it does superbly well. French cooking is based on more than gossamer sauces, *fines herbes*, snails and piglet tails. It is based on using every last bit of every last bite and using it in the grandest manner. Never is a morsel that can be salvaged and turned into an tasty tidbit ever banished to the garbage can. That last dry bit of leftover cheese is grated, that abandoned crust of bread is whirled into bread crumbs. Broths and bits of vegetables, that last spoonful of sour cream, that savory dill left too long alone in the refrigerator—all are, literally within seconds, a cold summer soup silky beyond belief. The Great Food Processors can transform you into a superb (yet thrifty in the European manner) cook . . . help you to attempt, and bring off, meals that would have heretofore been out of your culinary reach.

Why did I choose these three—the Cuisinart food processor, the KitchenAid, and the Starmix—from the multitude of machines on the market? First, I chose the Cuisinart machine because it is the most intriguing, the perfect performer, the hottest item on the cooking scene today. It is as indispensable to a gourmet kitchen as Scotch tape is to an office. It does take some getting used to . . . but it does the job. When I first acquired my Cuisinart food processor about three years ago, I used it frequently, mostly for slicing or grating summer vegetables or chopping a handful of this or that. Next came the quenelles and the mousses, and I marveled over its proficiency. But it wasn't until I began this book that I fully appreciated this small miracle maker. It was my job to experiment, and experiment I did. My Cuisinart container went from countertop to freezer. The machine did everything from cutting butter into *pâte brisée* to slicing shoestring potatoes, from mixing cookies in seven seconds to puréeing soups, from preparing gefilte fish to twirling *pâtés en terrine*. And each task I set for it, the more beautifully did it perform, until now I cannot imagine preparing a meal without its help.

---

* The Robot Coupe, a large restaurant-sized version of the Cuisinart food processor used widely in France, in general performs culinary tasks with the same dependable genius the Cuisinart machine displays. Two additional advantages, however, set it apart and make it my favorite of all the food preparers. First, it has the same virtues as the KitchenAid disc slicer in that it can slice whole vegetables. Second, a large container placed beneath the blades of this machine can comfortably hold enough slices or shreds to feed a houseful (or a restaurant full) of guests. If cooking and/or large-group entertaining is a passion of yours and price is no object, do purchase this most talented of all the machines.

To my knowledge no other machine can equal this processor's dexterity. It slices absolutely perfect, paper-thin wafers of vegetables unlike other food processors that slice less evenly and chop more haphazardly than this friendly kitchen wizard. The Cuisinart processor does have drawbacks. The motor, while powerful enough to slice with the skill of a magician, is really too fast for mixing doughs unless the utmost care is taken. If the motor had a rheostat to slow the monster down a bit when the occasion called for it, it would be infinitely improved. If it could whip egg whites and/or cream (at present the motor is so muscular that it breaks down the bubbles as it fluffs them up), it would truly be a dream machine. But as they say in the old song, "until the time that (one) comes along, I'll string along" with the Cuisinart processor. The darling of the kitchen . . . for a very good reason.

The KitchenAid is another love of mine, mainly because it too does the work it is called upon to do, and does it well, with a minimum of fuss, a great deal of finesse and a heap of dependability. It can absolutely be counted on to perform perfectly every time. While it doesn't chop, it will—with the proper attachment—slice, grate, whip, and knead bread *perfectly*. The KitchenAid K5A (and to a slightly lesser degree, the K45) is a must for every serious cook who can afford one. With its help, making bread can be a spur-of-the-moment decision rather than a muscle-bending ordeal. Egg whites whip up faster and in greater volume than with any other machine (including the Starmix, which is also quite competent). The strong and efficient flat mixing blade, backed up by an incredibly powerful (and blessedly silent) motor, can take on any mixing job no matter how strenuous. Its attachments are numerous, and for the most part are straightforward kitchen helpers. In the KitchenAid you have the perfect kitchen machine, one that rarely makes a mistake and can handle the most esoteric gourmet recipe or the most down-on-the-farm homey dish.

The Starmix food processor is included here because it encompasses the full range of kitchen needs. It chops, grates and purées (with a blender attachment). It whips cream and egg whites with a wire whipping attachment. It slices and grates vegetables with a slicing-grating disc, and it kneads bread with a dough hook. And best of all, these attachments are all included in the initial cost of the machine. The Starmix would at first glance seem to incorporate the best of both the Cuisinart food processor and the KitchenAid and therefore might be termed the one real all-around kitchen wonder. The drawback is that while the Starmix does perform a wider range of food processing chores, it neither chops, grates, nor slices with the clean-cut grace and skill of the Cuisinart processor, nor does it possess quite the solid professionalism of the KitchenAid machine. For anyone to whom quality of performance is more important than quantity of processes, the Cuisinart and the KitchenAid machines show more star quality than the Starmix. The additional-expense attachments available for the Starmix are, however, my favorites. The ice cream churn turns out supersoft, farm-rich ice cream in eight to ten minutes of actual turning time, and the attachment is small and easy to store when compared with the cumbersome (but larger capacity) KitchenAid churn. The liquefier attachment produces vegetable juices in seconds. And the *pomme frite* (French fry) cutter is truly a whiz.

Which machine, or combination of machines, you choose depends much upon your individual life style and its accompanying set of needs. If you lean toward gourmet foods, where you mince a handful of this or purée a soupçon of that . . . if your family (and/or your kitchen) is small and your entertaining is the gourmet sort . . . the Cuisinart machine is for you. Supplement it with a really good electric hand whipper (or a strong arm holding a wire whisk) and you'll get by admirably.

If, on the other hand, you have a large family with a kitchen to match, particularly if you are heavily into bread-baking and cake-making, mashing mounds of potatoes and churning buckets of home-made ice cream . . . the KitchenAid should be your kitchen aid. Supplement it with an efficient blender, and some expertise with a good chopping knife and it will take you all the way from the home front to the haute cuisine trail.

To my mind the ideal kitchen combination is the Cuisinart food processor with which you can mince, fine-chop, coarse-chop, purée, fine-grate, coarse-grate, thin-slice and thick-slice with incredible ease and the KitchenAid K5A with which you can beat egg whites and cream to soft or stiff points (or anything in between), knead large clumps of dough efficiently and well without so much as soiling your hands, juice oranges, churn ice cream in minutes, grind grain into natural, fresh flour, stuff sausage, or use the hot or cold jacket—an extra bowl which fits around the mixing bowl—to hold warm water for puffing petits fours batters or ice for your *crème pâtissière.*

This book is designed to take the mystery out of these wizards of the kitchen, and to put them to work for you. While it was in preparation I was besieged with requests for information, advice

. . . and recipes. Everyone, it seems, either has or intends to soon have one of these marvelous machines. The problem is that until recently the machines have been sent along to the purchaser without much in the way of instructions for use or recipes that can be prepared in them. The manuals tend to be literally translated outlines of the original language of the country of origin. The KitchenAid, the made-in-America processor, has the most helpful tips, but even this excellent manual has precious few recipes. What the food processor really needs, it seems, is a big, fat compilation of recipes, tips, hints, and instructions for use, including intricate charts giving exact seconds for grating, slicing, chopping and fine chopping for most ingredients. This is the book I have attempted to provide. The recipes are written in precise steps that outline the order in which the ingredients should be prepared/processed, the number of seconds most steps take as well as detailed instructions for baking, slicing, whipping, purée-ing, and so forth.

I like to feel you will no longer be left alone with your machine, to sink or swim in a morass of mousse. I have tried to imagine that I was at your side answering any question that might arise. Where procedures for the different machines differ slightly, I have made careful notes and included these in the recipe or as a footnote. The key letters C K S are used in place of the machine name to avoid repetition and/or confusion. When the C, K, or S is boxed, this indicates a footnote with an alternative procedure that should be followed by users of that particular machine. The next three chapters give evaluations of each of the three processors, a description of parts and how to use them, as well as tips and suggestions garnered from several years of intensive use.

THE CUISINART FOOD PROCESSOR

The clasping of the fantastic new food processors to the bosom of the American home is a culinary happening as notable (it seems to me) as the switching of kitchen fire-power from the hearth to the conventional in-kitchen stove. It's an easy matter to outdo yourself rather than merely make do with an assist from these speedy kitchen helpers. Suddenly those small but tedious niceties of gourmet cooking—the perfectly minced handful of fresh herbs tucked into a *beurre de fines herbes*, the finely chopped medley of celery, carrots, onion, plus the parsley, garlic, and lemon zest that lend magic to osso buco—become but a few seconds' worth of extra work. In these times when household help is frequently nonexistent and self-help is the order of the day, the speed-machines, those quiet and efficient helpers, free us for more rewarding pursuits.

Perhaps the outstanding attribute of the Cuisinart food processor in particular is that the problems inherent in designing a machine with its intended functions have been very intelligently solved. The food processor's primary purpose is to cut, and in this area the Cuisinart engineers have succeeded admirably. They have produced blades which are exceptionally sharp—not merely slashes stamped into a metal disc and then ground to an edge as in most food processors, but fine stainless-steel blades, honed razor-sharp and then spot-welded to the slicing disc.

The Cuisinart processor's main chopping blade is finely serrated stainless steel ground sword-sharp. This keen-edged blade is then coupled to a very fast, powerful motor and that, plus the larger cutting area of the two sides of the blade, is the secret of its great efficiency. No wonder it cuts so cleanly and so well.

APPEARANCE

Although what is important is not how this machine looks but how it works, this processor is a sturdy, attractive little space-age machine. It is better looking than most, but not as stunning as a few of the other kitchen machines (the Braun processor, for example, is a real looker, but beauty is as beauty does and what this beauty does best is to collect admiring glances as it decorates your kitchen counter). The Cuisinart processor stands about 13 inches high from its compact plastic (or more recently) metal base to its oval chimneyed top. Parts consist of a square motor housing, a see-through plastic container and a matching top cover with chimney-like spout and accompanying plunger. The plastic housing is as rugged as you could wish, and bowl, cover, and plunger are made from shatter-resistant plastic.

QUALITY OF CONSTRUCTION

Construction here simply cannot be faulted—no sloppy rough edges to snag your fingers, no flimsy plastic parts to fall apart. It is soundly and solidly constructed of Lexan, one of the toughest space-age plastics, the same material that it used for shatter-proof windows. Because this processor has a minimum of parts, it has a minimum of parts that can break. My own machine has been in constant use for several years and has never given me a hint of trouble.

CONVENIENCE

This machine, aside from performing every task assigned it with total authority, has obviously been masterminded by a real small-kitchen maven. There are only nine basic parts, counting the motor base itself, plus four optional parts. Each piece is of absolute minimum size, and all fit neatly into a small kitchen drawer, while the basic motor housing, plastic container, top, and plunger nestle in an unobtrusive corner of your kitchen counter. The container falls into place effortlessly over the metal shaft that protrudes from the motor housing, and with only a twist of your finger, the blades do the same. The container top easily twists less than a quarter-turn to turn the machine on and off. All in all, it couldn't be less complex—or more convenient.

EXCELLENCE OF RESULTS

Neither speed in itself, nor versatility, nor even convenience provides the true test of a machine. It is excellence of results that really counts, and in this respect the Cuisinart processor really outdoes itself. It goes with a hop, skip, and a jump from one cooking task to another, from gourmet to homespun and back again with never so much as a hesitation. From quenelles to mousses, from old-fashioned apple tarts to home-made sausages and scrapple, from *pâte à chou* to *pâtés en terrine*, from dough-nuts to duxelles, from *potage Saint-Germain* to baby foods . . . cookies, turnovers, baking-powder biscuits, dolmades, steak tartare, stir-fried beef and vegetables, mayonnaise, Hollandaise, pistou . . . This machine minces in seconds to produce the sharp-edged texture only hand-chopping heretofore was able to provide. It has other advantages as well—fewer large pieces left behind in coarse-chopping and *none* left uncut when the machine minces, as opposed to other machines, where ingredients are turned to liquid down near the blades while large pieces still remain on the top of the heap. There is none of this erratic be-havior with the well-behaved Cuisinart steel chopping blade that exposes the vegetable, meat, and so forth to so much more cutting surface.

In its capacity as a mixer *par excellence*, the Cuisinart machine with its tremendous muscle power often telescopes several indi-vidual processes into one swift whirl of blades. Flours generally need not be presifted, yeasts generally need no presoftening, purées generally require no straining (or when they do this oper-ation is blessedly easy, since the entire mass has been pulverized to a finer consistency than any other kitchen device can accom-plish).

The grating disc will tackle anything from cheese to potatoes to rutabagas and turn out perfect shreds with a minimum of effort. Of course no machine is perfect, and very occasionally a limp leaf of cabbage or such will catch in the blade and cause a bit of a fuss, but this is an easily handled and infrequent occurrence. In general, this food processor is an absolutely astounding suc-cess on every process it sets its blades to.

CLEANING

With only eleven parts to achieve every process, it follows that there are only eleven parts to wash. The base wipes clean in a jiffy, with only the small depression where the container rests when in the *on* position to fill with cake batter, bread crumbs, or whatever, but this too can easily be wiped clean with a damp cloth. The container top, made of super-tough Lexan plastic, also cleans in seconds. There is a convex switch housing that runs down one side of the container that occasionally fills with a few drops of water, but this has never affected the function of the machine in any way that I could perceive. All parts, with the exception of the plunger, are dishwasher-safe . . . a great advantage. One precaution—the blades are razor-sharp, and reasonable caution with these is recommended. I've planned the recipes in this book, wherever possible, so that ingredients that do not soil the container (such as bread crumbs) are processed first and other ingredients are added in order of messiness to preclude unnecessary washing of parts. Get in the habit of following this prescribed routine and you will save yourself hours of work over a period of time.

ADVANTAGES AND DISADVANTAGES

Many of the advantages of this machine are enumerated above and below and the rest you will discover for yourself as you use your machine, so there is no need here to reiterate.

Alas, the Cuisinart processor does make an occasional faux pas. The one most important flaw in this otherwise perfect performer is its inability to whip air bubbles into even the most cooperative ingredient. Egg whites simply roll over and play dead when the powerful motor starts showing off its muscle power. Speed, a quality that enhances most processes, becomes a liability in others. The whirling blades break down bubbles as quickly as they build them up. For this reason heavy cream remains heavy cream no matter how furiously the machine flourishes its blades. One turn of your head and onions become onion juice, meat is pulverized into a texture too fine for anything other than forcemeat, and doughs are overworked within a matter of a few excess seconds or so. You will understand why it is a good idea to have ingredients premeasured and lined up alongside the machine to *prevent* it from whirling too long in between each addition.

Another minus is the small overall capacity of the container bowl. If you are processing large quantities of anything, you must twirl, empty, and refill an inordinate amount of times. Also, the spout (and this is perhaps the biggest drawback) is quite narrow, requiring large vegetables and fruits to be precut before slicing or grating. This is particularly frustrating when outside edges must be cut from large cucumbers, leaving little left to slice except seeds, or when any recipe calls for whole slices of vegetables.

Finally, the machine does take a bit of getting used to, but it is so sparse in gadgets, attachments, and parts in general that it is easy to understand and therefore, in the long run, easy to work with. As with any other machine, the more you use it, the more adept you become.

BASIC PARTS

1 sturdy 8 × 7 × 5 inch plastic or metal base
1 plastic container bowl
1 plastic cover
1 plastic plunger that fits into feed tube
1 plastic spatula
1 plastic and stainless-steel knife blade
1 plastic mixing blade
1 metal and plastic medium slicing disc
1 metal and plastic medium shredding and grating disc

OPTIONAL PARTS/ATTACHMENTS

serrated slicing disc, fine
vegetable slicing disc, fine
fine shredding disc
pomme frite (French fry) cutter

USING YOUR CUISINART FOOD PROCESSOR

To operate your machine, place the container over the drive shaft with its protruding vertical ridge sitting a bit to the left of the small indented circle on the motor housing's top, then slide the container to the right until the bottom of the ridge locks snugly into the indentation. Set your working tool—the double-edged steel knife or the slicing or grating disc—directly over the drive shaft. Spin it slowly once or twice until it settles down into position—in any case, don't force it down. Next, slip the plunger into the spout and set the cover on the container so that the spout stands slightly to the left of the container's vertical ridge.

Now, with your hand on the spout, turn the cover to the right. This simultaneously locks the cover into the container and starts the motor, which will continue to run until you push the spout back to the left.

Dry ingredients are usually added to the container first so that any liquids added will be absorbed and will not run out of the container near the shaft.

To cut potatoes or other hard, round vegetables into julienne strips, cut them to fit the spout and slice in the usual way. Assemble the slices as though the vegetable were whole again, and run them through the slicing blade the other way so that the blade makes another series of cuts exactly perpendicular to the previous ones. It's easier than it sounds. Try it.

IMPORTANT TIPS AND SUGGESTIONS

• The usual way to process foods in the Cuisinart machine is to run it for the required number of seconds it takes to chop or grate or slice (see charts), then return the spout to its off position, wait until the blade or disc has come to a full stop, and lift off the cover. Occasionally, however, your recipe may direct you to turn the machine on and off by quickly twisting the spout back and forth in a smooth rapid motion. This important technique, the on-off method of chopping and mixing, slows the whirling of the motor and prevents overblending or overmixing of ingredients.

• Once your food is processed, turn the container back to the left and lift it off the base to avoid spillage on the surface of the machine.

When processing most foods, the cutting tool may be carefully removed when the cover is taken off and the food scraped out, but when you're mixing fairly liquid ingredients with the steel or plastic blades, you'll eliminate the risk of having these plunk into the pan (or bowl) with the batter (or soup) if you pour out the container's contents *before* removing the blade. Simply hold the blade in place by inserting the tip of your index finger through the hole in the container bottom and press against the blade's shaft.

• The processing tool you'll undoubtedly find handiest is the double-edged steel knife whose versatility extends to chopping, mixing, and blending, although the plastic mixing blade works well enough if you want to mix or blend ingredients without further reducing them. Please note that the steel cutting blade should be used at all times unless otherwise indicated.

• When preparing foods for processing, first pat them dry with paper towels, and make sure that the container and cutting tool are perfectly dry, too. Cut the vegetables, fruits, cheese, or meat you plan to mince or chop into 1-inch lengths or cubes. Aim for pieces as nearly equal size as possible so that chopping results will be even. Set the steel knife on the drive shaft *before* adding any ingredients to the container; otherwise the pieces underneath will keep the blade from settling into its accustomed place.

• Processing times vary, but all take a mere matter of seconds. The difference in time between coarse and fine chopping, for instance, may be no more than 2 or 3 seconds. Consult the charts for individual foods to learn how much time each will need to reach the degree of coarseness or fineness you prefer. You'll find it easier to estimate seconds by counting "one hundred and one, one hundred and two," and so on, figuring each group of numbers to represent one second. Try timing your counting with a stopwatch, if you happen to have one available; with a bit of practice, you'll get the feel of how long it takes to coarse- or fine-chop each individual food. It helps if you stop the motor once or twice during the processing to scrape down any large pieces from the container sides to where the blades can reach them.

• The machine will chop with super efficiency as little as an ounce of food at one time, or up to 2 cups. When you're working with large amounts of food, you'll find it's more efficient to process the pieces in several steps, 2 or 3 handfuls at a time, removing each batch as soon as it's processed before adding the next. This gives you a chance to pick out any large pieces and run them through with the next batch so all are evenly chopped. It also prevents the motor from dancing around on the counter, which occasionally happens when hard ingredients are added in large chunks and one piece sticks under the blade. When this occurs, anchor the motor by placing your hands on either side of the base until the chopping action reduces the pieces to more manageable and stabilizing size.

• Drain processed vegetables and/or fruits well unless these are to be added to liquid ingredients.

• When preparing your foods for slicing or grating, peel or don't peel according to recipe directions and cut into thicknesses or lengths specified in your recipe or, if not specified, sized to fit the spout. Set the slicing or grating blade in place on the drive shaft, put on the container cover, and pack the spout evenly in the manner outlined in the charts so that the food will not slip and pieces become elongated, especially when you are using the slicing blade. Use the plunger (again, not your fingers) to gently push the food against the cutting edge, bouncing it gently up and down if so directed in the charts.

• You may safely add hot foods to the container when your recipe so indicates, or ingredients may be added directly from the refrigerator; the steel blade will even pulverize ice cubes when crushed ice is called for.

• You may find that the motor will overheat if you've used the food processor for too long a time to chop hard foods or are mixing a particularly thick batch of ingredients. In some circumstances, the motor may click off altogether. This stoppage is due to a temperature-controlled circuit breaker within the base and does not mean that the motor of your machine has burned out. This is a built-in safety feature that's completely automatic—wait for 15 to 30 minutes to give the motor time to cool, then start it again.

• There are some recipes that call for foods to be coarsely chopped or diced, then served without further preparation, and these cannot, in my opinion, be properly chopped by machine, *any* machine. Take, for example, the vegetables that accompany that marvelous summer soup, gazpacho. This cooling broth is often served surrounded by small bowls of chopped fresh vegetables. While machine-chopped vegetables are adequate when served *in* the soup, they are simply not uniformly perfect enough in size and shape to be featured like a collection of jewels. There may be occasions when you are in a particular hurry and your guests are the sort that don't dwell on small perfections. In this case, by all means use your Cuisinart or Starmix machines. In any other case where perfectly cut ingredients are called for . . . chop by hand.

• Your Cuisinart food processor can be used to produce a flaky, tender pie crust . . . the secret is in the method. If you demand a tender, perfectly worked crust, it is best not to rely on the super-fast "whirl until the dough forms a ball" method. Following this procedure you may occasionally end up with a finished product with the consistency of cardboard. Until you have thoroughly mastered your machine's idiosyncrasies, the "works every time" way procedure is to whirl the dry ingredients for five seconds, turn off the machine, press *cold* shortening down against the blades, and turn the machine rapidly on and off until the mixture has the texture of coarse meal. Scoop this mixture into a bowl and stir in the ice water by hand with a fork until the dough cleans the sides of the bowl and forms a ball. This method takes 3 or 4 seconds longer but you're less likely to overwork the dough and produce an amateurish crust.

Another method for preparing pie dough is to follow the above directions up to the point where the water is added. Turn the machine off, then sprinkle in the water 2 tablespoons at a time, turning the machine rapidly on and off twice after each addition. Knead the dough on a heavily floured surface for 10 seconds or until well mixed.

My favorite, because of the superb and dependable results it produces, is the first method described. Other crusts require the slightly different modus operandi described in each recipe.

• Since the machine's prowess in chopping, slicing, grating, puréeing, mixing, blending and even kneading is ultimately due to its singularly sharp steel blades that are set into action by the machine's powerful motor, your pleasure—and safety—in using this food processor will be considerably greater if you take the following precautions when handling any of the blades:

1. Always set the container on the base *before* inserting any blade on the drive shaft.

2. Always wait until the knife or disc comes to a *complete* halt before taking off the container cover.

3. Always use the plunger—never your fingers—when working with the slicing or grating disc.

4. Always store these cutting tools in a safe place when they are not in use, especially if there are children about.

THE KITCHENAID FOOD PREPARER

Enshrined on its kitchen counter, the friendly dolphin-smooth head of the KitchenAid food preparer gleams as encouragingly at the brownies-and-ice-cream cook as it does in the direction of the gourmet cook who routinely whips up an ethereal *génoise* or sturdy kugelhopf. This is the recognized master American Kitchen Whiz, ready to lend a helping hand no matter how plain-Jane or esoteric the task. The KitchenAid is a machine made by Hobart, for many years manufacturers of first-rate heavyweight professional baking equipment. The makers have, happily, incorporated many of their fabricating and engineering techniques into their K5A and K45 home-help machines. The engineering is simple and direct All basic parts attach fairly easily and efficiently, with no tricky gadgetry or confusing coupling mechanisms. You never have that uneasy feeling you are dealing with a toy or gadget. With its powerful ten-speed motor, this machine gives the distinct impression of being a true professional . . . it's big, it's rugged, and it's obviously built to last. The paddle on the ice cream freezer, for example, and the entire surface of the ice or hot water jacket, are heavily tinned, just as their professional counterparts might be, and while the finish of some of the other attachments may not win any beauty prizes, you never get the impression you must pamper them or treat them gingerly. The housing and parts for the slicing equipment are die-cast of fairly heavy metal, and no effort has been made to plate, enamel or otherwise fancy them up. There is something comforting in all of this—at least for me—a kind of appearance-follows-function approach that is tremendously appealing.

The genius here lies in the wizardry of coupling a powerful motor with marvelous basic attachments, a combination unattainable in any other kitchen machine. The way these attachments interact with the five-quart stainless-steel bowl is a stroke of genius. The sleek, rather narrow sloping sides of the bowl serve to concentrate the ingredients where the beaters can easily reach them. The beaters themselves move around the stationary bowl and at the same time turn in the opposite direction on their own axis in what the KitchenAid people call "planetary action." The wire whip incorporates a sou'wester of air within the folds of egg whites or cream . . . result: a veritable Himalayan mound of meringue or whipped cream with not so much as a flick of the wrist. The sturdy flat beater strongarms the stiffest batter into submission, and the dough hook kneads with no help necessary.

The KitchenAid K45 and K5A both have a built-in power shaft to operate the many attachments available. Standard equipment for both includes the aforementioned stainless-steel bowl, flat

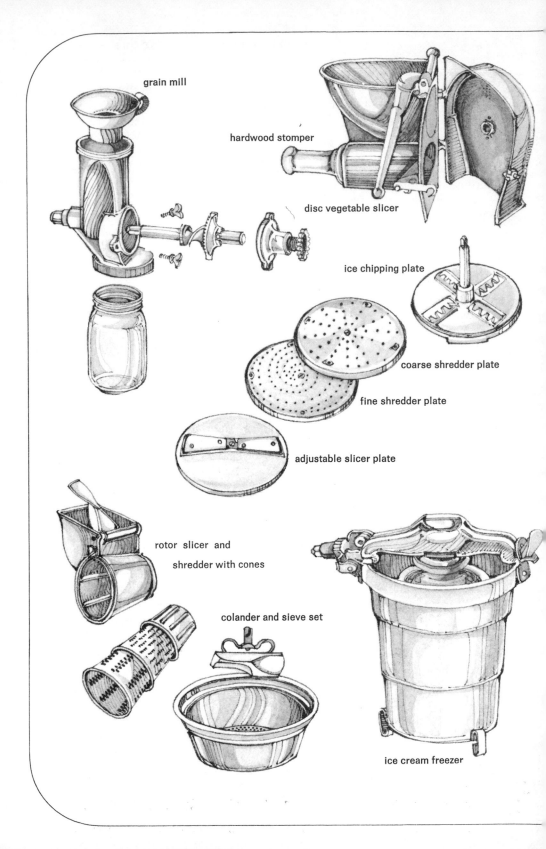

grain mill

hardwood stomper

disc vegetable slicer

ice chipping plate

coarse shredder plate

fine shredder plate

adjustable slicer plate

rotor slicer and
shredder with cones

colander and sieve set

ice cream freezer

pouring chute

splash guard

ice or hot water jacket

flat beater

juice extractor

dough hook

wire whip

5-quart bowl

base

food grinder

sausage stuffer

KitchenAid

KITCHENAID FOOD PREPARER

beater, dough hook and wire whip; optional equipment includes a food grinder, sausage stuffer, slicer and grater (either rotor or disc type), juice extractor, ice cream freezer, grain mill, can opener, pouring chute to make additions easier, splash guard to minimize splash-out, colander and sieve to ease the preparation of purées, jams, applesauce, and the like, and even a silver buffer to make your heirlooms gleam.

The main difference between the two models is that the K5A has more power for mixing and kneading, but there is also a difference in the bowl size—the K5A has a larger capacity. The K45 is somewhat easier to use because of the ease with which the bowl attaches, but the additional power and larger bowl capacity of the K5A are also important. Unlike the Cuisinart food processor, the KitchenAid food preparer will not chop your foods, but the grinding, grating, and slicing attachments work well and the disc-type slicer does what no other home machine can do—cut fruits and vegetables into beautiful, large whole slices. All in all, the KitchenAid is a strong, efficient machine, simply engineered and well constructed. It is relatively quiet in operation, utterly dependable, and as far as I can see should give quiet, efficient, trouble-free service for a long, long time.

APPEARANCE

While this machine, with its high motor housing and large stainless-steel bowl, may seem a bit ungainly at first, after you use it successfully for a few weeks it is bound to so endear itself that you'll feel, as I do, that it looks just right. Admittedly, my point of view is not quite as objective as it might be, since in general I find this a food preparer that can do little wrong.

It will sit on your counter or work table conveniently, and its workmanlike appearance—functional and efficient-looking—will surely prove no esthetic blight. The machine stands 16½ inches tall at its highest point, is about 10⅜ inches wide and 13½ inches long. It is too heavy to conveniently tuck out of sight after every use, but then there is no reason why you should do so. This is a kitchen aid, and it belongs where you can use it most efficiently.

However, the assorted optional attachments that make this the versatile food processor it is are, in the aggregate, rather space-consuming. The ice cream freezer, for example, is enormous.

Housed in a large, brightly colored fiberglass bucket about the size of a five-gallon pail, it has certainly not been designed for a small apartment kitchen but would be completely at home on the capacious shelf of a roomy country pantry. The other attachments—juicer, meat grinder and flour mill, etc.—are relatively small, but in total they do make a bulky and expensive load.

If space is a problem but cash isn't perhaps you should purchase a Cuisinart food processor in addition to your basic KitchenAid and buy those KitchenAid optional attachments that are 1) not too space-consuming and 2) not covered by the multitalented Cuisinart.

QUALITY OF CONSTRUCTION

Engineering here is simple, straightforward, and rugged. All parts attach easily and efficiently, with no tricky or confusing gadgetry or ingenious coupling mechanisms to break down. A heavy square shaft is an intrinsic and functional part of the machine. To use it, all you need do is pluck off a simple metal cap, slide in the attachment, and turn a knob to keep it in place. Most attachments will slide neatly into position, but several may require a rap or two with the heel of your hand, although once affixed you can count on them to stay where you want them to stay until you decide to detach them.

The KitchenAid is strong, well constructed, vibration-free, relatively quiet in operation, and utterly dependable.

CONVENIENCE

The KitchenAid K5A has eighteen attachments, and while there may be safety in numbers there is also invariably a certain amount of inconvenience. The slick beauty of performance in the Cuisinart is due in part to the simplicity of its design, with only a few small parts separate from the basic machine.

The basic KitchenAid machines, including the 4C, K45 and K5A, are also wonderfully functional when used for what I assume was their intended functions—mixing, whipping and kneading.

While the power unit built into the head of the KitchenAid machine does have sufficient muscle to drive all of the attachments with never so much as a hesitation, remember that each bit of equipment used must be taken from its storage place, fitted on the machine, detached, cleaned, and stored again until needed. In this respect, the KitchenAid is no less convenient than the Starmix or any other attachment-rich food preparer, but neither is it more convenient. Comments on the convenience of the various attachments can be found on pages 23 to 30, where each is discussed individually.

EXCELLENCE OF RESULTS

There is probably no home machine on earth as good as this one for whipping its whirling way across a complete repertoire of gourmet dishes. Use it to puff egg whites or whipping cream to heights unattainable by any other beater, then fold these resulting snowy mounds into mousses such as *mousse au chocolat, mousse au pralin de noisettes* and strawberry Bavarian cream, or *crème Saint-Honoré, génoise*, honey nut torte, carrot cake, and a dazzling variety of entrée and dessert soufflés.

For the stronger beating power needed to strongarm heavier ingredients into creamy mixtures, the flat beater of this machine has no peer. Sand tarts, spaetzle, pie fillings and crusts, walnut honey bread and other fruit-filled breads, mayonnaise, dressings and sauces—this attachment mixes them all . . . superbly.

The third partner of this gourmet trilogy of KitchenAid attachments is a dough hook that can bully *any* yeast bread dough into submission. Any bread, or for that matter any dough, that requires kneading: kugelhopf, pastries and pasta, pizza dough, bread doughnuts and hundreds and hundreds of others literally knead themselves into satiny smoothness.

CLEANING

All parts of your KitchenAid, with the exception of the sleek white motor housing, may be safely washed in hot, sudsy water, then rinsed well and thoroughly dried so that food or soap film won't build up and hamper operation. Keep the processor housing clean by wiping it after each use with a damp cloth, paying particular attention to the beater shaft where food occasionally accumulates.

ADVANTAGES AND DISADVANTAGES

The KitchenAid is a quiet, vibration-free machine. The motor whirls away with only the merest hum, the beaters do not clatter against the sides of the bowl, and the optional attachments do not chatter and clank as they slice, grate, grind, or churn. The overall noise factor is slightly higher than that of the Cuisinart processor and considerably lower than the rather unpleasantly garrulous Starmix processor.

The KitchenAid food preparer is such an all-around demon for beating, whipping, and kneading that, for the serious cook, it would be a bargain at almost any price. The only real drawback, as I see it, is the way the motor head hovers protectively over the steel bowl, making the addition of even the most cooperative ingredient a bit difficult. When it comes to incorporating a particularly troublesome one such as sifted flour, the bowl must be uprooted and set on a counter, the flour sifted over the combined ingredients, and then the bowl replaced within the embrace of the machine. If this procedure is ignored, the cook runs the risk of being fairly machine-gunned with fragments of flying flour. A large pouring chute to facilitate slipping ingredients past the large beating and whipping attachments is available at extra cost, but unfortunately even this doesn't solve the problem. This may be regarded as an imperfection, and it undoubtedly is one, but personally I would rather tolerate this inconvenience than tamper with the perfection of that dynamic duo (the attachments and the shape of the bowl) that work so well together. It would seem almost criminal to tamper with such success.

The basic machine and attachments, ice cream freezer, grain mill, juicer, etc., are quite expensive. While the optional attachments are intelligently engineered and sturdily constructed with hardly a plastic part in the lot, they occasionally require a bit of muscle to attach and detach. However, if you can afford it, have ample kitchen space, and are willing to do a little hand-wrestling on occasion, the relatively few disadvantages are more than compensated for by the overall excellence of the machine.

USING YOUR KITCHENAID FOOD PREPARER

Attaching the bowl in the K45 model is relatively simple. With the speed control in an off position, begin by tilting back the motor head, then set the bowl on the bowl-clamping plate and turn the bowl in a clockwise direction. Your beater, whip, or dough hook can then be slipped onto the beater shaft where, by pressing it upward as far as it will go and with a turn to the right, it should hook over the pin in the shaft. Lock the motor head into position by pushing the locking lever into the locked position, keeping it there until the mixing, beating, whipping, or kneading is completed; then push it to the unlock position, raise the motor head once more, and remove the tool by pressing it upward as far as possible and turning it to the left. To disengage the bowl, simply turn it in a counterclockwise direction.

To attach the bowl in the K5A model, keep the speed control in the off position and the bowl-lift handle in the down position. Line up the bowl supports over the locating pins on the sides of the bowl, then press down on the back of the bowl until the bowl pin snaps into the spring latch. Since the bowl must always be raised and in a locked position before any mixing can begin, raise it by rotating the bowl-lift handle found on the machine's neck until it snaps into place. To remove the bowl, lower it by rotating the handle back and down, then lift the back of the bowl to free the bowl pin from the spring latch and lift the bowl from its locating pins.

The beater, whip, and dough hook are all installed in the K5A in essentially the same way in which they are fitted to the K45. Begin with the bowl in the down position and the speed control at off. Slip the attachment onto the beater shaft, pressing upward as far as possible and turning to the right until it hooks over the pin in the shaft. Remove by pressing the tool upward as far as possible while simultaneously turning it to the left.

BASIC PARTS

1 powerful (300-watt motor) metal base
1 5-quart stainless-steel bowl
1 flat beater
1 wire whip
1 dough hook

OPTIONAL PARTS/ATTACHMENTS

rotor-slicer and shredder (comes with 4 cones: fine shredder and
  grater, coarse shredder and shoestringer, thick slicer, thin slicer)
disc vegetable slicer (comes with slicer plate and hardwood
  stomper)
coarse shredder plate (to be used with disc slicer)
fine shredder plate (to be used with disc slicer)
ice chipping plate (to be used with disc slicer)
grain mill
juice extractor
ice cream freezer
food grinder
sausage stuffer
colander and sieve set
splash guard
pouring chute
can opener
silver buffer
ice or hot water jacket

ATTACHMENTS

While attachments like the pouring chute, colander and sieve,
and the splash guard are designed to fit on the mixing bowl, most
KitchenAid attachments are fitted directly to the attachment hub
found on the motor head. It's generally a good idea to affix each
assembled attachment to the power shaft *before* fitting it into the
motor head's square wrench-hole socket. After removing the attachment hub cover, loosen the knob on the attachment hub by
turning it counterclockwise, then insert the shaft into the socket
by moving it back and forth until a smooth fit is achieved. You'll

know that the attachment is in its proper upright position when the bottom pin on the shaft housing fits easily into the notch on the attachment hub's rim. All that remains at this point is to tighten the attachment knob by turning it clockwise.

THE ROTOR-SLICER AND SHREDDER

This slicer-shredder comes complete with one fine and one coarse grating cone (usually called shredders), plus one thick and one thin slicing cone. This is similar in function to the Moulinex grater but is much faster and more efficient in turning out neat but concave slices of fruits, vegetables, meat, cheese, or whatever. This unusual shape presents something of a problem when arranging raw foods for eye appeal, but the slices do flatten out during cooking. The attachment expands the versatility of the KitchenAid machine to cover many of the same processes as the Cuisinart processor. It is more compact than the KitchenAid disc slicer-grater and is therefore easier to tuck out of the way between usings. While it performs well, one drawback the attachment does have is that sometimes the cones are slightly difficult to detach from the shaft. Although the square opening on the shaft housing is some help, it can still be somewhat of a bother. All cones, especially the one designed for fine grating, are *very* sharp (as they should be) but these can hurt your hand when you are turning them into and out of place. Also, when food is finely grated it tends to catch on the back of the blade and to drop in clumps, but this is more a nuisance factor than a serious drawback.

Before fitting any of the cones to the housing, loosen the knob on the attachment hub, insert the shaft housing into the wrench-hole, then tighten the knob. Next, attach the notched ends of the shaft into the appropriate holes in the back of the cone, and insert the square end of the shaft into the square opening you'll find on the housing; turn the cone in a clockwise direction until it tightens, then set the assembled cone unit into the housing and fit it into the square wrench-hole socket on the attachment hub. All that's left to do is to lock the cone unit into position with the latch directly behind the housing, and your machine is ready to work. To disassemble the cone unit or to change cones, raise the latch, pull out the cone and insert the square end of the shaft into the square hole on the housing, then rotate the cone in a counterclockwise direction until it loosens from the shaft.

To operate the rotor-type slicer or grater, prepare your ingredients as directed on the charts, lift the handle of the food hopper, and drop in the food. Set a bowl underneath to catch the food as it emerges, turn the machine to Speed 4, and push down on the handle. Always use the hopper plate—*never* your fingers or any other utensil—to push down the food.

THE DISC VEGETABLE SLICER

The disc-type slicer (and grater), unlike the rotor-type, comes equipped only with a slicer plate as standard equipment, although two graters (shredder plates) or an ice chipper are additionally available at extra cost.

I find the rotor attachment better for grating but the disc slicer does slice large whole vegetables beautifully. A marvelous and unique feature is a kind of dial-a-slice thickness selector, built into the attachment. Simply pull the shaft of the slicing plate toward you, turn the round nut on the shaft clockwise, and you'll get thin slices; for thicker slices turn the nut counterclockwise— easy as properly sliced apple pie. Wonderful! In fact, the only fault I can find is that there is a tendency to flip the finished shreds or slices about a bit if the bowl is not raised high enough and placed directly under the machine.

The disc-type slicer and grater housing is designed in one piece. To assemble it, all you have to do is fit it to the square wrench-hole on the attachment hub and tighten the knob. To set any of the plates in place, raise the latch and swing the front part of the housing away from the motor head, then insert the plate's shaft through the disc hole and into the hub's wrench-hole socket. Push the front of the housing back into position and secure it with the latch.

To slice or grate, prepare the food as directed in the charts, place in the hopper with the hopper cover handle in a raised position and set a bowl closely underneath; press down with hopper cover. Speeds 4 or 6 can be used for crisp, raw vegetables and fruits. Press lightly on the handle while the food is being processed. If you have long thin food like celery to slice or grate, slide it into the tube underneath the food hopper with its narrower end forward and use the stomper provided to press it in.

The disc slicing and grating plates, like all food processor tools, are beautifully sharp. Handle them with extreme care as you would any knife, and always use the hopper cover or the stomper —*never* your fingers or any other utensils—when slicing or grating.

GRAIN MILL

Given the present day preoccupation with the back-to-natural-products, plant-your-own-garden, bake-your-own-breads syndrome, the next step, naturally, is grind-your-own-grains. If this sparks your interest as it does mine, KitchenAid is the machine for you!

This sturdy little grain mill comes complete with a pint jar into which the grains are ground (and in which they may be stored) and a separate instruction booklet detailing the attachment's use and care, plus information on grains and basic whole-grain recipes. The mill will reduce wheat, corn rye, oats, buckwheat, or barley to a fairly fine flour, a coarse meal, or any texture in between. The resulting flour is not ground as finely as some mills will grind it and the machine is rather slow, but there is nothing for the baker to do but flick a switch. For the average home baking requirements, this attachment should do the job nicely.

JUICE EXTRACTOR

This is an odd juicer—most are horizontal, but this one is vertical. However, in true KitchenAid form it squeezes citrus fruits perfectly. The primary advantage is that it can be operated at very low speed. This makes it much easier to handle than juicer attachments of other machines which revolve at higher speeds and are difficult to handle if you have a weak grip or a small hand.

Assemble it by fitting the round end of its metal shaft into the reamer so that the pins on the shaft fit in the reamer's slots; push the square end of the shaft through the oval-shaped shield, then slide the strainer, narrow end first, into the slots on the shield. To attach the juicer to the attachment hub, loosen the attachment knob; fit the square end of the shaft into the square wrench-hole, and tighten the knob. Place a glass or pitcher under the juicer before turning the motor on. To use, cup the fruit firmly in your hand and press it lightly against the spinning reamer, moving it in all directions while simultaneously pushing inward and down.

ICE CREAM FREEZER

For anyone who loves homemade ice cream (and who doesn't?), a really superior ice cream churn is more of a necessity than a luxury. This frozen cream machine is powered by the hard-working and dependable KitchenAid motor, and that means no overheating, no mechanical breakdowns, and for the most part, no head (or back) aches. It's hard to believe but it's true . . . ten minutes from the time you start the motor, you have ready-to-eat soft ice cream.

The KitchenAid K45 model has a freezer with a 2-quart capacity, while the freezer designed for the K5A will supply you with 4 quarts at one time. This means more ice cream with little extra time or effort. If you wish, you may use the ice chipping plate (available separately), but small ice cubes seem to work just as well and are a lot less trouble.

This is a rather large, cumbersome attachment, so it uses a good deal of ice (about one and a half standard bags and hence more rock salt). I would suggest filling only half way up with ice and salt to minimize expense when you are making only two quarts in the four quart container. The machine is rather noisy, it spills a bit of water and it should be set on a cookie sheet with sides to catch any water that may overflow.

FOOD GRINDER

From the lofty pâté to home-style meatloaf, from *bifteck* to hamburger, for spaghetti sauces, tostadas, not to mention mincemeat, cranberry sauce, India relish, chutney, and of course, spicy fat sausages—the food grinder takes over where the whippers, beaters, slicers, and graters leave off.

The KitchenAid grinder has behind it all the muscle of that potent motor plus the sturdy construction and clear thinking design so prevalent in all Hobart products. There is never a hesitation or a shudder of vibration no matter how dense or fatty the ingredient.

Prepare the food for the grinder, particularly your meat, by cutting it into long strips before feeding it into the hopper. Make sure that you use the plunger, *never your fingers*, to press down each portion to be ground. Grind at as cold a temperature as possible—meats for sausages, for instance, are best ground by adding 1 ice cube with each pound of meat (see page 183)—and if you like you may put your cuts through the hopper twice for a better mix and more tender results.

To assemble the food grinder, set the grind worm inside the bottom of the grinder, then push the 4-bladed grinder knife onto the grind worm's exposed end so that the flat cutting edges are turned *outward*. Place either grinder plate in position; the notch in its edge should unite with the small pin in the grinder body. The last step is to screw the ring into the place, making sure that the fit is firm but not too tight.

SAUSAGE STUFFER

This small, inexpensive attachment is worth its weight in hot sizzling sausages. It fits easily into the food grinder and is made of tough, smooth plastic so that natural casings will not catch or stick on it.

COLANDER AND SIEVE SET

While the food processors purée in seconds with a whirlwind flash of their cleaver-sharp blades, this KitchenAid attachment follows the more classic procedure of forcing cooked fruits and vegetables through a finely perforated surface (in this case, sheet metal) with a pestlelike wooden bar. The action is rather slow, it is frequently necessary to stir the ingredients down from the sides of the colander, and only soft foods press through easily, but a sinew never need be strained in the process.

To use, simply attach the paddle to the beater shaft and fit the colander over the steel mixing bowl, then set the perforated disc (sieve) into the colander. As soon as your food is ready, place it

in the sieve and attach the bowl to the machine. Turn the motor
to the lowest speed as you start, increasing it afterwards to
Speed 2. Stop the machine once or twice during processing to
scrape down both paddle and colander sides.

SPLASH GUARD

This attachment is designed to minimize splash-out during the
mixing process. The light aluminum construction is adequate for
the job. However, it is meant to fit both the K45 and the K5A
bowls, and while it nestles into the K45 snugly and well, it fits
poorly into the narrower bowl of the K5A. Whether or not you're
using the splash guard, it's a good idea always to mix large
amounts of liquid ingredients at low speed, then increase the
speed gradually once the liquid has thickened.

POURING CHUTE

Meant to lend a helping hand when additional dry ingredients
must be added to a mixture while the beater, whip, or dough hook
is operating, this attachment is only moderately successful. Flour,
for example, still tends to spray both counter and cook if too much
is added too fast. Always turn the motor to the lowest speed and
add ingredients a bit at a time for best results.

CAN OPENER

This is a marvelous opener, easy to attach and operate. Simply
insert its shaft into the square wrench-hole on the attachment
hub, tighten the attachment knob, and turn the opener handle to
the right. Place the lid of the upright can under and back of the
round knife, then swing the handle back to the left. As soon as
the motor is turned to Speed 2, the knife will cut through the can
top and the magnet will grip the severed lid firmly. To release
the can, turn the motor off; hold the can and swing the handle
back to the right. The can opener performs efficiently on any size

can, but *never* use it to open a pressurized (aerosol-type) can or any cans containing flammable liquids.

SILVER BUFFER

Set the buffer into the attachment hub in the same manner as the can opener. To operate it, apply polish lightly to your silver pieces and let dry; a heavy application will cause the polish to roll up during the polishing process. Start on Speed 6 for a preliminary shine, then increase to Speed 10 to polish it to a high gleam. Be sure your silver is held against the buffer wheel so that the bristles rotate *away* from you, and for safety's sake, wear eye protection when operating the attachment. After polishing, wash, rinse, and dry each piece of silver thoroughly.

ICE OR HOT WATER JACKET

The water jacket surrounds the mixing bowl and should be filled with cold or ice water when preparing quenelles, whipping cream, etc., and with warm or boiling water when beating icings or mashed potatoes. Also used as a receptacle under the colander and sieve set.

IMPORTANT TIPS AND SUGGESTIONS

Each of the standard attachments—the flat beater, wire whip, and dough hook—is designed for specialized mixing. Use the flat beater for mixing cakes, cookies, biscuits, quick breads, pastry, and creamed icings, or for any recipe that calls for blending several ingredients. The wire whip's specialty is incorporating air quickly into such foods as eggs, egg whites, heavy cream, mayonnaise, waffle batters, sponge or angel cakes, or boiled frostings. The dough hook is of course superb for mixing and kneading yeast doughs.

The several speeds on the KitchenAid are also designed for specialized tasks:

Speed 1 Is the setting at which you should: begin all mixing procedures; add dry ingredients to dry batters; fold in dried fruits and nuts; blend heavy mixtures; or purée fruits. In general, Speed 1 is most suitable for any slow mixing, stirring, or folding.

Speed 2 Will mix, stir, or mash your ingredients a bit faster and is also the speed at which yeast doughs are mixed and kneaded. Use it to mash potatoes and other vegetables, cut shortening into flour, or to beat heavy or thin batters. The can opener and the colander and sieve attachment are also operated at this speed.

Speed 4 Will handle any medium-fast beating or creaming or slow whipping called for in your recipe. Cream your sugar and shortening together, begin to whip large amounts of cream, or add sugar to beaten egg whites at this speed. Attachments to be operated at Speed 4 include the food grinder, the ice cream freezer, and the slicing and grating cones and plates.

Speed 6 Is designed for fast beating or creaming, for medium-fast whipping or for finishing your batters. Use it to whip un-usually large amounts of egg whites (as in angel food cake), to whip cream or egg yolks or to prepare salad dressings, gelatin molds or sponge cakes, or to put the finishing touches on whipped potatoes. Attachments operated at this speed are the grain mill, juice extractor, and silver buffer.

Speed 8 Is a fast beating or whipping stage that should be reached in *gradual* steps through the previous speeds. It's also the speed at which egg whites for boiled frostings are whipped.

Speed 10 Duplicates the beating and whipping action described for Speed 8 at an even faster rate. You'll find it useful if you have small amounts of cream or only one egg white to whip, but be sure to advance the speed *gradually*. The silver buffer can also be operated on Speed 10.

(Note: A finer speed adjustment can be set, if desired, halfway between any of the above speeds. These intermediate settings would then correspond to Speeds 3, 5, 7 and 9.)

Always begin your mixing at the lowest speed, gradually increasing once the ingredients are fairly well blended. Because of the speed with which the KitchenAid attachments twirl, it's a good idea to keep a watchful eye on your mixture during the whole process. Operate only long enough for your batter, mixture or dough to reach the designated appearance: "well blended," "smooth and creamy," or "smooth and elastic."

Add eggs or small amounts of liquid ingredients as close to the side of the bowl as possible, keeping them away from the moving beater (the pouring chute, if you have one, simplifies matters somewhat). When you are adding large quantities or troublesome ingredients such as sifted flour, it's best to remove the bowl, add ingredients, replace bowl, restart the motor at the lowest speed, then gradually increase the speed. If the recipe indicates that scraping the sides of the bowl is necessary, be sure to turn the motor off first—otherwise, the beater may be damaged.

• Bring cold ingredients to room temperature (except butter as indicated) before mixing or adding them to other mixtures.

• When creaming ingredients, cream your butter, shortening, or cream cheese first—unless otherwise indicated—then add your other ingredients as directed.

• Add whole eggs one at a time, making sure that each is well mixed before adding the next.

• If your recipe calls for eggs to be separated, you may find it a help to do this directly after removing them from the refrigerator and allow them to warm in separate bowls.

• When your recipe indicates that nuts, dates, raisins and the like are to be folded in just before turning your batter or mixture out of the bowl, add them at the last minute at lowest speed. Other tips and information are included in the discussions of the individual attachments.

THE STARMIX FOOD PROCESSOR

The Starmix is the new machine in town, and perhaps the most versatile food processor on the culinary horizon. It shows off its star quality in a dazzling display of food-processing functions. No other machine, to my knowledge, chops, minces, blends, purées, slices, grates, kneads, mixes, churns ice cream, and whips clouds of egg whites and cream. It is billed by the makers as a "universal kitchen machine," and it does, but for a few imperfections, come very close to being just that.

While the basic Starmix machine performs well, the attachments are particularly exciting. I sometimes think that processing attachments are as much a liability as they are an advantage. They are usually large, cumbersome, and a nuisance to clean and store. My idea of the perfect machine is one that does everything with no additional parts. But since this is, unfortunately, still only a dream, there are three marvelous Starmix attachments which I would be reluctant to give up.

A superb attachment that arrives at no extra cost with your machine is the small whirling-dervish whipping device that fastens to the top of the shaft of the steel kneading-slicing bowl. This attractively designed double-beater rotates carousel-fashion, producing frothy mounds of egg whites or whipped cream in far less time than usual. These whisklike whips are so effective that egg whites must be carefully watched to prevent them from turning from soft peaks to stiff to dry before you can so much as blink an eye.

The ice cream freezer is an amazing machine that makes the actual churning of frozen cream easier and less time-consuming than preparing a bowl of Jello. With this small and convenient attachment in your kitchen you can whip up ice cream as offhandedly as you might stir up a tray of brownies.

Another superb Starmix attachment is the compact and easy-to-use juice extractor. In seconds almost any hard vegetable or fruit can be twirled into a vitamin-rich cocktail. Your kitchen becomes a nutrition center with a flick of the Starmix switch.

APPEARANCE

The Starmix comes with two tops: one a standard blender and the other a sturdy and functional-looking stainless-steel bowl. When either of these is in place on the gray and white plastic base, the machine looks as it should—like a heavy-duty kitchen helper. While this processor would not win design awards, it is attractive enough to decorate your kitchen counter in an unobtrusive way.

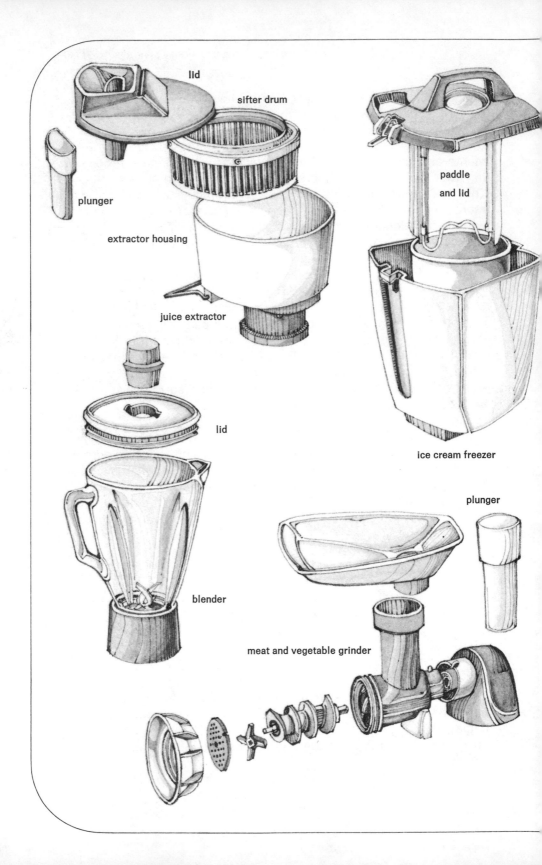

lid

sifter drum

plunger

paddle
and lid

extractor housing

juice extractor

ice cream freezer

lid

plunger

blender

meat and vegetable grinder

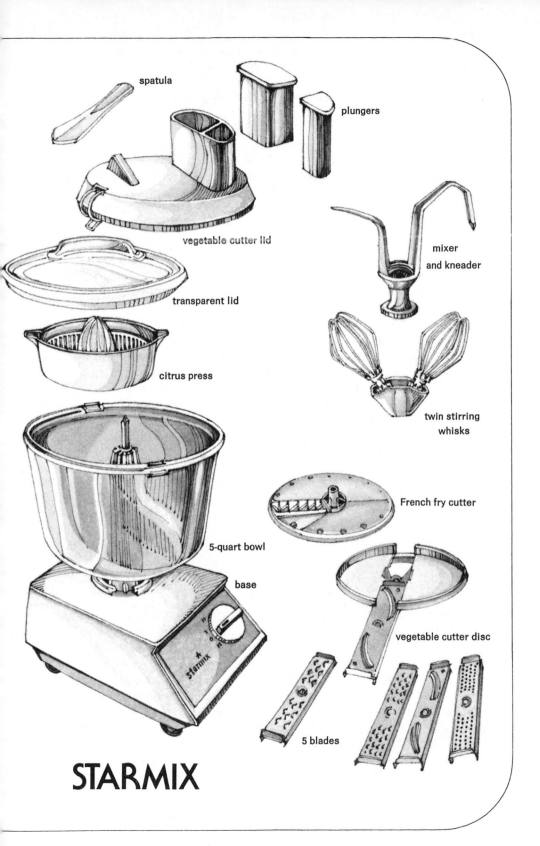

spatula

plungers

vegetable cutter lid

mixer and kneader

transparent lid

citrus press

twin stirring whisks

5-quart bowl

French fry cutter

base

vegetable cutter disc

5 blades

STARMIX

QUALITY OF CONSTRUCTION

The Starmix is certainly a competently made machine. The plastic is heavy and well molded, as you would expect any superior appliance to be in this plastic age. The metal parts are well cast and the stainless-steel bowl is made from the heaviest gauge of any kitchen machine, assuring that this should be around at least as long as the sun continues to shine. Every part that should fit together does so efficiently and in most cases with a minimum of bother. The entire mechanism is based on double action at the central shaft, about which a gear slowly revolves, in a manner similar to what the KitchenAid people call "planetary action." The main coupling device—which joins the various parts to the motor housing, whence springs the power—is reminiscent of the manner in which a camera lens is fastened into a camera. This appears to be well thought out, and in general, it does perform well. However, to my mind it doesn't click reassuringly enough into place to give a feeling of absolute dependability, a feeling reinforced when the juice extractor once flew off the shaft and spun across the counter like a top. This is admittedly the only such unpleasant experience I have had with the machine and should perhaps be discounted.

One more serious shortcoming, at least in my estimation, is the relative lack of keenness of the slicing and grating blades. These are merely sharpened extensions of the part itself, and not, as in the Cuisinart, separate sharp blades spot-welded to the attachment.

CONVENIENCE

Smaller and more conveniently sized than the KitchenAid, this machine is probably the best all-around processor for nongourmet, small family cooking. This is not to demean the Starmix as unequal to more sophisticated menus but rather to emphasize the jack-of-all-trades convenience of this versatile machine. Since plastic and lightweight metal are the primary construction materials, weight poses no special problem. The base, which is essentially a large motor in a streamlined plastic housing, is the only heavy part, but even this is not excessively so.

The attachments are easy to understand and to affix, and are moderate in size, so storage is less of a problem than with some of the other machines.

CLEANING

All parts except the motor housing and juice extractor may be washed in hot sudsy water. Blender parts should be washed, preferably right after each use. Rinse and dry thoroughly before using again, paying particular attention to the inside of the cone where water has a tendency to collect. When working with dry ingredients, make sure that the blender jug is also completely dry.

All parts of the mixer and kneader attachment are washable. The clamping cap that covers the twin stirring whisks may be detached if cleaning is necessary; all you need do is squeeze the ends together lightly. Should the spindle need a washing, unscrew it, using the dough hook as a lever.

When using the juice extractor, each time you juice three or four small apples (or their equivalent) remove the filter strip, then scrape off and discard the pulpy residue. Although the drum and filter strip of this attachment are completely washable, take special care when cleaning the extractor—its bottom should not be submerged in water. Clean the interior of the extractor under running water, wiping off the bottom afterward with a damp cloth.

ADVANTAGES AND DISADVANTAGES

A good deal of research and thought have obviously gone into the Starmix processor and its attachments, as witness its tremendous versatility of functions. Helpful details have been added such as the see-through plastic tops of the mixer-kneader attachment and the ice cream freezer. These serve a far more than decorative purpose. It is unusually helpful to be able to follow the progress of the mixing and kneading of bread and the thickening and freezing of ice cream to their successful conclusions. How much more convenient this is than wrestling with paddle and top, ice and salt water only to find the cream is still partially frozen.

Another plus is the well-conceived blender jar with its small opening in the blender top to allow the addition of ingredients without splashing kitchen walls and ceiling, and its twist-apart base to permit easy cleaning.

Along with the positive, there are a few negative aspects to the Starmix processor as well. The process with which I had the most trouble was the clamping and unclamping of the super-strong steel-wire holders on the sides of the plastic top to the slicer attachment. Until these are well broken in, they must be struck sharply with the heel of the hand to facilitate opening and closing. As the clamps loosen up a bit, this becomes less of a problem, but not before your hand has given, and taken, a few nasty blows.

The noise factor here is also a problem. The Starmix machine does clatter more than either the Cuisinart or the KitchenAid, but it is still less garrulous than quite a few of the other machines on the market. All in all, however, the Starmix processor with its attachments is still highly recommended.

BASIC PARTS

1 solid plastic-housed two-speed motor ($\frac{1}{2}$–$\frac{3}{4}$ horsepower)
1 plastic spatula
1 1$\frac{1}{2}$-quart blender and lid
1 mixer and kneader (consists of a 5-quart seamless stainless-steel bowl with a built-in spindle, twin stirring whisks, a dough hook, and a transparent plastic lid)
1 vegetable cutter disc with five blades

OPTIONAL PARTS/ATTACHMENTS

French fry cutter
meat and vegetable grinder
juice extractor
citrus press
ice cream freezer

USING YOUR STARMIX FOOD PROCESSOR

A wealth of the Starmix attachments—the blender jug, mixer and kneader, vegetable cutter disc and blades and plastic spatula are standard equipment, while the grinder, ice cream maker, juice extractor, citrus press, and French fry cutter are optional—may be mounted individually on the same powerful motor base, where a simple switch sends them immediately into action.

All the attachments sit directly on the power drive where, by twisting either to the left or right as indicated for each below, they will lock into position. A built-in safety feature is that none of the attachments will work until its cover is set in place; conversely, only when the motor has completely stopped can the cover be removed. Should you overload the machine or run the motor too long, an automatic switch-off is also built in. If the motor shuts itself off, simply turn the switch to off, take out the excess ingredients, and give the motor a chance to cool before proceeding.

There are two working speeds on the Starmix machine. Speed II is the normal setting and should be used for most operations and for the vegetable cutter and other optional attachments as well. Speed I is provided in case you prefer a low working speed. There is also an instant-action switch designated by the letter M, the purpose of which is to let you fold stiffly beaten egg whites, cream, flour, and so on into other ingredients and to aid you in mounting the blender jug and fruit juice attachments. The M switch is automatic: the motor will shut off as soon as you release it.

Instructions for using the assorted attachments are given here under the descriptions of each that follow.

ATTACHMENTS

BLENDER JUG

The blender jug, frequently referred to in recipes as "the container," will handle all chopping, blending, mixing, or puréeing operations. As the crossed blades go into action, they create a strong suction that pulls the contents of the jug within their cutting sphere and simultaneously forces the food upward against the jug's walls so that chopping or mixing takes place evenly. In most cases, only a few seconds are necessary for coarse chopping, while fine chopping takes a second or two longer. Until you get used to your machine you'll probably find it is better to switch off the motor one or two seconds sooner than the time indicated in an individual recipe or the charts.

To assemble the blender jug, turn the jug upside down and set in the crossed blades. Top these with the sealing ring and cone, twisting to secure the cone at its base. Lock the base into the motor drive by turning it to the left. Affix the cover to start the motor. The jug is fashioned from high-quality plastic and will withstand temperatures of 200 degrees F. or 95 degrees centigrade (hot but not boiling).

Chopping and puréeing take place when ingredients are placed in the blender jug and whirled to the required degree of fineness. The Starmix manual is a little confusing here because it refers to grinding or grating specific ingredients in the blender jug. The grinding action involved is actually chopping; food is put in the blender against the blades and processed as long as indicated in the recipes or charts. Hard ingredients like cheese, chocolate, carrots, potatoes, or even pieces of stale bread can also be chopped—although the manual calls this grating—by being dropped through the opening in the blender cover with the motor running. Vegetables with a low liquid content may be easier to chop if you use this method, but empty the blender jug when it is one-third full; otherwise the contents will become puréed. Fine and coarse grating are actually best undertaken with the grating attachments for the vegetable cutter (see below). Consult the charts to learn which foods are suitable for processing in the blender.

When vegetables are being cut for recipes such as fine cole-slaw or vegetable soup, where speed is more important than perfection of processing, liquid may be added to facilitate cutting, then drained off and discarded, or in the case of soup, retained and used as part of the amount called for in your recipe.

Work with small amounts of nuts or poppy seeds when crushing in the blender; otherwise some will gather beneath the blades in a mass while the rest will remain practically whole. Chocolate, too, should be chopped in small amounts because heat from the motor may cause the pieces to stick or melt. Your spices or citrus peel will reduce to powder much more easily if you blend them with a little sugar. When preparing drinks in the blender jug, add the ice cubes last so they won't be reduced to liquid.

Most standard blender recipes (including those for alcoholic and nonalcoholic drinks and baby foods) may be prepared in this attachment.

MIXER AND KNEADER

The mixing and kneading attachment consists of a steel bowl with a built-in spindle, twin stirring whisks, a kneader (generally referred to as a dough hook), and a plastic lid. To set the mixing bowl into place, twist it slightly until it fits over the raised notches on the motor base, then lock the bowl on by sliding it to the right. Both dough hook and twin stirrers attach easily—simply set them on the spindle.

Use the twin stirring whisks for such operations as mixing cake batters, sauces, and mayonnaise, and for whipping cream or egg whites when you are preparing mousses, meringues, *génoise*, etc. The dough hook will handle yeast and other doughs, pie and chou pastries, or any stiff batters.

VEGETABLE CUTTER

The vegetable cutter goes directly on the mixing bowl spindle, but the plastic cover that sits on the mixing bowl during mixing and kneading is supplanted by a double-spouted cover formed from thicker plastic and complete with all-too-sturdy clamps. All vegetable-cutter parts are completely washable in hot, soapy water.

To use the vegetable cutter, slide the appropriate cutting plate —thick or thin slicer, coarse or fine grater, or fine-holed grater— onto the flat disc. Set disc and cutting plate over the mixing bowl spindle, rim side up, then place the bowl on the motor base and lock it by turning to the right. Clamp the cover on and proceed to slice or grate your ingredients through either of the two spouts (the third opening in the cover is the bean snipper, a most amusing and useful feature). Each spout has its own separate plunger; close the spout not in use when the motor is running or food will force its way up this unused opening. Slice or grate through the larger spout when preparing large vegetables or several small vegetables at one time; use the smaller spout to process small amounts or more slender foods. Always use the appropriate plunger—*never* your fingers or any other utensil—to push the food down against the blades.

FRENCH FRY CUTTER

This optional attachment makes preparing any quantity of potatoes for French frying quick and easy. To use, set the cutting plate on the mixing bowl spindle and cover with the vegetable cutter lid. Turn the motor to Speed II (never use this attachment at Speed I) and use the plunger to push the potatoes through the large spout.

GRINDER

The Starmix grinding attachment will process cooked and un-cooked meat, fish, hard-cooked eggs, fruit, cheese, and most other foods. Cut each ingredient you plan to grind into long strips, then arrange the pieces on the plastic feeding plate and push down with the specially designed plunger.

To assemble the grinder, slip the grind worm into the grinder housing with its longer shaft end outwards. Slip on the knife so the cutting edge faces outwards, place the steel grinding disc over the knife, positioning it by fitting its notches into the corres-ponding notches on the grinder housing, and screw on the locking ring. Join grinder and gear component by twisting until the pin on the grinder housing locks into position, then lock the whole attachment on the motor base by turning it to the right. All grinder parts are washable, but dry well after each use. This grinder is rather curious-looking and quite attractive, but ingredients tend to stick in the small disc and must be cleaned by pushing through each hole with a nutpick. This fine disc is the only standard part of the attachment; a coarse grinder blade is available, but at extra cost.

JUICE EXTRACTOR

This optional attachment is designed to help you prepare nutri-tious juices from most fresh vegetables in a matter of seconds. The machine works very well, but its capacity is rather limited. It will juice leafy as well as root vegetables, although the former should be rolled up before being passed through the cover open-ing into the machine: herbs should also be handled in this manner. Most fruits—including peeled and seeded citrus fruits and even berries if they are firm and you juice them in small amounts—can also be processed.

This extractor is a bit tricky to puzzle out at first: the lid must be in just the right position before the metal bar can be locked in place. For ease of operation, set the sifting drum on the drive shaft in the extractor housing. Place the filter strip in position and attach the lid. The assembled extractor will lock on the motor with a turn to the right; it is correctly mounted when the pouring spout is at your right as you face the machine. Cut the fruits or vegetables to be processed into segments small enough to pass through the opening in the cover. Place a *tall* glass under the pouring spout, set the machine at Speed II and tamp down the ingredients through the opening with the plunger provided, *never* with your fingers.

CITRUS PRESS

This particular juicer is geared only for citrus fruits. In my opinion the attachment spins too fast to be practical. Fruits are hard to hold in place if you have a small hand or a weak grip. The press fits over the mixing bowl on the motor base and must be washed along with your juice glass . . . quite a bit of work, especially if you are making only a small amount of juice.

To assemble, fit the mixing bowl on the motor base. Place the one-piece pressing cone and attached sieve basket into the juice container, then set both on the mixing bowl spindle. Operate by pressing the fruit halves gently and evenly on the cone. If you are making large amounts of juice or are adding juice directly to ingredients already in the mixing bowl, use the pressing cone without the juice container.

ICE CREAM FREEZER

This is a marvelous attachment—one of my favorites from all the machines I've tested. Absolutely perfect for churning up one quart of ice cream in roughly ten minutes, it performs with no excess of ice or salt and has a plastic top through which you can see exactly how quickly your cream is freezing. The one-quart capacity means that less ice and salt are required when making ice cream and also that the freezer itself is smaller and hence easier to store.

One small drawback is the small opening through which additional ice must be fed one cube or tablespoon of crushed ice at a time. This also means that additional salt cannot be added in layers but must be premeasured and added more or less by whim as the machine revolves.

FRUITS, VEGETABLES & NUTS

	seconds	yield	notes
Apple (1 Medium: 5–6 oz.)			
CUISINART			
Chop	3	½ Cup	Peel and core; cut in eighths. Coarsely chopped: stop once, scrape down
	5	½ Cup	Finely chopped: stop twice, scrape down.
	6	½ Cup	Minced: stop twice, scrape down. Pick out any large pieces and chop separately.
Grate	1	1 Cup	Coarsely grated (with skin): very nice 1-inch shreds, but better to peel because some skin sticks on top of blade.
	2	¾ Cup	Finely grated (without skin): very thin, nicely done, peeling necessary here.
Slice	2	½ Cup plus	Thin slicing: peel, core and cut to fit spout. Arrange cut side against the blade.
	2	¾ Cup	Thick slicing: peel, core and cut in quarters; nice size for apple tart.
KITCHENAID (Disc)			
Chop			Doesn't chop.
Grate	8		Not really practical; pulp catches in back of blade.
Slice	8	1 Cup	Peel and core or peel whole apple; slices whole fruit in perfect slices. No other machine will do this except Robot Coupe.
KITCHENAID (Rotor)			
Chop			Doesn't chop.
Grate	3	¾ Cup	Coarsely grated: peel and core; very nice shoestring pieces 1 inch long: if unpeeled, some pieces of peel remain in machine.
	3	½ Cup plus	Finely grated: peel and core; performs beautifully, fine threads of apple 1 inch long..

	seconds	yield	notes
Slice	1½	¾ Cup	Coarsely sliced (peeled): very nice slices, good for pie.
	1½	¾ Cup	Coarsely sliced (unpeeled): slightly ragged, some peel remains in machine, so peeling is suggested.
	2	½ Cup	Thinly sliced: a bit ragged; coarse slicing is recommended.

STARMIX			Peel and core; cut in eighths.
Chop (Blender)	2	½ Cup plus	Coarsely chopped: turn quickly on and off, stir up pieces from bottom; turn quickly on and off again.
	4	⅓ Cup	Finely chopped: turn quickly on and off, stir up pieces from bottom, turn quickly on and off again 3 times more.
Grate			Performs well with or without peel, but is best peeled; cut in quarters.
	3	1¼ Cups	Coarsely grated: put cut side down; makes somewhat ragged shoestring strips.
	8		Finely grated: results are akin to apple sauce: not practical.
Slice			Peel, core and cut in quarters, do 2 or 3 quarters at a time.
	3	¾ Cup	Coarsely sliced: Slices are basically the same when either speed is used—slightly ragged, but highly usable.
	8	½ Cup	Finely sliced: results are paper-thin and broken; not really practical.

Banana (1 Ripe, firm, peeled fruit)

CUISINART			
Slice	3	1 Cup	Thin perfect slices.

KITCHENAID (Disc)			
Slice	8	1 Cup	Performs nicely; don't press too hard.

KITCHENAID (Rotor) Slice	3	1 Cup	Performs well with both coarse and thin blades; cut fruit in half crosswise and put cut ends next to blade. Press gently.

STARMIX			
Slice	6	1 Cup	Use coarse slicer; nice slices.

	seconds	yield	notes

Beets (3 Medium: about 2 oz. each)

CUISINART

			Peel, cut in quarters; place in spout cut side down.
Grate			
(Uncooked)	8	1½ Cups	Coarsely grated: bounce plunger gently up and down.
	16	1⅓ Cups	Finely grated: bounce plunger lightly.
(Cooked)	1½	¾ Cup	Fine grater recommended.
Slice			
(Uncooked)	6	2 Cups	Trim to fit; performs beautifully with both coarse and thin blades.
(Cooked)	5	2 Cups	Same as above.

KITCHENAID

(Disc)			Peel.
Grate			
(Uncooked)	12	1½ Cups	Use fine disc; does nice job; finely shredded.
(Cooked)	8	¾ Cup	Nicely shredded.
Slice			
(Uncooked)	9	2¼ Cups	Adequate; slices slightly ragged.
(Cooked)	3	2¼ Cups	Adequate; slices slightly ragged.

KITCHENAID

(Rotor)			Peel.
Grate			
(Uncooked)	6	2 Cups	Coarsely grated: interesting shoestring pieces.
	4	1½ Cups	Finely grated: performs well; nice fine threads.
(Cooked)	6	1 Cup	Peel. Coarsely grated: shoestring pieces.
	4	1 Cup	Finely grated: Beautiful thin shreds.
Slice			
(Cooked)	5	2 Cups	Coarsely sliced: nicely cut.
	5	1½ Cups	Finely sliced: nicely cut.
(Uncooked)	6	2 Cups	Both coarse and fine blades perform well.

STARMIX

			Peel.
Grate			
(Uncooked)	7	2 Cups plus	Coarsely grated: performs well.
	14	2 Cups	Finely grated: good job, but 1 piece is generally left behind the blade.
(Cooked)	4	1¼ Cups	Coarsely grated: performs well.
	8	¾ Cup plus	Finely grated; performs well.

	seconds	yield	notes
Slice (Uncooked)	3	2 Cups	Peel. Coarsely sliced: performs well.
		1½ Cups	Finely sliced: performs well.
(Cooked)	3	1¾ Cups	Coarsely sliced: nicely cut.
	6	1½ Cups	Finely sliced: nicely cut.

Broccoli Stems, for Soup

CUISINART			Stems only.
Slice	1½	⅔ Cup	Fit 3 into spout at once; beautiful, even pieces suitable for soup.

KITCHENAID (Disc) Slice	2½	1¼ Cup	Stems only. Fit 6 into spout at once; nicely cut.

KITCHENAID (Rotor) Slice	1½	1¼ Cup	Florets: Slices after a fashion but not really practical. Stems only. Coarsely slices 6 pieces quite nicely.

STARMIX Slice	2	1¼ Cup	Stems only. Use coarse blade; nicely sliced.

Cabbage (¼ Medium head)

CUISINART Chop			Cut in 1-inch squares; chop 2 handfuls at a time; pick out large pieces and redo.
	1	1 Cup	Coarsely chopped: performs very well.
	2	1 Cup	Finely chopped: stop once to scrape down.
	3	¾ Cup	Minced: stop once to scrape down.
Grate			Cut to fit spout, put cut edge against blade; bounce plunger up and down.
	4	2 Cups	Coarsely grated: beautifully cut; good for coleslaw.
	16	1⅓ Cups	Finely grated: beautifully cut, good for coleslaw.
Slice			Trim to fit spout, put cut edge against blade.
	13	1½ Cups	Thinly sliced: good for coleslaw.
	2	1½ Cups	Thickly sliced: ⅛ inch strips; good for Cabbage Curry (see page 237).

	seconds	yield	notes
KITCHENAID			
(Disc)			
Chop			Doesn't chop.
Grate	8	1 Cup	Coarsely grated: nicely done.
			Fine grating disc: not practical.
Slice			Put cut end against blade.
	6	2 Cups	Shredded very nicely, perfect for coleslaw.
KITCHENAID			
(Motor)			
Chop			Doesn't chop.
Grate			
	5	1½ Cups	Coarsely grated: very nice for coleslaw.
	15	1½ Cups	Finely grated: works very well, nicely grated.
Slice			Cut in half.
	3	2 Cups	Thinly sliced: shreds nicely.
	8	2½ Cups	Thickly sliced: coarsely shredded, but thin slicing is better for coleslaw.
STARMIX			Cut in 1-inch squares; chop 2 handfuls at a time.
Chop			
(Blender)		1 Cup	Coarsely chopped: (Without liquid) turn machine on and off until desired coarseness is reached; stop as necessary to push pieces down.
			Finely chopped: not practical: pieces range from ½ inch to liquid; use grater.
Grate			Cut to fit spout.
	10	2 Cups	Coarsely grated; nicely shredded.
	48	1 Cup	Very finely grated; adequate job; press hard to force through; limp leaves catch in machine.
Slice			Cut cabbage in eighths; place cut edges against blade.
	12	2½ Cups	Coarsely sliced: nicely cut.

Carrots (1 Medium)

	seconds	yield	notes
CUISINART			
Chop			Scraps, quarter lengthwise; cut in 1-inch pieces; chop only 2 or 3 handfuls at one time when chopping more than **one** carrot.
	4	½ Cup	Coarsely chopped: stop once, scrape down.

	seconds	yield	notes
	6	½ Cup	Finely chopped: stop once, scrape down.
	9	½ Cup	Minced: stop 3 times, scrape down.
Grate			Scrape, cut in pieces; arrange on sides in spout, fill spout; lightly bounce plunger up and down for best results
	4	½ Cup plus	Coarsely grated.
	9	½ Cup plus	Finely grated. Good for tea sandwiches.
Slice			Scrape, cut in half crosswise, arrange in spout cut sides against blade. If slicing two at one time, arrange with two top side down, one top side up.
	6	½ Cup	Thinly sliced.

KITCHENAID
  (Disc)

	seconds	yield	notes
Chop			Doesn't chop; use grater.
Grate			Scrape.
	15	½ Cup	Use fine disc, apply pressure firmly; makes nice, thin shreds ½ to 1 inch long.
Slice			Scrape; use top speed for neater cutting.
	6	½ Cup	Performs well, but last pieces are usually elongated.

KITCHENAID
  (Rotor)

	seconds	yield	notes
			Scrape.
Chop			Doesn't chop; use grater.
Grate			
	3	½ Cup	Coarse grater produces shoestring pieces.
Slice			Cut in half.
	2	½ Cup	Thinly sliced: good slices, but best when slicing 3 halves at once; otherwise last slices are large because carrot slips sideways. When slicing one carrot use narrow Tube.
	5	½ Cup	Thickly sliced: very nicely done.

STARMIX

	seconds	yield	notes
Chop			Scrape: cut in 1-inch pieces.
	2	⅓ Cup	Coarsely chopped: (Without liquid) difficult to get pieces a uniform size. (With liquid: see page 40). For fine chopping it's best to use grater.

	seconds	yield	notes
Grate			Scrape; put broad end down in small opening in spout.
	7	½ Cup	Coarse grated: nicely shredded.
	54	⅓ Cup plus	Finely grated: nicely shredded.
Slice			Use small opening in spout.
	5	1 Cup	Coarsely sliced: very nicely cut.
	16	1 Cup	Finely sliced: very nicely cut.

Celery (2 Ribs; Note—Use only firm ribs and remove all strings. After processing, drain before using in recipe.)

	seconds	yield	notes
CUISINART			Cut in 1-inch pieces.
Chop			
	2	¾ Cup	Coarsely chopped: stop once to scrape down.
	3	¾ Cup	Finely chopped: stop twice to scrape down.
	4	¾ Cup	Minced: stop three times to scrape down.
Grate			Cut to fit spout and arrange horizontally; results are very usable shreds, but not actually grated.
	2	¾ Cup	
Slice	6	¾ Cup	Cut in same length pieces to fit spout.
KITCHENAID (Disc)			
Chop			Doesn't chop.
Grate			Not practical, catches behind blade.
Slice			
	24	¾ Cup	Rather ragged, stringy slices but does work.
KITCHENAID (Rotor)			
Chop			Doesn't chop; use grater.
Grate			Arrange cut side against blade.
	3	⅔ Cup	Coarsely grated: shoestring pieces 1 inch long; not a terribly practical size.
	3	⅔ Cup	Finely grated: nice thin threads, pick out any long pieces; works best with back of celery against blade.
Slice			Cut in equal-length pieces; arrange cut sides against blade; fill hopper to top for best results.
	3	1¼ Cups	Coarse slicing: slightly ragged but adequate.
	7	1 Cup	Fine slicing: slightly ragged but adequate.

	seconds	yield	notes
STARMIX			Cut in 1-inch pieces.
Chop			
(Blender)	2	⅔ Cup	Performs adequately.
Grate			
	6	¾ Cup plus	Performs adequately.
Slice			Cut to fit in equal-size pieces; coarse slicer does cut nicely; fine slicing is not practical.
	4	¾ Cup	

Chocolate (1 1–oz. square)

	seconds	yield	notes
CUISINART			
Chop			Cut square in half.
	15	¼ Cup	Coarsely chopped; performs very well.
	30	¼ Cup	Finely chopped. Performs well.
Grate			Arrange with cut side against blade.
	20	¼ Cup	Will do job but slowly; chopping is better for most recipes.

	seconds	yield	notes
KITCHENAID			
(Disc)			
Chop			Doesn't chop; use grater.
Grate			Use fine disc at Speed 2, then Speed 8.
	8	⅓ Cup	Very nice, light thin curls.

	seconds	yield	notes
KITCHENAID			
(Rotor)			
Chop			Doesn't chop; use coarse or fine grater.
Grate			
	9	¼ Cup	Coarsely grated: performs very well.
	5	¼ Cup	Finely grated: performs very well.

	seconds	yield	notes
STARMIX			
Chop	10	3 Tablespoons	Drop in top with motor running; results are fine powder with some larger pieces.
(Blender)			
Grate			
	3	3 Tablespoons	Use coarse grater at Speed II; fine grater not practical.
	16	3 Tablespoons	Nut grater at Speed II; fine powder but does the job.

	seconds	yield	notes

Coconut (Fresh, 2½ Oz.)

CUISINART

Cut in 1-inch pieces.

	seconds	yield	notes
Chop			
	25	⅔ Cup	Coarsely chopped. Performs well in all instances.
	1½ minutes	⅔ Cup	Fairly finely chopped.
	2 minutes	⅔ Cup	Finely chopped.
Grate			
	20	1 Cup	Coarsely grated.
	25	⅔ Cup	Finely grated.

KITCHENAID (Disc)

	seconds	yield	notes
Chop			Doesn't chop; grate instead.
Grate			Cut in ½-inch strips, press hard.
	30	⅔ Cup	Some chunks result, but most is finely grated; performs well.

KITCHENAID (Rotor)

	seconds	yield	notes
Chop			Doesn't chop; grate instead.
Grate			Cut in ½-inch strips; place in hopper.
	5	⅔ Cup	Coarsely grated: shoestring pieces.
	3	½ Cup	Finely grated: small pieces catch in machine but in general shreds beautifully.

STARMIX

Cut in 1 X ½ inch strips; use Speed II.

	seconds	yield	notes
Chop			
	2	⅔ Cup	Coarsely chopped: stop once to scrape down.
	9	⅔ Cup	Finely chopped: stop twice to stir and push down.
			Starmix is best machine for finely chopped coconut.
Grate			Cut in ½-inch pieces; use fine grater; bounce plunger up and down.
	20	⅔ Cup	Produces perfectly beautiful shreds, which no other machine can do. Nut grater: not practical.

Cucumber (1 Large: 9–11 oz., peeled. After processing, drain before using in recipe.)

	seconds	yield	notes
CUISINART			Remove and discard seeds; cut in 1-inch pieces.
Chop			
	3	1⅓ Cups (1 Cup drained)	Coarsely chopped: pick out large pieces.
	5	1⅓ Cups (1 Cup drained)	Finely chopped: stop once to scrape down.
Grate			Remove and discard seeds; cut to fit spout.
	1½	1⅓ Cups	Coarsely grated: nice job.
	4	1 Cup	Finely grated: perfect shreds, not at all mushy.
Slice			Trim to fit spout.
	4	1½ Cups	Thinly sliced: beautiful.
KITCHENAID (Disc)			
Chop			Doesn't chop.
Grate			Not practical; results in a mushy mass.
Slice			
	5	2 Cups	Coarsely sliced: nice whole slices.
	4	2 Cups	Thinly sliced: nice whole slices.
KITCHENAID (Rotor)			
Chop			Doesn't chop; grate instead.
Grate			Remove and discard seeds.
	4	1⅓ Cups	Coarsely grated: shoestring shreds: 1 inch long.
	3	1⅓ Cups	Finely grated: fine, beautiful threads.
Slice			
	5	2 Cups	Coarsely sliced: nice slices.
	4	2 Cups	Thinly sliced: nice slices.
STARMIX			Cut in 1-inch cubes and place in blender (don't drop in top or results will be purée).
Chop (Blender)	2	1 Cup	Coarsely chopped (at Speed I): coarse and fine pieces, some juice.
Grate			Use coarse grater; shoestring strips; fine not practical.
	6	2 Cups	

	seconds	yield	notes
Slice			
	3	1 Cup	Coarsely sliced: these slices not as clean-cut as Cuisinart machine but more perfect than KitchenAid.
	5	1 Cup	Thinly sliced: makes ribbons; very interesting texture.

Eggs (1 Hard-cooked, chilled and shelled)

	seconds	yield	notes
CUISINART			Dry eggs well; cut in quarters.
Chop	Turn on/ off once quickly	¾ Cup	Coarsely chopped: performs nicely in every instance.
	Turn on/ off twice quickly	⅔ Cup	Finely chopped.
	Turn on/ off quickly three times	⅔ Cup	Minced.
Grate			
	1	½ Cup	These attachments will do the job but not as efficiently as the chopping blade. Yolk clings to top of machine.
Slice			Unsatisfactory broken slices.
KITCHENAID (Disc)			
Chop			Doesn't chop.
Grate			
	3	½ Cup	Coarse grater: whites in shoestring pieces, yolks coarsely chopped.
	4	⅓ Cup	Fine grater: nice fine threads; interesting texture.
Slice			Not practical.
KITCHENAID (Rotor)			
Chop			Doesn't chop.
Grate			Coarse grater not practical. Results from fine grater not perfect, but will serve for egg salad if you do a bit of hand-chopping. Recommended only when cooking for a crowd.
Slice			Not practical.

	seconds	yield	notes
STARMIX			Cut in quarters.
Chop (Blender)	1	⅓ Cup plus	Push egg down against blade, then turn motor quickly on and off twice; finely chopped, does perfect job.
Grate			Not practical.
Slice			Not practical.

Eggplant (1 Medium: 12 oz., peeled)

	seconds	yield	notes
CUISINART			Will chop and grate with its usual ease, but eggplant is most frequently cooked cut in cubes or sliced and consequently these operations are not too practical.
Slice	12	2 Cups	Cut in quarters: very nicely sliced.

	seconds	yield	notes
KITCHENAID (Disc)			
Slice	13	2 Cups	Slices not as beautiful as in the Cuisinart machine, but advantage is you can put a *whole* (medium) eggplant in without cutting it and adjust the blade to the thickness you prefer.

	seconds	yield	notes
KITCHENAID (Rotor)			
Grate	7	2 Cups	Use coarse grater; fine grater not practical.
Slice	4	2 Cups	Coarse slicer: fairly efficient; fine slicing not practical.

	seconds	yield	notes
STARMIX			
Slice	3	2 Cups	Coarsely sliced: somewhat ragged slices; quite usable. Fine slicing impractical.
French Fry Cutter	2½	2 Cups	Works quite well: for French-fried eggplant.

Green Beans (20 Beans)

	seconds	yield	notes
CUISINART			
Slice	2	1 Cup	To French-cut, remove ends and strings, cut to fit spout and arrange in spout lengthwise; shorter pieces than KitchenAid makes but well cut.

	seconds	yield	notes
KITCHENAID (Disc) Slice	3	1 Cup	To French-cut, remove ends and strings; stack upright against blade; bring plunger down carefully.
KITCHENAID (Rotor) Slice			Cut beans to fit hopper; results are ragged julienne strips; not really practical.
STARMIX	25	1 Cup	Use Bean Chipper Hole; very amusing and also quite efficient. No other machine has this feature.

Green Peppers (1 Medium: 6–7 oz. After processing, drain before using in recipe.)

	seconds	yield	notes
CUISINART			Seed and cut in 1-inch pieces; after chopping pick out any large pieces and redo.
Chop			
	2	1 Cup	Coarsely chopped: stop once to scrape down.
	3	1 Cup	Finely chopped: stop twice to scrape down.
	4	1 Cup	Minced: Stop twice to scrape down.
			Manual: on and off 4 times: coarsely chopped. On and off 5 times: finely chopped. On and off 6 times: minced. Drain before using in recipes.
Grate			Seed and cut to fit; arrange in spout, cut edge down.
	2	½ Cup	Coarsely grated: performs fairly well but a few pieces are left on top of blade.
	1	⅓ Cup	Finely grated: does grate, but most liquefies; not really too practical.
Slice			Seed and cut in 2-inch pieces; arrange on sides in spout.
	2	¾ Cup plus	Very nicely cut.
KITCHENAID (Disc)			
Chop			Doesn't chop.
Grate			Not practical.
Slice	10	1 Cup	Cut around top and pull out seeds, then carefully slice away any white pith without cutting pepper; slices are U-shaped, not perfect rings.

	seconds	yield	notes
KITCHENAID			
(Rotor)			
Chop			Doesn't chop; use grater instead.
Grate			Seed and cut in quarters.
	3	½ Cup	Coarsely grated: results are similar to chopping but some skin remains behind on blade.
	2	¼ Cup	Finely grated: results are more like minced; again, some skin remains on blade.
Slice	2	½ Cup	Seed and cut in quarters: Slices are ragged; some skin comes through; better results with disc blade.
STARMIX			Seed and cut in 1-inch pieces: place in blender. After processing, pick out larger pieces and redo.
Chop			
		¾ Cup	Manual: Turn on and off 6 times: results are adequate.
		½ Cup	Drop through spout with machine on: very finely chopped, some liquid.
Grate			Use manual chop or grater: see above.
Slice			Seed and cut in quarters; arrange cut side down against blade.
	4	⅔ Cup	Slices are fragmented; recommended only when there's no need for perfect slices and some quantity need be processed.

Herbs (⅓ Cup tightly packed, with tough stems removed)

	seconds	yield	notes
CUISINART			
Chop	7–15	⅓ Cup	Will finely chop or mince most fresh herbs in fair-sized amounts; however, chives must be chopped by hand, since these tend to sliver unless processed with other ingredients.
KITCHENAID			
(Disc)			Not practical.
KITCHENAID			
(Rotor)			Not practical.
STARMIX			
Chop		⅓ Cup	Will finely and nicely chop most herbs; however, chives must be chopped by hand unless processed with other ingredients.
(Blender)			

	seconds	yield	notes

Leeks (1 Medium)

CUISINART

Split, wash and cut in ½-inch pieces. These tend to sliver, as do chives and scallions.

	seconds	yield	notes
Chop			Not really practical except for fine chopping.
Slice	2	⅓ Cup plus	Not perfect slices, but usable for soups, etc; white part slices best; wash after slicing.

KITCHENAID (Disc)

	seconds	yield	notes
Chop			Doesn't chop.
Slice			Not really practical.

KITCHENAID (Rotor)

	seconds	yield	notes
Chop			Doesn't chop.
Slice	4	¼ Cup	Cut in half (not lengthwise). Not really practical unless you're slicing white part only; wash after slicing.

STARMIX

Split to clean; cut in 1-inch pieces.

	seconds	yield	notes
Chop			Manual chop: place in blender, turn on and off, scraping down each time, twice for coarse and three times for minced (does not coarse-chop well).
Slice			Will slice white part only, but results are very thin slices; slice tops by hand and wash after slicing.

Lemons and Limes (Small)

CUISINART

Trim top, bottom and sides to fit spout— the master-slicer does it again.

	seconds	yield	notes
Slice	2	25 thin slices	Thinly sliced: thin and beautiful.
	1½		Thickly sliced: for perfect slices, use small fruit.

KITCHENAID (Disc)

	seconds	yield	notes
Slice			Not practical.

KITCHENAID (Rotor)

	seconds	yield	notes
Slice			Not practical.

STARMIX

	seconds	yield	notes
Slice			Not practical.

	seconds	yield	notes

Lettuce (¼ Firm head, drain well)

	seconds	yield	notes
CUISINART			Cut to fit spout; drain well.
Slice	2	1¼ Cup	Thin slices or shreds.

	seconds	yield	notes
KITCHENAID (Disc)			Not really recommended unless you are cooking for a crowd.
Grate	2	1½ Cups	Coarse grater: shreds. Fine grater: not practical.
Slice	4	1½ Cups	Adjust blade to fairly wide slice; performs quite well.

	seconds	yield	notes
KITCHENAID (Rotor)			Performs well in all instances.
Grate	2	1¼ Cups	Coarse grater: finely chopped.
	2	¾ Cup	Fine grater: minces.
Slice	3	1½ Cups	Coarsely shredded.
	3	1½ Cups	Finely shredded.

	seconds	yield	notes
STARMIX			
Grate	3	1½ Cups	Cut the ¼ head in half and place cut edges against blade. Coarse grater: finely chops. Fine grater: not practical.
Slice	3	1½ Cups	Cut to fit; drain well. Coarsely sliced: finely shredded with some big pieces. Fine slicing not practical.

Mushrooms (3 Large)

	seconds	yield	notes
CUISINART			Arrange in spout on sides.
Grate	2	1 Cup	Coarse grater: good job.
	3		Fine grater: beautiful thin shreds.
Slice			Arrange neatly in spout on sides.
	3	¾ Cup	Coarsely sliced: beautiful when mushrooms stay in place, otherwise diagonal slices.
	4	½ Cup	Finely sliced: same as above.

	seconds	yield	notes
KITCHENAID (Disc) Grate	4	½ Cup	Coarse grater: roughly the equivalent of coarsely chopped.
	6	⅓ Cup	Fine grater: thin threads; beautiful, but I'm not sure for what use.
Slice	10	½ Cup	Push down gently so as not to break mushrooms.

	seconds	yield	notes
KITCHENAID			
(Rotor)			
Grate	2	½ Cup	Coarsely grated.
	3	½ Cup	Finely grated.
			Both work quite well.
Slice			Remove stems.
	3	½ Cup	Coarsely sliced: performs well.
	3	½ Cup	Thinly sliced: works well, too; stack sides toward blade for best results; do two large at one time.
STARMIX			Cut in half and place cut side down.
Grate	2	½ Cup	Coarse grater: equal to coarsely chopped.
	6	½ Cup	Fine grater: nice thin shreds.
Slice			Cut stems flush with caps; push down lightly.
	2	¾ Cup	Coarsely sliced: quite nice slices.
	4	½ Cup	Thinly sliced: very thin, fragmented slices; coarse slicing recommended.

Nuts (Hard nuts, such as almonds. Soft nuts, such as pecans or walnuts) ½ Cup

	seconds	yield	notes
CUISINART			*Hard nuts*
Chop			Coarsely chopped: impossible to do; result is fine crumbs and large pieces.
	8	⅔ Cup	Finely chopped: nicely done.
			Soft nuts
	4	½ Cup	Coarsely chopped: nicely done (1 or 2 large pieces left unchopped).
	7	½ Cup	Finely chopped: nicely done.
	On/off 11 times		Manual: on and off 11 times.
		½ Cup	Coarsely chopped: same results as when whirled steadily—see above.
Grate			*Hard nuts*
	2	½ Cup	Coarsely grated.
	5	⅔ Cup	Finely grated. Performs efficiently when either coarsely or finely grating, but a few pieces do get caught in spout.
			Soft nuts
	1	½ Cup	Coarsely grated: coarse texture, perfect.
	2	½ Cup	Finely grated: also perfectly processed. Some pieces catch in spout in either grater.

	seconds	yield	notes
KITCHENAID			
(Disc)			
Chop			Doesn't chop.
Grate			*Hard nuts*
	8	½ Cup	Very fine and powdery; a few whole nuts may slip by, but easier to grate by machine than by hand.
			Soft Nuts
			Coarse grater: not practical.
	8	½ Cup	Fine grater: does grate finely but some large pieces slip through.
KITCHENAID			
(Rotor)			
Chop			Doesn't chop.
Grate			*Hard nuts*
	5	⅔ Cup	Coarsely grated.
	3	⅔ Cup	Finely grated: some large pieces come through on both kinds of grating, but in general both do a very good job.
			Soft nuts
	2	½ Cup	Coarsely grated.
	3	½ Cup	Finely grated. Both perform well.
STARMIX			
Chop			*Hard nuts*: in blender.
	8	⅔ Cup	Fine chopping only; not possible to do coarse chopping well.
			Soft nuts: in blender.
	4	½ Cup	Fine chopping only; not possible to do coarse chopping well.
Grate			*Hard nuts*:
	8	⅔ Cup	In Nut Grater (at Speed II); finely grated, almost powder.
	4	½ Cup	Coarsely grated (at Speed II): satisfactory.
			Soft nuts:
	3	½ Cup	Coarsely grated (at Speed I): coarsely chopped, very satisfactory.
	9	½ Cup	Finely grated (at Speed I); very satisfactory.
	6	½ Cup	In Nut grater: reduces nuts to powder.

	seconds	yield	notes
Olives			
CUISINART			
Chop			*10 Extra-large stuffed green olives*
	1	½ Cup	Coarsely chopped: on/off twice, stop once to scrape down.
	2	½ Cup	Finely chopped: stop twice to scrape down.
	3	½ Cup	Minced: stop 3 times to scrape down. Beautifully done in all cases.
			15 large, pitted black olives
	1	¼ Cup	Coarsely chopped: beautifully done.
	2	¼ Cup	Finely chopped: beautifully done.
Slice			Carefully arrange 4 extra-large green olives with pimento against blades.
	1	¼ Cup	Some pimento is dislodged, but slices are nice both with the coarse and the fine blades; the coarse blade performs better. Pitted black olives tend to break when sliced. Not really practical.
KITCHENAID (Disc)			*10 Extra-large stuffed green olives*
Chop			Doesn't chop.
Grate			Not practical.
Slice			Carefully arrange pimento against blade.
	2	¼ Cup	Coarse and fine slice: fairly nice job; more pimento stays in place than in the Cuisinart machine, but slices are more ragged. Not really practical.
			15 Large, pitted black olives Same results as green.
KITCHENAID (Rotor)			
Chop			Doesn't chop.
Grate			*10 Extra-large stuffed green olives*
	2	⅔ Cup	Coarsely grated: coarsely chopped.
	3	½ Cup	Finely grated: minced.
			15 Large, pitted black olives Same results as green.
Slice			*10 Extra-large stuffed green olives*
	2	½ Cup	Coarsely sliced: will slice, but slices are a bit ragged; not really practical because olives should look attractive.
			15 Large, pitted black olives Same results as green.

	seconds	yield	notes
STARMIX			
Chop			*10 Extra-large stuffed green olives*
		½ Cup	Coarse chopping: turn on and off twice; stop once to scrape down sides; some big pieces.
		⅔ Cup	Fine chopping: turn on and off 6 times; stop each time to push down; results adequate.
			15 Large, pitted black olives Same results as green.
Slice			Fractured slices; not practical.

Onions (1 Medium, 3–4 oz., peeled and with 1 slice cut from both top and bottom. Drain if necessary after processing.)

	seconds	yield	notes
CUISINART			Cut in quarters.
Chop	2	⅓ Cup plus	Coarsely chopped.
	3	½ Cup	Finely chopped: stop once to scrape down.
	4	½ Cup	Minced: stop once to scrape down.
			Manual chopping (turning on and off). Produces same results as above.
	On and off		
	5 times	⅓ Cup plus	Coarsely chopped.
	7 times	½ Cup	Finely chopped.
	10 times	½ Cup	Minced.
Grate			Cut in quarters; arrange cut side down in spout.
	1	½ Cup	Coarsely grated; some pieces catch in spout, but perfect grating.
	5	⅓ Cup	Finely grated: too fine and mushy; coarse blade gives better results.
Slice			Trim ends and sides to fit or cut in quarters.
	1½	½ Cup plus	Does good job, but doesn't slice in round rings.
KITCHENAID			
(Disc)			
Chop			Doesn't chop.
Grate			Not practical; mostly juice.
Slice	5	1 Cup	Works very well; rings are whole, but some do break.

	seconds	yield	notes
KITCHENAID			
(Rotor)			
Chop			Doesn't chop.
Grate	6	¼ Cup	Coarsely grated: some pieces stick; not easy to grate; disc attachment recommended.
	3	¼ Cup	Finely grated: much sticks on blade; not really practical.
Slice	3		Thin, fractured slices; not really practical because curve of slicer doesn't lend itself to slicing onions.
STARMIX			
Chop	4		In blender: (at Speed I) cut in quarters; uneven pieces, some large, some small.
			Drop in blender with motor running (at Speed II); not practical; almost puréed.
Grate	2	½ Cup	Coarsely grated: shoestring pieces.
			Fine grating not practical.
Slice	2	½ Cup	Coarsely sliced: works better with two onions.
			Finely sliced: doesn't work well; outside layers get caught.

Pickles (2 Medium, 2 oz. each)

	seconds	yield	notes
CUISINART			
Chop			Cut in 1-inch pieces.
	2	½ Cup	Coarsely chopped.
	2½	½ Cup	Finely chopped.
	3	½ Cup	Minced: performs perfectly at each stage.
Slice			Cut off ends; do two at a time to fill spout; place upright.
	1½	¾ Cup	Perfect slices for hamburgers, etc.
KITCHENAID			
(Disc)			
Chop			Doesn't chop.
Grate	2	½ Cup	Coarse grater: shoestring ribbons; nicely done; interesting shape.
	5	⅓ Cup	Fine grater: fine threads of pickle but large piece of skin remained in disc; not really practical.
Slice	3	¾ Cup	Very nicely done.

	seconds	yield	notes
KITCHENAID			
(Rotor)			
Chop			Doesn't chop; use grater.
Grate			Cut in 1-inch pieces.
	2	½ Cup	Coarsely grated: shoestring shreds.
	2	½ Cup	Finely grated: could be used for finely chopped.
Slice			Cut in half; put cut side against blade.
	1½	1 Cup	Coarsely sliced; fairly nice slices; definitely practical.
	1½	1 Cup	Finely sliced: usable slices.
STARMIX			
Chop			Cut in 1-inch pieces: place in blender; turn machine quickly on and off.
	On and off twice	½ Cup	Coarsely chopped: stop, stir and scrape down once.
	On and off 3 times	½ Cup	Finely chopped: stop, stir and scrape down once.
Slice			Put through small hole in container top.
	3	½ Cup	Coarsely sliced: very good job.
	5	⅓ Cup	Thinly sliced; some ragged slices, but most are fine.

Potatoes (1 Medium, 4 oz., peeled. Drop processed vegetable in cold water to prevent darkening. Drain.)

	seconds	yield	notes
CUISINART			
Chop			Cut in quarters.
	2	¾ Cup	Coarsely chopped: stop once to scrape down.
	4	¾ Cup	Finely chopped: stop once to scrape down.
Grate			Cut in quarters; arrange in spout; bounce plunger up and down lightly.
	3	1 Cup	Coarsely grated: beautiful.
	6	½ Cup	Finely grated: beautiful.
Slice			Slice off sides to fit spout or cut in quarters.
	1	½ Cup	Thinly sliced: beautiful.
French Fry Cutter			A perfect performer.

	seconds	yield	notes
KITCHENAID (Disc)			
Chop			Doesn't chop; use grater.
Grate	10	¾ Cup	Very good for potato pancakes; finely shredded.
Slice	5	¾ Cup	Slices beautifully; advantage is you can put whole vegetable in and adjust slices to thickness desired.
KITCHENAID (Rotor)			
Chop			Doesn't chop; use grater.
Grate	5	¾ Cup	Coarsely grated: very nice shoestring pieces.
	9	¾ Cup	Finely grated: very nicely done.
Slice	2	¾ Cup	Coarse slicing: beautiful, whole slices; the Cuisinart machine slices more cleanly, but these are perfectly adequate.
STARMIX			
Chop			In blender: cut in quarters or 1-inch pieces.
	3	1 Cup	Coarsely chopped (at Speed I).
	1½	1 Cup	Finely chopped (at Speed II).
Grate			Cut in half.
	2½	1 Cup	Coarsely grated: shoestring fries.
	15	1 Cup	Finely grated: for potato pancakes; press down hard on plunger.
Slice	3	¾ Cup	Coarsely sliced: very nice.
	5	¾ Cup	Finely sliced: paper-thin.
French Fry Cutter			
	2	1½ Cups	Cutter is fast and efficient, better than cutting by hand, but pieces frequently get caught in blades at end of slicing.

Rutabagas (Yellow turnips; ¼ Small, 5 oz., peeled)

	seconds	yield	notes
CUISINART			
Grate			Cut in quarters; cut side down; bounce plunger up and down lightly.
	3	1¼ Cups	Coarsely grated: beautiful.
	6	1 Cup	Finely grated: beautiful, fine shreds.

	seconds	yield	notes
Slice			Cut thin slice from bottom and top; then cut to fit spout.
	1½	1 Cup	Both coarse and fine blades work well.

KITCHENAID (Disc)	seconds	yield	notes
Grate	50	1⅓ Cups	Grates very nicely; apply very firm pressure.
Slice	14 slow 7 fast		Slices beautifully at either speed; this machine makes large slices, exactly the thickness you prefer; a definite advantage.

KITCHENAID (Rotor)	seconds	yield	notes
Grate	3	1⅓ Cups	Coarsely grated: nice, shoestring pieces.
	3	1⅓ Cups	Finely grated: beautiful, thin threads.
Slice	2	¾ Cup	Coarse slicing: nicely done.
	3	¾ Cup	Fine slicing: nicely cut concave slices that will flatten out when cooked.

STARMIX	seconds	yield	notes
Grate	4	1⅓ Cups	Coarsely grated: nicely cut, shoestring pieces.
	30	¾ Cup	Finely grated: beautiful fine threads.
Slice	5	1 Cup plus	Coarse slicing: good job.
	9	¾ Cup	Fine slicing: good job.

Scallions* (5 Medium, with 3 inches green top)

CUISINART	seconds	yield	notes
Chop			Cut in ½ inch pieces.
	2	½ Cup	Coarsely chopped: stop twice to scrape down.
	3	⅓ Cup	Finely chopped: stop three times to scrape down.
	5	⅓ Cup	Minced: stop once to scrape down.
			All result in slightly elongated pieces.

KITCHENAID (Disc)			
			Doesn't chop.

KITCHENAID (Rotor)			
			Doesn't chop.

* Note: Scallions do not chop really well in any machine unless processed with other ingredients.

	seconds	yield	notes
STARMIX			Cut in ½-inch pieces; put in blender.
Chop	3	⅓ Cup	Turn on and off four times; results are mostly mush and large pieces; not really practical.

Shallots (5 Whole, peeled)

	seconds	yield	notes
CUISINART			
Chop	2	¼ Cup	Coarsely chopped.
	3	¼ Cup	Finely chopped: stop once to scrape down.
	4	¼ Cup	Minced: stop once to scrape down. Perfect job for all.

KITCHENAID (Disc)			Doesn't chop.

KITCHENAID (Rotor)			Doesn't chop.

STARMIX Chop			Put in blender.
	Turn on and off 3 times	3 Tablespoons	Coarsely chopped: stop twice to scrape down; works well.

Strawberries (6 Medium, hulled firm berries)

	seconds	yield	notes
CUISINART			Arrange carefully with sides down against blade, press gently with plunger.
Slice	1	⅔ Cup	Coarse slicing: perfect slices.
	1	⅔ Cup	Thin slicing: perfect slices. Using firm berries, it does a perfect job with both blades.

KITCHENAID (Disc) Slice	3	⅔ Cup	Slices adequately on disc slicer; performs as well as Starmix, but not as well as the Cuisinart machine.

KITCHENAID (Rotor)	2	⅔ Cup	Not recommended.
Slice			Will slice on coarse, but disc does a better job; half the slices are mutilated.

	seconds	yield	notes
STARMIX Slice	2	⅔ Cup	Good, but not as good as the Cuisinart machine; use coarse slicer; fine slicer not practical.

Summer Squash (Yellow Squash, Zucchini; 1 Medium, 5 oz.)

	seconds	yield	notes
CUISINART			
Chop			Cut in 1-inch pieces.
	3	1¼ Cups	Finely chopped: beautiful job.
Grate			Cut to fit spout; lay on side.
	2	1 Cup	Coarsely grated: beautiful.
	3	1 Cup	Finely grated: beautiful.
Slice	3	1 Cup	Cut to fit spout; lay on side (works well with cut end down but better if arranged horizontally); perfect slices.
KITCHENAID **(Disc)**			
Chop			Doesn't chop.
Grate			Apply firm pressure.
	24	¾ Cup	Nice thin shreds, for squash pancakes, etc.
Slice			Slice off ends, put through whole; perfect slices, not as beautiful as the Cuisinart machine but better than Starmix.
	12	1⅓ Cups	
KITCHENAID **(Rotor)**			
Chop			Doesn't chop.
Grate	4	1⅓ Cups	Coarsely grated: shoestring pieces, 1 inch long; beautiful.
	5	1⅓ Cups	Finely grated: some skin may fail to grate, but results are beautiful threads of squash; peeling recommended.
Slice	3	1¾ Cups	Coarse slicer.
	4	1¾ Cups	Fine slicer. Both slice beautifully; better than disc slicer; slightly concave, perfect pieces either way.
STARMIX			
Chop			Split lengthwise; cut in ½-inch pieces.
	Turn on and off twice	¾ Cup	Coarsely chopped: stop once to push pieces down.
	Turn on and off four times	¾ Cup	Finely chopped: stop once to push pieces down.

	seconds	yield	notes
Grate			Peeling recommended, since skin often catches in blade.
	6	1½ Cups	Coarsely grated: nice shoestring pieces.
	30	⅔ Cup	Finely grated: interesting, thin threads; perfect for zucchini pancakes.
Slice			Cut and fit two pieces at a time; one piece alone causes diagonal slicing.
	5	1¼ Cups	Coarse slicing: slices are twice the thickness of those sliced on the Cuisinart machine; are fine, but occasionally ragged

Sweet Potatoes (1 Medium, 6½ oz., peeled)
CUISINART

	seconds	yield	notes
Grate			Cut to fit spout.
	4	1 Cup	Coarse grater.
	7	¾ Cup	Fine grater.
Slice			Cut slice from bottom to fit spout.
	2½	1½ Cups	Coarse slicing.
	1½	1½ Cups	Fine slicing.
			Small slices, but perfect on both.

KITCHENAID (Disc)

	seconds	yield	notes
Grate	5	1½ Cups	Coarse grater: shoestring shreds.
	8	1¼ Cups	Fine grater: beautiful threads; delicious fried in butter with a squeeze of lime juice.
Slice			Cut off ends.
	7	1¼ Cups	Slices nicely, but not as beautifully as the Cuisinart machine.

KITCHENAID (Rotor)

	seconds	yield	notes
Grate	9	1½ Cups	Coarsely grated: nice shoestring pieces.
	4	1¼ Cups	Finely grated: nice threads.
Slice	3	1¼ Cups	Coarse slicing: good job; not as clean-cut as the Cuisinart machine.
	3	1¼ Cups	Fine slicing: good job.

STARMIX

	seconds	yield	notes
Grate			Cut in half lengthwise; fit in machine.
	6	1½ Cups	Coarsely grated: shoestring strips.
	12	1 Cup	Finely grated: does beautiful job.
Slice	8	1½ Cups	Coarse slicing: trim to fit.
	7	1 Cup	Thin slicing.
			Slices occasionally get caught but otherwise both blades slice very well.

	seconds	yield	notes

Tomato (1 Medium, firm, peeled)

It's best to hand-slice your beautiful tomatoes for salads, sandwiches, etc. Your machine will come in handy, though, when you are preparing soups, sauces, purées or relishes.

CUISINART

	seconds	yield	notes
Chop	5	⅔ Cup	Seed, cut in quarters.
			Turn motor on and off 10 times; coarsely chopped with juice; not recommended except as mentioned above.

KITCHENAID
(Disc)

			Not practical.

KITCHENAID
(Rotor)

			Not practical.

STARMIX

	seconds	yield	notes
	On and off quickly	⅔ Cup pulp	Seed, cut in quarters, put in blender. Mostly mush, not really practical except as mentioned above.

Turnips (3 Small, 2 oz. each, peeled)

CUISINART

	seconds	yield	notes
			Cut in quarters.
Chop	5	1 Cup	Coarsely chopped.
	7	1 Cup	Finely chopped.
	10	1 Cup	Minced: performs well for all. Pick out any large pieces and reprocess.
Grate			Cut in quarters; lay cut side down with small end on top.
	1½	1¼ Cups	Coarsely grated: beautiful.
	9	1¼ Cups	Finely grated: bounce plunger up and down; grates beautifully.
Slice			Trim to fit spout.
	4	1½ Cups	Coarse slicing: performs perfectly for both.
	6	1¼ Cups	Fine slicing: very thin slices.

KITCHENAID
(Disc)

	seconds	yield	notes
Chop			Doesn't chop.
Grate			
	5	1¼ Cups	Coarse grating: performs perfectly.
	10	1 Cup	Fine grating: very thin shreds, do more than one turnip at a time.
Slice	4	1 Cup	Slices very well.

	seconds	yield	notes
KITCHENAID			
(Rotor)			
Chop			Doesn't chop.
Grate			Put in whole.
	3	2 Cups	Coarsely grated: perfect job, shoestring pieces.
	2	1½ Cups	Finely grated: beautiful job, perfect threads.
Slice			Put in whole.
	1½	1⅓ Cups	Coarse slicing: quite nice, concave slices.
	2	1⅓ Cups	Fine slicing: concave, slightly ragged.
STARMIX			Cut in quarters, put in blender.
Chop	1½	1 Cup	Coarsely chopped (at Speed II).
	2½	1 Cup	Finely chopped (at Speed II); Speed I not practical.
Grate	3	1⅓ Cups	Coarsely grated: heavy, shoestring pieces; ragged.
	14	1¼ Cups	Finely grated: very nice threads, good job, but press down hard.
Slice	6	1⅓ Cups	Coarse slicing: beautiful slices.
	2	1 Cup	Fine slicing: beautiful thin slices.

Watercress (¼ Cup, tightly packed, with all stems removed)

	seconds	yield	notes
CUISINART			
Chop	3	¼ Cup	Nicely done.
KITCHENAID			
(Disc)			Not practical unless done with other ingredients.
KITCHENAID			
(Rotor)			
Grate	4	2 Tablespoons	Will finely chop, but not really practical unless done with other ingredients; a lot is lost on blade.
STARMIX			
	Turn on and off	¼ Cup	Turn motor on and off twice; stop once to stir pieces up and push down against blade; turn on and off, push down, then turn on and off once more; results are a little watery but can be used.

	seconds	yield	notes

Winter Squash (Acorn, Butternut, Hubbard; ½ of 18 oz. squash, peeled)

CUISINART

	seconds	yield	notes
Chop	6	⅔ Cup	Coarsely chopped: good job.
	10	⅔ Cup	Finely chopped: good job.
			Bounce plunger up and down.
Grate	16	1⅔ Cup	Coarse grater: beautiful job.
	32	1 Cup	Fine grater: beautiful thin threads.
Slice	3	1⅓ Cup	Coarse slicing: good job.
	4	1⅓ Cup	Fine slicing: beautiful thin slices.

KITCHENAID (Disc)

	seconds	yield	notes
Chop			Doesn't chop.
Grate	12	1⅓ Cup	Coarse grater: shoestring shreds about 1 inch long.
	28	1 Cup	Fine grater: fine threads.
Slice	12	2 Cups	Good job.

KITCHENAID (Rotor)

	seconds	yield	notes
Chop			Doesn't chop.
Grate			Cut in pieces to fit.
	8	1¼ Cup	Coarsely grated: shoestring size; works perfectly.
	3	⅔ Cup	Finely grated: beautiful shreds; very fine.
Slice			Cut in pieces to fit.
	2	1 Cup	Thick slicing: good job.
	3	1 Cup	Thin slicing: good job.

STARMIX

	seconds	yield	notes
			Cut in 1-inch pieces, put in blender a handful at a time.
Chop	1½	1 Cup	Coarsely chopped (at Speed II). Pick out large pieces and process separately.
	2½	1 Cup	Finely chopped (at Speed II). Speed I not practical.
Grate	12	1¼ Cups	Coarse grater: interesting shoestring curls.
	56	⅔ Cup	Fine grater: press down hard; does a good job; makes fine threads.
Slice	8	1¼ Cups	Coarsely sliced: very nicely done.
	20	⅔ Cup	Finely sliced: beautiful thin slices.

CHEESE & MEATS

	seconds	yield	notes

Cheese* (Hard, such as Parmesan; soft, such as Cheddar and Swiss; 1½ oz. piece)

CUISINART

	seconds	yield	notes
Chop			*Hard cheese*: cut in ½-inch pieces.
	15	¼ Cup	Coarsely chopped.
	23	¼ Cup	Finely chopped: processes beautifully in both cases.
			Soft cheese: cut in 1-inch pieces.
	5	⅓ Cup	Coarsely chopped: grating is better.
Grate			*Hard cheese*: doesn't work; chop instead.
	10–14	⅓ Cup	*Soft cheese*: nicely grated, very thin.
Slice			*Soft cheese*: cut to fit spout.
	2	½ Cup	Thin slicing: thin, not perfect slices.
	2	½ Cup	Thick slicing: perfect slices ⅛ inch thick.

KITCHENAID (Disc)

	seconds	yield	notes
Chop			Doesn't chop.
Grate			Use fine disc at Speed 2, then Speed 6. *Hard cheese*
	8	⅓ Cup	Makes thin shreds (½ inch long); very nice.
			Soft cheese
	7	½ Cup plus	Makes fine shreds (½ to 1 inch long); very nice.
Slice			Performs well.

KITCHENAID (Rotor)

	seconds	yield	notes
Chop			Doesn't chop.
Grate			*Hard cheese*: cut in small pieces, put in hopper.
	4½		Coarsely grated: large pieces; fine grating is better.
	4	⅓ Cup plus	Finely grated: fine threads; can be crumbled and used.
			Soft cheese
	4	½ Cup plus	Coarsely grated: shoestring pieces; good for cooked dishes.

* Note: Cheese generally processes best when it is cold.

	seconds	yield	notes
	4	⅓ Cup plus	Finely grated: nice threads; not exactly grated but could be used in dishes calling for grated cheese.
Slice			*Soft cheese*
	1½	⅓ Cup plus	Thick slicing: very nice.
	3	⅓ Cup plus	Thin slicing: nice slices, slightly concave.

STARMIX

	seconds	yield	notes
			Hard cheese: cut in small pieces; works well.
			Soft cheese: cut in pieces and coarsely chop.
Chop	Turn on and off twice	⅓ Cup	Cannot finely chop; merely pulverizes, makes a paste.
Grate			*Hard cheese*: use Nut Grater at Speed II.
	20	¼ Cup	Very finely grated.
			Soft cheese
	3	⅓ Cup	Coarsely grated (at Speed II): good for pizza.
	15	⅓ Cup	Finely grated (at Speed II): very nice; put pieces that are left over through with next large piece; press down hard.
Slice			*Soft cheese*
	3	⅓ Cup	Thin slicing: usable, slightly broken pieces.
	2	⅓ Cup plus	Thick slicing: does slice, but some crumbling results; adequate, but not great.

NOTE: Mozzarella cheese, which has a consistency different from the cheeses listed above, can also be sliced on each machine, although the results on any of the machines are only fair.

Uncooked Meat (8 oz. Chuck)

CUISINART

	seconds	yield	notes
Chop			Cut away gristle between fat and meat (see instructions for making hamburger, page 195), as well as all separate streaks of gristle.
			Cut in 1-inch cubes; chop half the amount at one time.
	7	1 Cup	Coarsely chopped: some large pieces left.
	9	1 Cup	Finely chopped: very well.

	seconds	yield	notes
Slice			Meat should be partially frozen. Cut away all gristle; cut in pieces 1 inch wide; use thick slicing blade.
	2	¾ Cup	Machine may vibrate a little but slices are good for Sukiyaki.

NOTE: The Cuisinart machine will chop uncooked bacon, but not perfectly; turn on and off 3 times to chop coarsely, on and off 4 times to chop finely; 4 slices will make ⅔ cup coarsely chopped bacon, ½ cup finely chopped; bacon should be *cold*.

	seconds	yield	notes
KITCHENAID (Disc) Chop			Doesn't chop.

	seconds	yield	notes
KITCHENAID (Rotor) Chop			Doesn't chop.

	seconds	yield	notes
STARMIX Chop			Cut away all gristle; leave small amount of fat; cut in 1-inch cubes.
	8	¾ Cup	Chopping in blender not practical; turning motor on and dropping pieces in will work, but not as well as the Cuisinart machine; has separate grinder attachment.

Cooked Meat (Beef, Lamb, Veal, Chicken, Turkey, Ham)

	seconds	yield	notes
CUISINART Chop			Cut in 1-inch pieces; cut away any gristle.
	5	1 Cup	Coarsely chopped.
	7	1 Cup	Finely chopped.
	9	1 Cup	Minced.
			Performs all of the above tasks perfectly.

	seconds	yield	notes
STARMIX Chop			Cut in 1-inch pieces; cut away all gristle.
		1 Cup	For best results, drop in blender while motor is running, a few pieces at a time; finely chopped or minced meats are good for salad or croquettes.

Grating and slicing cooked meats not practical in all cases.

	seconds	yield	notes

Making Bread Crumbs (1 cup stale bread, broken in 1-inch pieces; for deep frying, remove crusts to insure even browning of fried foods)

	seconds	yield	notes
CUISINART			
Chop	17	¼ Cup	Fine bread crumbs; turning machine quickly on and off for 18 seconds gives same results as steady whirling; Starmix is better for making bread crumbs, however.
KITCHENAID			
(Disc)			
Chop			Doesn't chop.
Grate			Performs well.
KITCHENAID			
(Rotor)			
Chop			Doesn't chop.
Grate			*Hard Italian bread*
	3	½ Cup	Coarsely grated.
	3	⅓ Cup	Finely grated: very good job.
			Hard brown bread
	7	⅓ Cup	Finely grated: very good job.
			Soft Italian bread: cut into cubes.
	5	⅔ Cup	Coarsely grated: press down; not practical.
STARMIX			
Chop			For fine bread crumbs:
	8	¼ Cup	Finely chopped (at Speed II).
	6	¼ Cup	Finely chopped (turn on and off quickly at Speed II).
Grate	8	¼ Cup	Finely grated (at Speed II): turn on machine and drop through top.
			All methods are equally efficient.

Note on Using Uncooked Egg Whites

Because uncooked egg whites have been found to be a source of salmonella infection, I prefer not to use them or recommend their use. However, if you do decide to do otherwise, be sure that the eggshells are perfectly clean before you crack and separate whites from yolks, and keep any dish that includes these well chilled.

Note on Measuring Herbs

If fresh herbs are not available when called for in any recipe, you may substitute 1 teaspoon dried for each tablespoon of fresh.

How to Whip Egg Whites

Egg whites whip up in a matter of seconds in your KitchenAid or Starmix food processor. As a preliminary procedure, be sure that your bowl and beaters are sparkling clean and thoroughly dry before beginning; any greasy residue will hamper the whipping process.

To whip egg whites in the KitchenAid, turn the motor gradually to Speed 8 and whip until the desired stage is reached. To use the Starmix, allow the twin stirring whisks to operate as long as necessary at Speed II. Until you become more familiar with your machine, it's a good idea to stop once or twice during the process to observe the progress of your egg whites.

Whipping Stages

The mixture is at the *frothy stage* when large air bubbles appear on the surface. When the bubbles are reduced in size and slight whip marks appear, the whites have *begun to hold their shape.*

The *soft peak* stage is reached when the mixture stands in peaks which recede as soon as they are formed.

As soon as the whites form pointed but soft peaks, *almost stiff* is the description that best fits them.

The stage known as *stiff but not dry* takes the whites one step further. Here the peaks are stiff and sharply pointed, but their surfaces glisten and their color is uniformly white.

The *stiff and dry* stage is reached when the peaks resemble soapsuds, take on a dull sheen, and break apart in chunks when lifted with a fork.

Add cream of tartar or any flavoring to egg whites when they reach the frothy stage. When making meringues, add sugar as soon as the whites form soft peaks (use Speed 4 with your KitchenAid machine).

Whipping Cream

Best for whipping is very cold cream that's at least one day old. Chill the bowl, too, before you start. If your recipe calls for folding the whipped cream into other ingredients, beat it only until it forms soft peaks. When toppings or fillings are needed, whip the cream to a stiff consistency that holds its shape well. Should your recipe call for a sweetened or flavored cream, fold in the sugar or flavoring as soon as the cream has been whipped to the desired consistency.

Follow the general instructions for whipping cream that come with your machine, taking care not to overbeat, since the various whipped-cream stages are separated only by seconds.

How to Deep-Fry

Successful deep-frying requires that the cooking fat reach a sufficiently high temperature before any food is actually added. Uncooked foods will deep-fry best when the fat is at 370 degrees F.; precooked foods require a temperature of 390 degrees F.

Deep-frying is easy with an electric deep fryer or frying pan with its built-in thermostat, but if you lack either of these conveniences, try testing cooking temperatures this easy way. Simply drop a small cube of bread into the hot fat: at 370 degrees F., the bread will brown in 60 seconds; at 390 degrees F., you'll have a nicely toasted cube in 40 seconds.

HORS D'OEUVRES, DIPS, & CANAPÉS

HORS D'OEUVRES

HOT FILLED HORS D'OEUVRES

RISSOLES · FRIED PASTRIES

Roll out dough for Pie Pastry (see page 357) and cut into small circles with a 2½-inch cutter. Place spoonfuls of any of the fillings for croquettes (see pages 180–182) or crêpes (see pages 147–148) or one of the vegetable purées (see pages 217–223) on one half of each circle; then fold the circle in half and press the edges together with a fork. Fry in deep, hot vegetable oil until golden brown on both sides, turning once. Drain briefly on paper towels before serving hot.

PROFITEROLES · LITTLE CREAM PUFFS

Make small cream puffs, following the recipe for Pâte à Chou (see page 358). Press down centers of each puff when hot or cut a small piece from the top of each cooled one; then fill with any of the fillings suggested in the above recipe.

CRÊPES · LITTLE PANCAKES

Follow recipe and directions for making crêpes described on page 146, but use less batter and make smaller crêpes. Arrange small amounts of any of the suggested crêpe fillings (see pages 147–148) across the hot mini-pancakes, and then roll up and serve.

PETITES CROQUETTES · LITTLE CROQUETTES

Delicious hot hors d'oeuvres can be made from any of the croquette mixtures on pages 180 through 182. Simply shape chilled croquette mixture into balls the size of walnuts, roll in flour, and dip first in beaten egg and then in bread crumbs. Heat several inches of vegetable or salad oil in a deep heavy saucepan or electric deep fryer until it reaches a temperature of 370° F., and fry croquettes to a golden brown. Drain briefly on paper towels. Serve hot.

CHEESE PUFFS

(YIELD: ABOUT 2 DOZEN)

1/4   Cup milk
1   Tablespoon butter
1/2   Cup sifted all-purpose flour
1/4   Teaspoon salt
2   Eggs
1/3   Cup grated C K S Parmesan cheese
    Vegetable oil for frying

I   Place milk and butter in a heavy saucepan and bring to a boil. Immediately add the flour and salt and stir rapidly over very low heat for 1 minute or until mixture cleans sides of pan.

II   Remove from heat and place in container C or bowl K S. Start motor and beat in the eggs one at a time. When both eggs are well incorporated, add the cheese and whirl only long enough to blend well.

III Heat oil to a depth of one inch. Drop cheese mixture by half teaspoons into the hot oil, and then fry until golden brown. Drain puffs briefly on paper towels before serving hot.

CROÛTES AU FROMAGE · CHEESE TOASTS

(YIELD: ENOUGH TO SERVE 6)

    ¾ Cup hot thick Basic White Sauce (see page 271)
    ¼ Cup grated C K S Swiss cheese
    1 Egg
       Pinch each freshly ground black pepper and cayenne
    1 Loaf of French bread cut in ½-inch slices
    2 Tablespoons each butter and oil

I Whirl C K S the white sauce, cheese, egg, pepper and cayenne for 10 seconds, or until well blended.

II Refrigerate for 30 minutes.

III Meanwhile, fry the bread slices to a golden brown on both sides in the hot butter and oil. Cool.

IV Spread one side of each fried bread slice with the chilled cheese mixture. Place under broiler until puffed and lightly browned. Serve hot.

RAMEQUIN DE FROMAGE

(YIELD: ENOUGH TO SERVE 4 TO 6)

    ¾   pound piece of Swiss cheese
    3   eggs
    1½ cups milk
    ⅛   Teaspoon each salt and cayenne pepper
        Generous pinch ground nutmeg
    6   Slices white bread, with crusts removed

I   Slice C K S cheese. Preheat oven to 375 degrees F.

II   Mix C K S eggs, milk, and spices until well blended.

III   Cut bread slices in half and arrange in an overlapping ring in the bottom of a shallow, round earthenware casserole or glass pie plate, sandwiching some of the cheese in between the slices.

IV   Pour egg mixture over all and arrange remaining cheese slices on top.

V   Place casserole or pie plate in a larger pan. Pour hot water into the larger pan to a depth of one inch. Bake for 35 minutes or until top is lightly browned. Serve hot.

PARMESAN CHEESE TWISTS

(YIELD: ABOUT 2½ DOZEN TWISTS)

1   Recipe Parmesan Cheese Dough (see page 369)

I   Prepare dough as directed. Chill.

II   Preheat oven to 350 degrees F.

III   Roll out dough to ½-inch thickness on a lightly floured board. Cut in strips ½ inch wide and 5 inches long. Form the twists by pinching each strip in alternating directions along its length. Give each patterned strip a slight twist before setting on a well-greased baking sheet. Sprinkle the twists lightly with paprika and bake for 15 to 20 minutes or until nicely browned. Remove from baking sheet with a spatula and cool 2 minutes on a wire rack. Serve warm.

FROMAGE ÉMILIE

(YIELD: ABOUT 1¼ CUPS)

8 Ounces Cheddar cheese
1 8-Ounce package cream cheese
3 Tablespoons mint leaves, with all stems removed*
½ Teaspoon salt
2–3 Tablespoons brandy
¼ Cup each toasted almonds and pecans, chopped or grated C K S

I Place the cheeses, mint leaves, and salt in container C S or bowl K. Whirl for 5 or 6 seconds, stopping machine once or twice to scrape down sides; then turn on machine, pour in enough brandy to make a stiff mixture, and whirl for 2 or 3 seconds more or until ingredients are well mixed.

II Scrape cheese mixture onto wax paper and shape into ball. Chill well.

III Roll ball of cheese in nuts, then refrigerate until serving time. Surround with crackers before serving cold.

* KitchenAid users: hand-mince mint.

QUICHE

(YIELD: ENOUGH TO SERVE 6—ONE 10-INCH QUICHE)

½ Recipe Pie Pastry (see page 357)
1 4½-Ounce piece Swiss cheese
4 Eggs
1 Cup heavy cream
1 Cup milk
½ Teaspoon salt
 Dash each nutmeg and black or cayenne pepper

I Prepare and refrigerate pastry as directed.

II Preheat oven to 375 degrees F. Roll out the dough to ⅛ inch thick and about 12 inches wide. Arrange in a 10-inch quiche mold or pie plate; crimp the edges, taking care to attach the pastry firmly to the sides. Lightly prick the entire bottom surface with a fork and bake in the middle rack of the oven for 5 to 8 minutes.

III Meanwhile, grate C K S cheese. Combine with eggs, cream, milk, and seasonings in container C S or bowl K; mix only long enough to blend well.

IV Pour cheese-egg mixture into partially baked pastry shell. Place on the middle rack of the oven and bake at 375 degrees F. about 30 minutes or until the quiche is set and a knife inserted in the center comes out clean. Serve warm or at room temperature.

QUICHE LORRAINE

Arrange 5 strips of sliced country-cured bacon, cut in quarters and lightly browned over medium heat, over the bottom of the partially baked pastry shell and cover with the cheese-egg mixture. Dot with 1 or 2 tablespoons butter and bake as directed.

OTHER QUICHE VARIATIONS

The custard-like basic quiche filling adapts beautifully to a variety of ingredients. Try varying both taste and texture by including any of the following:

• Thinly sliced C K S onions, mushrooms, zucchini, etc., sautéed in butter until transparent.

• Fresh spinach leaves, cooked and drained, then finely chopped and puréed.

• ¼ Cup grated Parmesan cheese, either as an addition to basic ingredients or as a substitute for part of the grated Swiss.

• Chopped cooked ham, sautéed in butter until lightly browned.

HOMMOS • CHICKPEA PUREE

Serve hommos, this beautiful Near Eastern purée, with warm pita. Break off a piece of the bread, scoop up a bit of hommos, and enjoy.

(YIELD: ABOUT 3½ CUPS)

> 2 Cups dried chickpeas
> Tahini Dressing (see page 261)
> Salt, freshly ground black pepper, and cayenne pepper
> 3 Tablespoons fresh parsley leaves, with all tough stems removed
> Pita

I Cover chickpeas with water and allow to soak overnight. Drain well, add fresh water to cover, and cook for 2 to 3 hours or until peas are tender and the skins begin to flake off.

II Drain well, then purée in container C S or rub through a fine sieve K. Blend in dressing and spices to taste. Sprinkle with finely chopped C S parsley and serve warm with pita.

OLD STOVE PUB TARAMOSALATA

(YIELD: ENOUGH TO SERVE 10 TO 12)

> 5 Ounces Fantis Russian-style carp roe caviar
> 10 Slices dry homemade-type white bread, trimmed
> Juice of 2 lemons
> ½–1 Cup olive oil
> Greek olives
> Parsley sprigs
> Pita or Toast Points (see page 304)

I Soak all but 2 slices of the bread for 5 minutes in water to cover, and then squeeze out excess moisture.

II Add roe and moist bread to container or bowl. Process by turning machine on and off until roe and bread are well mixed.

IV Turn on machine and add oil and lemon juice alternately in a thin stream until enough oil has been added to produce a mixture the consistency of mayonnaise. Chill well and serve in a bowl, garnished with Greek olives and parsley, and surrounded with warm pita or buttered toast points.

MUSHROOM CAVIAR

(YIELD: ENOUGH TO SERVE 6)

2 *Small onions, peeled and cut in quarters*
3 *Tablespoons olive oil*
¾ *Pound fresh mushrooms, trimmed and cut in half*
1½ *Tablespoons each lemon juice and sour cream*
2 *Tablespoons minced fresh chives*
Salt and freshly ground black pepper
Watercress sprigs
Toast Points (see page 304)

I   Whirl onions in container C S for 4 seconds, stopping once to scrape down container sides, or finely chop K by hand. Heat oil and sauté onions until soft but not brown.

II   Meanwhile, whirl C S or finely chop by hand K mushrooms; add to pan with onions and cook, stirring frequently, until moisture has evaporated.

III   Remove from heat and blend in lemon juice, sour cream, chives, and salt and pepper to taste. Chill thoroughly. Garnish with watercress and serve on toast points.

CAROTTE RAPÉE · SHREDDED CARROT APPETIZER

(YIELD: ABOUT 2 CUPS)

4 *Medium carrots, scraped and cut to fit spout*
3 *Tablespoons olive oil*
1 *Tablespoon lemon juice*
Salt and freshly ground black pepper

I   Finely grate C K S carrots. Combine with oil and lemon juice, season to taste with salt and pepper, and toss lightly.

HAROSET

Now everyone can have their fill of Haroset at the Passover table. This recipe takes less than a minute to prepare in your Cuisinart processor.

(YIELD: ABOUT 3 CUPS)

2	Large McIntosh apples, peeled, cored, and cut in quarters
½	Cup raisins
¼	Cup each unblanched almonds and walnuts (or ½ cup of one or the other)
½	Cup pitted dates (optional) *
½	Teaspoon each ground ginger and cinnamon
4 to 6	Tablespoons sweet red wine

I   Place raisins and nuts in container. Whirl until finely chopped, stopping once to scrape down sides of container. Remove from container and set aside.

II   Coarsely chop C S apples.

III   Mix together fruits, nuts, spices, and as much of the wine as necessary to make a spreadable mixture. Ideally, the mixture should be refrigerated for at least 4 hours before serving.

* If using dates, chop by hand.

GEFILTE FISH

(YIELD: ENOUGH TO SERVE 6)

3	Pounds whole fish (pike and carp or pike and whitefish are best)
	Salt
4	Large onions, peeled
¼	Cup Matzo Meal (see page 303)
1	Teaspoon salt
	Freshly ground black pepper
2	Eggs
¼	Cup cold water
1	Large carrot, scraped
1	Large rib celery, with all strings removed

3   Sprigs parsley
Preserved Horseradish (see page 242) or prepared
bottled horseradish

I   Use a very sharp knife to cut the fish in 2-inch slices;
carefully cut away the bones and flesh, leaving the skin intact.
(If desired, you may cut away the flesh only, leaving the bones
attached to each section of skin.) Place the skin and bones in a
large bowl, sprinkle with salt, then cover and refrigerate for 20
minutes

II   Cut the flesh and two of the onions into 1-inch pieces;
finely chop C S or grind K S together, 2 or 3 handfuls at a time.

III   Return the fish and onion mixture to the container, add
the matzo meal, 1 teaspoon salt, pepper to taste, eggs and enough
cold water to bind the ingredients lightly together, and whirl C S
until smooth, or mix lightly by hand until thoroughly blended.
Moisten your hands with cold water and fill the reserved skin
sections with the fish mixture.

IV   Place the reserved bones in the bottom of a large
soup kettle or other large saucepan. Thickly slice C K S the
remaining onions, the carrot, and celery and add to the kettle
along with the parsley sprigs. Add cold water to cover, cover the
kettle and bring to a boil. Carefully add the stuffed fish sections,
lower the heat, and simmer, covered, for 1½ to 2 hours, or until
liquid is reduced to half its original quantity.

V   Allow fish to cool slightly before removing from
cooking liquid. Serve warm or chilled, garnished with sliced cooked
carrots and horseradish on the side. If desired, strain cooking
liquid and serve cold as a jellied sauce to accompany the cold
gefilte fish.

WHOLE GEFILTE FISH

Keep the skin, including the head and tail intact, but
remove all bones along with the flesh. Prepare filling as directed
and use mixture to fill the skin. Sprinkle skin with salt and pepper
before setting the fish in the kettle with the vegetables and water.
Whole fish retain the shape better, and are easier to remove, if

you set them on a heatproof plate before placing them in the kettle and cooking as directed.

FISH BALLS

Section, fillet, and grind fish flesh as directed, but shape fish and onion mixture into balls. Arrange skin and bones on bottom of the kettle, then add vegetables and fish balls and cook as directed.

DIPS

LIPTAUER CHEESE
(YIELD: ABOUT 2 CUPS)

1 8-Ounce package cream cheese, at room temperature
8 Tablespoons (1 stick) butter, at room temperature
1 Cup cottage cheese
4 Flat anchovy fillets, cut in pieces
3 Tablespoons well-drained capers
2 Tablespoons each sweet Hungarian paprika and caraway seeds
1 Teaspoon dry mustard
1/2 Teaspoon each salt and white pepper
2 Tablespoons gin
1/4 Cup chopped fresh chives

I Cut cream cheese and butter in 1-inch pieces and place in container C S or bowl K. Cream together for 10 seconds or until well blended, stopping once to scrape down sides. Add cottage cheese, anchovies, capers, and spices. Whirl for 5 or 6 seconds, then add the gin with the motor running, stopping once to scrape down container sides.

II Keep chilled for a few days to age. Stir in chopped chives before using.

PAPRIKA CHEESE DIP

Serve with halved fresh mushrooms, cauliflower florets, and whole, fresh young green beans.

(YIELD: ABOUT 1¼ CUPS)

1   8-Ounce package cream cheese, at room temperature, cut in pieces
4   Tablespoons sweet butter
2   Tablespoons sweet paprika
4   Tablespoons whole caraway seeds
1   Tablespoon chopped fresh chives
1   Teaspoon salt
¾   Teaspoon dry mustard
¼   Cup sour cream

I   Place all ingredients except sour cream in container C S or bowl K. Process for 5 or 6 seconds or until well blended, stopping once to scrape down container sides. Add sour cream and mix until well blended.

II   Keep chilled.

SOUR CREAM AND BLUE CHEESE DIP

Serve with carrot sticks, celery, and other raw vegetables.

(YIELD: ABOUT 1½ TO 2 CUPS)

¼   Pound blue cheese
½   Small onion, peeled and cut in half
1   Cup sour cream
    Freshly ground black pepper

I   Place cheese, onion, and sour cream in container C S. Season to taste with pepper and whirl for 5 or 6 seconds, stopping if necessary to scrape down container sides. KitchenAid users: hand-mince onion; then mix all ingredients thoroughly.

II   Keep chilled.

THREE-CHEESE AND NUT COCKTAIL SPREAD

(YIELD: 1 POUND)

8 Ounces sharp Cheddar cheese, cut in pieces
4 Ounces each Roquefort and cream cheese,
    cut in pieces
4 Tablespoons butter, cut in pieces
1 Cup pecans
3 Tablespoons heavy cream
1 Teaspoon Tabasco sauce
1 Clove garlic, peeled
    Crackers or Toast Points (see page 304)

I Have all ingredients at room temperature. Cream
C K S together the cheeses, butter, nuts,* heavy cream, Tabasco
and garlic until well mixed. Stop machine 2 or 3 times to scrape
down container or bowl sides.

II Pack mixture into oiled mold and chill until firm.
Then unmold on a serving plate, or store in crocks. Serve with
crackers or toast points.

* KitchenAid users: hand-mince or grate nuts and mix these in last.

CONFETTI COTTAGE CHEESE DIP

Whirl all ingredients (except chopped tomato) for
Confetti Cottage Cheese (see page 249) in your container C S,
adding as much sour cream as necessary to bring mixture to the
consistency you prefer for dipping.
Stir in tomato bits just before serving cold.

CLAM DIP

Serve with celery sticks, cherry tomatoes, scallions, potato chips, or crackers.

(YIELD: ABOUT 2 CUPS)

> 1 Cup sour cream
> 6 Ounces cream cheese, cut in pieces
> ½ Small onion, peeled and cut in quarters
> 1 Teaspoon salt
> ½ Teaspoon Tabasco sauce
> 1 Cup cooked clams, with their liquor

I Place sour cream, cream cheese, onion, salt, and Tabasco in container C S. Whirl for 5 or 6 seconds. KitchenAid users: hand-chop onion and clams and mix well.

II Drain clams, reserving liquor. Add clam juice to container if necessary, to bring dip to desired consistency. Then add clams quickly and process by turning machine on and off twice—the clams should be finely chopped, not minced.

III Keep chilled.

SALMON AND SMOKED SALMON DIPS

Prepare Salmon or Smoked Salmon Filling (see page 208) as directed, adding as much sour cream as necessary to bring mixture to proper consistency for dipping. Mince 2 scallions with 3 inches green top by hand, and stir into dip. Serve cold.

Crabmeat Filling, Shrimp Filling, Lobster Filling, Mushroom Filling, and many of the other fillings listed on pages 203 to 212 can be turned into appetizing dips when thinned to the proper consistency with sour cream.

Experiment—and add variety to the cocktail hour.

GUACAMOLE DIP

(YIELD: ABOUT 2 CUPS)

    2   Ripe avocados, peeled and pitted
    2   Cloves garlic, peeled and cut in half
    1/2 Small onion, peeled and cut in quarters
    4   Teaspoons lemon juice
    1/2 Teaspoon Tabasco sauce
        Salt and freshly ground black pepper
    1   Medium tomato, peeled, seeded, and finely chopped
    2   Tablespoons Foolproof Mayonnaise (see page 252)

I Cut avocados in quarters, reserving 1 quarter.

II Place remaining avocados, garlic, onion, lemon juice, Tabasco, and salt and pepper to taste in container C S. Turn the machine quickly on and off 5 or 6 times, stopping once to scrape down container sides. KitchenAid users: hand-mince all solid ingredients, mix well, and then continue with Step IV.

III Finely chop the remaining avocado and the tomato by hand and stir into the Guacamole.

IV Turn mixture into a bowl and spread the top with mayonnaise, then chill until serving time.

V At serving time, stir mayonnaise into dip and serve cold with corn chips.

DEVILISH-HOT DIP

Serve with tiny meatballs, vegetable cubes, shrimp, or tortilla chips.

(YIELD: ABOUT 2 CUPS)

    2   Ripe avocados, peeled, seeded and cut in 1-inch pieces
    1/2 4-Ounce can hot green chili peppers, cut in 1-inch pieces
    1/2 Medium onion, peeled and cut in pieces
    1   Clove garlic, peeled and cut in half

¼   Cup Foolproof Mayonnaise (see page 252)
1   Tablespoon lime juice
1   Teaspoon salt

I   Combine avocado, chili peppers, onion, garlic, mayonnaise, lime juice, and salt in container C S. Whirl for 6 or 8 seconds, stopping machine once or twice to scrape down sides. KitchenAid users: hand-mince all ingredients and mix well.

II   Keep chilled.

TOMATO-CUCUMBER DIP

(YIELD: ABOUT 2½ CUPS)

  1   Large cucumber, peeled and seeded
1½   Teaspoons salt
  2   Hard-cooked eggs
  1   Recipe Tomato Cream Sauce (see page 269)
  2   Tablespoons capers, drained

I   Finely grate C K S cucumber. Then place in a colander, sprinkle with the salt, and allow to drain for 15 to 20 minutes, stirring from time to time.

II   Chop C or grind K S eggs.

III   Rinse cucumbers under cold water, squeeze dry with paper towels, and place in container C* Ⓚ Ⓢ. Add eggs, sauce, and capers, and whirl only long enough to mix well.

IV   Keep chilled.

* Cuisinart machine users: use plastic blade.
Ⓚ Ⓢ KitchenAid and Starmix users: mix by hand.

FRESH HERB DIP

Serve with an assortment of vegetables, and/or lobster pieces and shrimp.

(YIELD: ABOUT 2 CUPS)

8 Ounces cream cheese, cut in pieces
½ Cup sour cream
3 Cloves garlic, peeled and cut in half
¼ Cup fresh parsley, with all stems removed
¼ Cup fresh chopped chives
Salt and freshly ground black pepper
Heavy cream

I Place cream cheese, sour cream, garlic, and herbs in container C S. Season to taste with salt and pepper, and then whirl for 5 or 6 seconds, stopping once or twice to scrape down container sides. KitchenAid users: hand-mince solid ingredients and then blend all ingredients well.

II Turn on machine and pour in as much heavy cream as necessary to bring dip to consistency you prefer; then shut off machine immediately.

III Keep chilled.

MUSTARD DIP

Serve with shrimp or an assortment of tiny beef, pork, and lamb balls.

(YIELD: ABOUT 2 CUPS)

¼ Cup Dijon-style mustard
¼ Cup chopped fresh chives
¼ Cup well-drained capers
2 Cups sour cream
½ Teaspoon dry mustard

I Place all ingredients in container C S or bowl K. Process for 5 or 6 seconds, or until thoroughly blended.

II Keep chilled.

CHUTNEY NUT DIP

Prepare Chutney Nut Filling as directed (see page 205). Trim and mince by hand 3 scallions with 3 inches green top; then stir in along with as much heavy cream as necessary to bring mixture to proper consistency. Serve cold with shrimp and/ or assorted cocktail meatballs.

CANAPÉS

Attractive canapés, each spread with a flavorful compound butter and highlighted with a contrasting tidbit or colorful garnish, make an elegant nibble to accompany cocktails. Prepare these miniature open-faced sandwiches by slicing a trimmed, *uncut* bread loaf lengthwise in ¼-inch slices; then cut each slice into triangles, circles, rectangles, or crescents. Toast lightly or sauté on one side in butter to help the canapés retain their crispness longer. Decorate as elaborately—or as simply—as you wish, following the combinations suggested below or whatever your fancy dictates. Just remember to chill the compound butters well before spreading or piping them through a pastry tube as a garnish, and keep the finished canapés cold until serving time.

ANCHOVY-EGG CANAPÉS

Toast thin slices of white bread on one side and spread with Anchovy Butter (see page 103). Top each with a slice of hard-cooked egg. Cut pimentos into thin strips and arrange in latticework fashion over sliced egg, then garnish with capers.

ARTICHOKE CANAPÉS

Toast thin circles of white bread on one side. Spread with Curry Butter (see page 106) and center each canapé with ½ small artichoke heart. Garnish with a border of Shrimp Butter (see page 105) piped through a pastry bag.

CANAPÉS LIEGEOISE

Peel and very thinly slice C K S 1 small eggplant. Soak in salted water to cover for 2 hours, then pat dry with paper towels and cut into small rounds. Cut toast rounds of the same size and number and brush lightly with Anchovy Butter (see page 103).

Spread toast with cooked chopped C S tongue mixed with enough mayonnaise to bind. Dip eggplant rounds in melted butter, then place over tongue mixture. Sprinkle each round with grated C K S Swiss cheese and a caper. Broil until cheese bubbles and lightly browns. Serve hot.

CANAPÉS MICHELINE

Cut thinly sliced pumpernickel into squares and spread with Horseradish Butter (see page 104). Cover the corners of each square with a bit of black caviar, top with oysters poached in white wine for 2 or 3 minutes, and garnish with pipettes of Foolproof Mayonnaise (see page 252) flavored to taste with mustard and Tabasco and squeezed through a pastry tube.

CANAPÉS POUR BOIRE · HAM CANAPÉS

Cut bread slices into rounds and toast on one side. Spread untoasted sides with Mustard Butter (see page 105). Cover with thin slices of cold ham, then top with well-drained horseradish. Decorate edges with mayonnaise mixed with a little anchovy paste and piped through a pastry tube. Garnish with finely chopped pimentos, chives, capers, and onion.

CAVIAR CANAPÉS

Toast bread rounds on one side and spread with Smoked Salmon Butter (see page 105). Dot with a bit of black caviar and sprinkle with minced hard-cooked egg and fresh parsley.

CRABMEAT OR SHRIMP CANAPÉS

Toast bread triangles on one side and spread with Lobster Butter (see page 104). Cover with flaked, well-drained crabmeat, then garnish with a dollop of mayonnaise and red caviar. For Shrimp Canapés, substitute for the crabmeat ½ shrimp cooked, peeled, and sliced lengthwise.

LOBSTER CANAPÉS

Toast thin slices of white bread on one side. Cut into shapes and spread with Deviled Butter (see page 104), then top each with thinly sliced C K S peeled cucumber. Mince C S cooked lobster meat and the white part of scallions and heap over cucumber slices. Top each canapé with a dollop of mayonnaise and a slice of stuffed olive before serving cold.

OYSTER OR MUSSEL CANAPÉS

Toast circles of thinly sliced dark bread on one side, then spread with Horseradish Butter (see page 104). Top the circles with oysters poached for 2 or 3 minutes in their own juices, drained and cooled, and then dipped in mayonnaise flavored with mustard. Garnish with bits of crisp bacon. Substitute cooked mussels for the oysters to prepare Mussel Canapés.

PALM CANAPÉS

Cut thinly sliced white bread into circles, toast on one side, and spread with Chivry Butter (see page 103). Top with hard-cooked egg slices and place a small piece of heart of palm on the center of each yolk. Crisscross with thin pimento strips.

TURKEY CANAPÉS

Cut thin slices of white bread into squares, toast on one side, and spread with Tarragon Butter (see page 107). Arrange over this squares of thinly sliced turkey breast or tongue. Garnish with a border of cream cheese blended with chutney and piped through a pastry tube. Decorate the center of each with a slice of stuffed olive.

POTATO CHIPS

2   All-purpose potatoes, about 7 ounces each, peeled
    Vegetable oil for deep-frying
    Salt

I   Slice C K S potatoes very thinly.

II   Arrange on paper towels. Cover with additional paper towels and press out excess moisture.

III   Heat 1½ inches oil to 375 degrees F. in a large skillet (see How to Deep-Fry, at end of charts). Slip in potato slices, one at a time, until surface of oil is covered. Stir with a slotted spoon until slices are golden brown; do not overbrown.

IV   Remove potato chips with a slotted spoon and drain on several thicknesses of paper towels. Salt to taste just before serving.

BANANA CHIPS

(YIELD: 6 CUPS)

8   Large green bananas, peeled
    Vegetable oil for deep frying
    Salt

I   Follow directions for Potato Chips.

COMPOUND BUTTERS

MAKING YOUR OWN BUTTER

(YIELD: ¼ POUND)

If you bake your own bread, you most certainly should whip your own butter. Your wonderful food processor makes this feasible.

> 1 Cup heavy cream
> Cold water
> Ice cubes

I Let the cream stand at room temperature for a day to ripen, then refrigerate for 2 hours or until cream has a thick, glossy look.

II Chill the container C, blender S, or bowl K (as well as the metal blade or whip) in the refrigerator, to help the butter "come" more readily. Whirl the cream* until the butter forms. Pour off the buttermilk and save for cooking or drinking.

III Leave the butter in the container and add 1 cup water and 2 ice cubes. Whirl until the water is milky. Discard the water

---

* KitchenAid users: beat the cream on Speed 4, then gradually increase speed to high. As the cream changes to butter gradually decrease speed. Omit the ice in Step III, but use ice-cold water.

and repeat the process until the last drop of cream has been washed away. Refill the container as many times as is necessary for the water to come perfectly clear. Discard water.

IV Whirl 30 seconds, then discard any water that accumulates in the container. Repeat this process until the butter is water-free.

V If you like your butter salted, sprinkle some over the butter and whirl 30 seconds more.

VI Pack the butter in crocks or shape into a bar and cover it tightly with moisture-resistant wrap. Refrigerate. Remember that butter, like milk, will develop off-flavors if not tightly covered. To freeze, cover the original wrappings with aluminum foil.

COMPOUND BUTTERS

These distinctive butters, which form the basis of many a tasty canapé, may also be used to enhance the flavor of fish, meat, or vegetables. Your food processor C S prepares them in seconds. The KitchenAid machine will also perform this task but rather less efficiently, since solid ingredients must be hand-minced. Begin with cold butter and chill finished butters until ready for use.

USES FOR COMPOUND BUTTERS

Anchovy Butter Broiled or sautéed fish.
Bercy Butter Broiled steaks or chops.
Carlton Butter Broiled or sautéed fish.
Chivry Butter Mussel Canapés.
Corn Butter Freshly cooked corn or any hot vegetable.
Curry Butter Artichoke Canapés.
Deviled Butter Lobster Canapés.
Garlic Butter Garlic bread, fish, or baked oysters.
Green Butter Broiled or sautéed fish or for finishing cream sauce
   for broiled poultry.

Horseradish Butter Canapés Micheline.
Lobster Butter Finishing fish sauces—canapés.
Maître d'Hôtel Butter Broiled meat, poultry, fish.
Marchands de Vins Butter Broiled steaks or chops.
Mustard Butter Canapés pour Boire.
Nut Butter Spread over hamburgers or steaks before grilling.
Paprika Butter Broiled poultry or fish or to finish paprika sauce.
Shallot Butter Broiled meat, poultry, fish.
Shrimp Butter Hot fish or to finish hot fish sauces.
Smoked Salmon Butter Lobster Canapés.
Tarragon Butter Broiled meat, poultry, fish.
Watercress Butter Cooked vegetables.
White Butter Poached fresh-water fish.

The following butters may be easily prepared by placing all ingredients in container and processing until well incorporated. Stop once or twice as necessary to scrape down sides of container. Keep finished butters chilled.

BEURRE D'ANCHOIS · ANCHOVY BUTTER

2 *Flat anchovy fillets, cut in pieces*
6 *Tablespoons sweet butter, cut in pieces*

BEURRE CARLTON · CARLTON BUTTER

8 *Tablespoons butter, cut in pieces*
1 *Tablespoon each chopped chutney and chili sauce*
1 *Teaspoon Worcestershire sauce*

CHIVRY BUTTER

1 *Shallot, peeled and sliced*
1½ *Teaspoons each chopped fresh chives, chervil, parsley, and tarragon, with all stems removed*
6 *Tablespoons butter, cut in pieces*

CORN BUTTER

8	Tablespoons butter, cut in pieces
½ to 1	Teaspoon of any one of the following herbs or spices: celery salt, chili powder, nutmeg, oregano, savory or tarragon

DEVILED BUTTER

6	Tablespoons butter, cut in pieces
3	Tablespoons Worcestershire sauce
2	Tablespoons Tabasco sauce
2	Teaspoons each dry mustard, chopped onion, and chopped fresh chives

BEURRE D'AIL • GARLIC BUTTER

2	Large cloves garlic, peeled and cut in half
6	Tablespoons butter, cut in pieces

HORSERADISH BUTTER

1	1-Inch piece horseradish root, scraped and cut in pieces
6	Tablespoons butter, cut in pieces

BEURRE DE HOMARD • LOBSTER BUTTER

8	Tablespoons sweet butter, cut in pieces
3	Tablespoons lobster coral or roe

BEURRE À LA MAÎTRE D'HÔTEL · MAÎTRE D'HÔTEL BUTTER

½ Teaspoon fresh parsley leaves, with all stems removed
Salt and freshly ground black pepper
8 Tablespoons butter, cut in pieces
Juice of ½ lemon

MUSTARD BUTTER

8 Tablespoons butter, cut in pieces
1½ Teaspoons prepared mustard

NUT BUTTER

½ Cup walnuts or pecans
12 Tablespoons butter
2 Teaspoons chopped fresh chives
¼ Teaspoon Tabasco sauce

BEURRE DE CREVETTES · SHRIMP BUTTER

12 Cooked shelled shrimp, cut in half
8 Tablespoons butter, cut in pieces

SMOKED SALMON BUTTER

1 2-Inch slice smoked salmon
6 Tablespoons sweet butter, cut in pieces

BEURRE D'ESCARGOT · SNAIL BUTTER

½ Pound (2 sticks) cold butter, cut in pieces
6 Shallots, peeled and cut in half
2 Cloves garlic, peeled and cut in half
2 Tablespoons fresh parsley leaves, with all tough stems removed
½ Teaspoon salt
¼ Teaspoon white pepper

WATERCRESS BUTTER

6 Tablespoons sweet butter, cut in pieces
⅓ Cup watercress leaves, with all stems removed
1 Flat anchovy fillet, cut in pieces

Many recipes for compound butters call for several ingredients (such as shallots, herbs, and/or vegetables) to be precooked in several tablespoons of butter or water to cover. In such cases merely cook the solid ingredients until tender, drain them well, cool to room temperature, and process with cold butter and any remaining listed ingredients. Keep finished butters chilled until needed.

CURRY BUTTER

3 Shallots, peeled and sliced
8 Tablespoons butter
¾ Teaspoon curry powder

BEURRE VERT · GREEN BUTTER

6 to 8 Spinach leaves, with all stems removed
2 Small shallots, peeled and sliced
1 Tablespoon fresh parsley leaves, with all stems removed

1   Teaspoon each *fresh chervil and tarragon leaves*
    Water to cover the above
8   Tablespoons butter, cut in pieces

BEURRE DE PAPRIKA · PAPRIKA BUTTER

½   Small onion, peeled and coarsely chopped
1½ Teaspoons paprika
8   Tablespoons butter, cut in pieces

BEURRE D'ECHALOTE · SHALLOT BUTTER

6   Small shallots, peeled and sliced
8   Tablespoons butter
½   Teaspoon chopped fresh chives

BEURRE D'ESTRAGON · TARRAGON BUTTER

6   Tablespoons fresh tarragon leaves, with all stems
    removed
    Water to cover the above
6   Tablespoons butter, cut in pieces

To prepare the following butters, cook the shallots in wine or vinegar until the liquid is reduced to one-fourth of its original volume. Cool to room temperature. Whirl the cold butter with any remaining ingredients, add the shallot mixture while the motor is turning. Process until ingredients are well incorporated.

BEURRE BERCY · BERCY BUTTER

1   Cup dry white wine
8   Shallots, peeled and sliced
8   Tablespoons butter, cut in pieces
2   Tablespoons fresh parsley leaves, with all stems
    removed
    Salt and freshly ground pepper

BEURRE MARCHAND DE VINS · MARCHAND DE VINS BUTTER

1 Cup red wine
8 Shallots, peeled and sliced
8 Tablespoons butter, cut in pieces
1 Tablespoon fresh parsley leaves, with all stems removed
  Salt and freshly ground pepper

BEURRE BLANC · WHITE BUTTER

½ Cup vinegar
2 Shallots, peeled and sliced
6 Tablespoons butter, cut in pieces
1 Teaspoon finely chopped fresh parsley leaves
  Salt and freshly ground black pepper

PÂTÉS

TERRINE DE PORC · TERRINE OF PORK

(YIELD: ENOUGH TO SERVE 8 TO 10)

- 1   *Pound fresh pork breast, half fat and half lean, cut in 1-inch pieces*
- ¾   *Pound boiled ham, cut in 1-inch pieces*
- 1   *¾-Pound piece smoked tongue*
- 1   *⅓-Inch thick slice prosciutto*
- 3   *Large cloves garlic, peeled and cut in half*
- ½   *Cup mixed fresh sage, tarragon, rosemary, and parsley leaves, with all tough stems removed*
- 1   *Small bay leaf*
- 2   *Medium onions, peeled and cut in quarters*
- 3   *Tablespoons vegetable oil*
- 1   *Pound lettuce leaves*
- 1   *Pound spinach leaves, with all tough stems removed*
- ½   *Teaspoon salt*
-    *Freshly ground black pepper*
- 1   *Egg*
- 3   *Tablespoons brandy*
-    *Pinch allspice*
-    *Dash cayenne pepper*
- ½   *Pound country-cured bacon*
- 1   *Cup all-purpose flour*
- ¼   *Cup water*

I Processing 2 or 3 handfuls at a time, coarsely chop C S or grind K the pork breast; finely chop C S or grind K the boiled ham. Combine meats and set aside.

II Using a large sharp knife, cut the tongue and prosciutto into thin strips about ⅓ inch wide. Set aside.

III Whirl garlic, herbs, and bay leaf in container C K S for 3 seconds; add onions and whirl mixture for 5 or 6 seconds longer.

IV Heat the oil in a large skillet and sauté the onion-garlic mixture until the onions are soft but not brown. Meanwhile, chop C S or grate K the lettuce and spinach leaves. Add to the skillet, then cover and cook over low heat for 5 minutes. Remove from the heat and season with ½ teaspoon salt and black pepper to taste. Set aside.

V Lightly beat the egg and stir, together with the brandy, into the combined chopped pork and ham; season with the all-spice, cayenne pepper, and salt and black pepper to taste.

VI Preheat the oven to 375 degrees F. Line a 2½-quart terrine equipped with a lid with strips of bacon crossing in both directions; the ends of the bacon should overlap the edges of the terrine. Arrange ⅓ of the vegetable-herb mixture over the bacon, cover with a layer of half the chopped pork and ham and top this with half the tongue and prosciutto strips placed lengthwise. Push the layers down gently with your fingers, then add half the remaining vegetable-herb mixture, the remaining chopped pork and ham, and the rest of the tongue and prosciutto strips, in that order. Top with the remaining vegetables and herbs.

VII Gently tap the terrine to firm up the layers, then bring up the overlapping ends of the bacon strips, side ends first, so that the terrine's top layer is covered. Put the lid on the terrine and seal the edges where top and bottom meet by brushing with a thick paste made by combining the flour and water.

VIII Set the tightly sealed terrine in a shallow pan; add enough boiling water to the pan to bring it to a level at least 1½ inches up the sides of the terrine. Bake for 1 hour, then reduce the heat to 350 degrees F. and bake 1 hour longer. The terrine is done if the juices run dark brown when you prick the meat mixture with

K KitchenAid users: hand-chop garlic, herbs and onion; crumble bay leaf.

a fork. If necessary, reseal the terrine as before and return to the oven to bake longer.

IX Remove the lid and weight down the meat mixture with a heavy plate. Allow to stand for 12 hours, then refrigerate, still weighted, for another 24 hours. To serve, remove and reserve the bacon for another use, then cut the terrine into serving portions.

TERRINE DE VEAU, D'ALSACE

2	*Pounds boneless pork*
1	*Cup dry white wine*
5	*Chicken livers, trimmed*
2	*Ounces rum*
1½	*Pounds boneless veal*
½	*Teaspoon salt*
¼	*Teaspoon coarsely ground black pepper*
⅛	*Teaspoon each powdered cinnamon, cloves, ginger, and nutmeg*
1½	*Ounces cognac*
2–3	*Truffles, diced (optional)* *
½	*Pound lean country-cured bacon slices, cut in quarters*
1	*Bay leaf*

I Marinate the pork in the wine and the chicken livers in the rum, both for 2 days.

II Cut several ¼-inch slices from the veal and reserve.

III Cut the remaining veal and the drained, marinated pork into 1-inch pieces. Finely chop C S (but do not reduce to forcemeat) or grind K these pieces of pork and veal. Mix the chopped meats with the spices and the cognac. Preheat oven to 300 degrees F.

IV Line the bottom of a deep, earthenware pâté dish or terrine with half the chopped meat mixture. Imbed the chicken livers in this (reserve the rum). Cover with the truffles (or pepper-

---

* A tablespoon of well-drained green peppercorns make a nice substitution here.

corns), the bacon slices, and the reserved veal slices. Lightly press the remaining chopped meat mixture over all and smooth with the back of a spoon that has been dipped in the reserved rum marinade. Cover tightly, set in a pan of warm water, and bake for 2 hours.

V Replace the lid of the terrine with a weighted board and chill for 24 hours. Serve *cold*.

PURÉE DE FOIE GRAS · PURÉED CHICKEN LIVERS
(YIELD: ABOUT 1 CUP)

½ *Pound chicken livers*
  Water
½ *Cup softened butter or chicken fat*
1 *Tablespoon sherry*
  Dash each salt and freshly ground black pepper
  Toast Points (see page 304)
  Finely chopped onion

I Simmer the livers in water to cover for 15 minutes, turning them once. Drain well.

II Purée C K S the warm (not hot) livers with the butter or fat, sherry, salt, and pepper.

III Pack in a crock and chill in the refrigerator. Serve cold with toast points and chopped onion.

QUICK AND EASY CHOPPED CHICKEN LIVERS
(YIELD: 1½ TO 2 CUPS)

1 *Pound chicken livers*
2 *Medium onions, peeled and sliced C K S*
2 *Tablespoons butter*
2 *Eggs*
2 *Tablespoons softened butter*
¼ *Teaspoon salt*
⅛ *Teaspoon freshly ground black pepper*

1   Tablespoon brandy, cognac, or sherry
1   Tablespoon chopped fresh chives

I Cook livers and sliced onions in butter until livers are cooked through. Remove from pan and place in container C S. (K users run all cooked ingredients through fine blade of your grinder; then hand-mix all ingredients.)

II Beat eggs together lightly and scramble In pan In which livers were cooked until eggs are just set. Remove from heat and add to container. Cool to room temperature.

III Add softened butter, salt, and pepper to container, sprinkle brandy over ingredients, and then process by quickly turning machine on and off 6 to 8 times or until well mixed, stopping twice to scrape down container sides.

IV Keep chilled. Serve cold, garnished with chopped chives and a sprinkling of freshly ground black pepper.

CHUTNEY-CHEESE PÂTÉ

(YIELD: ENOUGH TO SERVE 6)

5   Ounces Cheddar cheese, cut in 1-inch cubes
8   Ounces cream cheese, cut in pieces
4   Tablespoons dry sherry
1   Teaspoon curry powder
Salt
½   Cup chutney
2   Tablespoons minced chives

I Whirl C S together Cheddar cheese, cream cheese, sherry, curry powder, and salt to taste along with ¼ cup of the chutney until well blended, or grate K Cheddar and blend in bowl with these ingredients.

II Spoon ¾ of the cheese mixture into a small pâté terrine. Combine remaining cheese mixture with remaining chutney; whirl until well blended, then spread over pâté in dish. Chill several hours or overnight. Serve cold, sprinkled with chives and accompanied by crisp wheat wafers or Toast Points (see page 304).

SOUPS

FAITH FESSLER'S FRESH CUCUMBER SOUP
(YIELD: ENOUGH TO SERVE 6)

  1 *Large cucumber, peeled and seeded*
 12 *Ounces cream cheese*
 10 *Scallions, with 3 inches green top, cut into thin slices*
  1 *Cup tightly packed watercress leaves, with all stems removed*
  1 *Cup tightly packed fresh parsley leaves, with all stems removed*
  3 *Tablespoons sour cream*
 ¾ *Teaspoon salt*
     Heavy sweet cream
     Freshly ground black pepper

I Cut the cucumber and cream cheese in 1-inch pieces and place with the scallions, watercress, parsley, sour cream, and salt in the container C Ⓚ S. Whirl for 6 seconds. Scrape down the container's sides and whirl for 1 or 2 seconds more if necessary to achieve a fairly smooth texture.

II Refrigerate this base at least 4 hours before serving cold. To serve, thin with heavy sweet cream to the consistency you prefer. Pour into well-chilled bowls and sprinkle each portion with freshly ground black pepper.

Ⓚ KitchenAid users: put cucumber, scallions, watercress, and parsley through the fine blade of food grinder and mix into soup by hand.

CHILLED ALMOND-AVOCADO SOUP

(YIELD: ENOUGH TO SERVE 6–8)

    2   *Cups blanched almonds*
    1   *Large ripe avocado, peeled, pitted, and cut in 1-inch*
        pieces
    5   *Cups chicken broth*
    1   *Teaspoon lemon juice*
        Salt and white pepper
  1/8   *Teaspoon ground nutmeg*
    2   *Cups light cream*
  1/2   *Cup heavy cream*
    1   *Tablespoon vegetable oil*

I   Set 1/4 cup almonds aside and chop C S or grate K the rest.

II   Add avocado and 1/4 cup broth to container C Ⓚ S. Whirl until mixture is smooth, stopping once or twice to scrape down container sides.

III   Place almond-avocado mixture in large saucepan and stir in remaining broth, lemon juice, salt and white pepper to taste, and nutmeg. Bring almost to a boil, then lower heat and simmer for 5 minutes.

IV   Stir in light cream and simmer until soup is just heated through. Refrigerate for at least 2 hours.

V   Whip the heavy cream.* Chill.

VI   Sliver remaining 1/4 cup almonds by hand, toss with 1 tablespoon oil, and toast in a preheated 400 degrees F. oven for 15 minutes, or until lightly browned. Cool to room temperature. To serve, top each plate of soup with a dollop of whipped cream and a sprinkle of toasted almonds.

Ⓚ KitchenAid users: mash avocado with a fork and mix by hand.
* Cuisinart users: Whip by hand or by using electric mixer.

VICHYSSOISE

A classic . . . with the work time cut to seconds.

(YIELD: ENOUGH TO SERVE 8)

1 Medium onion, peeled and cut in quarters
5 Leeks, white part only, cut in 1-inch pieces
4 Tablespoons butter
4 Medium potatoes, peeled
4 Cups chicken broth or water
1 Teaspoon salt
2 Cups milk
  Heavy cream
  Freshly ground black pepper
2 Tablespoons minced fresh chives

I Chop C S or grind K S onion and leeks, then sauté in the butter until onions are translucent.

II Thinly slice C K S potatoes and add to the vegetables along with the broth and salt. Cook over medium heat until potatoes are tender.

III In two or three stages, place vegetables and broth in container C S or special attachment K and purée until smooth. Refrigerate until well chilled.

IV Just before serving, stir in milk and cream to the consistency you prefer, season to taste with salt and pepper, and garnish with chives.

HLODNIK

One of the most cooling of summer soups is this handsome Russian import. The rich, pink beet broth creates a perfect backdrop for hard-cooked egg quarters and lemon slices.

(YIELD: ENOUGH TO SERVE 6)

6 Small beets, peeled and cut in quarters
1/2 Cup young beet tops (use only the very small new green leaves)

1½   Cups water
 2   Scallions with 3 inches green top, cut in 1-inch pieces
 1   Tablespoon fresh dill leaves, with all tough stems
     removed
 4   Cups chicken broth
1¼   Cups sour cream
 4   Tablespoons lemon juice
 2   Teaspoons vinegar
 1   Teaspoon salt
 2   Medium cucumbers, peeled, seeded, and cut in 1-inch
     pieces
 1   Cup cooked ham, cut in 1-inch pieces
 1   Cup cooked shrimp
     Freshly ground black pepper
 6   Hard-cooked eggs, cut in quarters
 1   Small lemon, thinly sliced C Ⓚ Ⓢ with the skin intact

I   Grate beets C K S. Finely chop beet tops in container
C Ⓚ S. Cover and cook beets and tops in 1½ cups water until
beets are tender; then set aside to cool.

II   Chop together C S scallions and dill. Stir into beets
and cooking liquid along with broth, lemon juice, vinegar, and salt.
Whirl the sour cream with ½ cup beet soup C S and stir this into
the soup. Refrigerate for at least 3 hours.

III   Chop C S cucumbers and set aside to drain thoroughly. Coarsely chop C S the ham and shrimp. Stir cucumbers,
ham, and shrimp into soup.

IV   To serve, ladle soup into well-chilled soup plates and
season to taste with freshly ground black pepper. Garnish with
egg quarters and thin slices of lemon.

Ⓚ Ⓢ KitchenAid and Starmix users: slice lemon by hand.
Ⓚ KitchenAid users: chop vegetables, ham, and shrimp by hand.

ICED FISH, MEAT, AND CUCUMBER SOUP

This chilled yogurt soup requires no cooking. Mix it in less than five minutes, then set it aside in your refrigerator to await your guests.

(YIELD: ENOUGH TO SERVE 6)

1	Cup cooked chicken, cut in 1-inch pieces
1	Cup cooked shrimp
2	Medium cucumbers, peeled, seeded, and cut in 1-inch pieces
2	Small dill pickles, peeled and cut in half
1	Medium leek, trimmed and cut in 1-inch pieces
1/4	Cup fresh parsley leaves, with all tough stems removed
2	Tablespoons fresh fennel leaves, with all tough stems removed
3 1/2	Cups each unflavored yogurt and milk
2 1/2	Tablespoons lemon juice
	Salt and freshly ground black pepper to taste
6	Hard-cooked eggs, cut in quarters

I Coarsely chop C S or grind K S together chicken and shrimp. Set aside.

II Coarsely chop C S or grind K S together cucumbers and pickles, then set aside to drain.

III Finely chop together C S or grind K S leek, parsley, and fennel.

IV Combine yogurt and milk and stir in chicken, shrimp, cucumbers, pickles, leeks, fresh herbs, and lemon juice. Season to taste with salt and pepper and refrigerate for at least 4 hours. Serve cold, garnished with egg quarters.

CREAM OF CARROT SOUP

(YIELD: ENOUGH TO SERVE 6)

7	Medium carrots, scraped
6	Tablespoons butter
1 1/2	Teaspoons granulated sugar
1/4	Teaspoon salt
1/2	Cup water
3	Tablespoons all-purpose flour

⅓   Teaspoon salt
     Pinch freshly ground black pepper
     Pinch ground nutmeg
3½   Cups milk
     Heavy cream

I   Slice C K S carrots.

II   Melt 3 tablespoons butter in a saucepan. Add carrots, sugar, ¼ teaspoon salt, and water. Simmer, covered, for 25 minutes

III   Meanwhile, melt remaining butter in a heavy saucepan, then stir in the flour, ⅓ teaspoon salt, pepper, nutmeg, and milk. Continue to cook, stirring constantly, until the mixture is smooth and thick. Cover the sauce and cook over low heat for 5 minutes, then remove and set aside.

IV   Remove carrots from heat. Set ¼ cup aside. Purée C K S the remaining carrots.

V   Mix white sauce and puréed carrots either by hand or machine (in several steps).

VI   Pour carrot mixture into saucepan. Simmer over low heat for 30 minutes. Just before serving, stir in cream to the consistency you prefer. Serve hot, garnished with reserved carrot slices.

CREAM CHEESE SOUP

(YIELD: ENOUGH TO SERVE 6)

3   Ribs celery, with all strings removed, peeled and chopped
6   Medium leeks, white parts only, hand-chopped
4   Tablespoons butter
4½   Tablespoons all-purpose flour
3⅓   Cups chicken broth
2   Cups water
1   Teaspoon salt
12   Ounces cream cheese, at room temperature
1½   Cups plain yogurt
3   Egg yolks
     White pepper
⅓   Cup minced leek tops C S

I Sauté the celery and white part of leeks in the butter over low heat, stirring occasionally. When the leeks are soft but not brown, stir in the flour, broth, water, and salt.

II Bring the mixture to a boil, stirring constantly; allow to simmer for 15 minutes. Remove from the heat and cool for 5 minutes.

III Meanwhile, blend together C K S cream cheese, yogurt, and egg yolks. Blend with the cooled vegetable mixture. This will have to be done in several steps.

IV To serve, return soup to saucepan and simmer over low heat, stirring constantly, until the soup is just heated through. Take care not to let it boil or the egg yolks will curdle. Season to taste with white pepper. Serve hot, garnished with leek tops.

CREAM OF TOMATO SOUP

(YIELD: ENOUGH TO SERVE 6)

2	Medium onions, peeled and cut in quarters
1	Tablespoon each fresh basil and thyme leaves, with all tough stems removed
2	Tablespoons each butter and olive oil
	Salt and freshly ground black pepper
6	Medium tomatoes, peeled, seeded and cut in quarters
3	Tablespoons tomato paste
4	Cups chicken broth
4	Tablespoons all-purpose flour
1½	Teaspoons granulated sugar
1½	Cups heavy cream

I Chop C S or grind K together onions and fresh herbs.

II Heat butter and oil in a large soup kettle, add onions and herbs, then season to taste with salt and pepper and sauté until onions are golden and transparent.

III Coarsely chop C S tomatoes 3 at a time by quickly turning machine on and off 3 or 4 times, or chop by hand K. Add to onions along with tomato paste and simmer for 10 minutes, stirring occasionally.

IV Blend ½ cup broth with the flour and stir into the tomato mixture. Add remaining broth and cook for 30 minutes, stirring frequently with a wooden spoon.

V Remove soup from heat and purée in container C S or using special attachment K. Return puréed soup to a clean kettle. Add sugar and cream and simmer over low heat, stirring frequently until soup is hot. If desired, stir 1 or 2 tablespoons butter into soup before serving.

POTAGE SAINT-GERMAIN · CREAM OF PEA SOUP

(YIELD: ENOUGH TO SERVE 6)

2	Cups (1 pound) dried split peas
4	Cups water
1	Teaspoon salt
1	Large carrot, scraped
1	Medium onion, peeled
⅓	Cup salt pork, cut in ½-inch pieces
2½	Tablespoons butter
1	Large leek, green part only, well-washed
5	Lettuce leaves
1	Small bay leaf
	Pinch dried thyme leaves
1	Cup fresh green peas, cooked
1½	Cups chicken broth
1	Teaspoon granulated sugar
1	Tablespoon butter
1	Cup heavy cream
	Salt and freshly ground black pepper
	Croutons (see page 303)

I Cover split peas with cold water and soak several hours or as directed on the package.

II Drain split peas, discard water, and set in a large saucepan. Add 4 cups fresh water and 1 teaspoon salt and bring peas to a boil, removing any froth that rises to the surface, then cover and simmer over low heat until partially cooked.

III Meanwhile, grate C K S carrot and onion. Set aside. Finely chop C or grind K S salt pork and heat with the butter in a large, heavy soup kettle. Add carrot and onion and sauté vegetables until onion is soft.

IV Shred or slice C K S leek and lettuce and add to the sautéed vegetable mixture along with the bay leaf and thyme. Cook for 3 or 4 minutes, stirring occasionally.

V Add the partially cooked split peas and the cooking liquid to the kettle and cook for about 1 hour or until the peas are very soft.

VI Discard the bay leaf and purée the soup and fresh cooked green peas together in container C Ⓚ S. This will have to be done in 3 or 4 steps.

VII Return puréed soup to kettle, add broth, and bring to a boil; reduce heat and simmer for 10 minutes. Stir in sugar, butter, and heavy cream. Season to taste with salt and pepper before serving hot with croutons.

Ⓚ KitchenAid users: purée in a blender or press through a sieve.

CREAM OF PEANUT BUTTER SOUP
(YIELD: ENOUGH TO SERVE 6)

1	Medium onion, peeled and cut in quarters
2	Ribs celery, with all strings removed, cut in 1-inch pieces
2	Tablespoons butter
2½	Tablespoons all-purpose flour
5	Cups chicken broth
⅔	Cup Spanish-Peanut Butter (see page 376)
1⅔	Cups heavy cream
1	Cup sour cream
	Salt
¾	Cup coarsely crumbled tostados (or Fritos)

I Chop onions and celery in container C Ⓚ S.

II Heat butter in a large saucepan, add the chopped vegetables, and sauté until onions are golden and transparent. Blend in the flour and cook for 2 minutes.

Ⓚ KitchenAid users: hand-chop vegetables.

III Place the vegetable-flour mixture, and the peanut butter in container C S or bowl K and whirl until well mixed. Add ½ cup of the chicken broth 2 tablespoons at a time with motor running.

IV Return this mixture to the kettle, add the remaining chicken broth, and bring to a boil, stirring constantly. Remove from the heat and set aside for 5 minutes. Spoon off and discard any peanut oil that rises to the surface.

V Stir in the sour cream, add salt to taste, and reheat over very low flame until soup reaches serving temperature. Garnish each portion with a generous spoonful of sour cream topped with tostados or Fritos before serving hot.

CREAM SOUPS

Elegant but easy cream soups can also be made by diluting nearly any vegetable purée (see pages 217 to 223) with enough light cream to bring mixture to the consistency you like best.

MULLIGATAWNY
(YIELD: ENOUGH TO SERVE 8)

  1 *3½-Pound chicken, cut in serving pieces*
  3 *Tablespoons butter*
  1 *Medium onion, peeled and cut in quarters*
  1 *Small carrot, scraped and cut in 1-inch pieces*
  1 *Medium green pepper, blanched in boiling water for 2 minutes, then seeded and cut in 1-inch pieces*
  2 *Sour green apples, peeled and cut in quarters*
  2 *Tablespoons each curry powder and all-purpose flour*
1½ *Quarts chicken broth*
 ½ *Cup finely chopped C S or grated K coconut*
  1 *Tablespoon granulated sugar*
  1 *Teaspoon salt*
  4 *whole cloves*
  3 *Small tomatoes, peeled, seeded, and cut in quarters*
  1 *Tablespoon fresh parsley leaves, with all stems removed*
1½ *Cups cooked rice*

I   Brown chicken pieces in butter in a large soup kettle.

II   Meanwhile, finely chop C S or grind K S onion, carrot, green pepper, and apples.

III   Add chopped vegetables and apple to the browned chicken and cook, stirring occasionally, until onion is lightly browned.

IV   Blend in curry powder and flour, then add broth and coconut and stir over low heat for 5 minutes. Add sugar, salt, and cloves and simmer until chicken is nearly tender (about 15 to 20 minutes).

V   Chop together C S or grind K tomatoes and parsley. Add to soup and cook at low boil for 15 minutes.

VI   Remove chicken from kettle, discard skin and bones and cube meat by hand. Set aside.

VII   Purée soup C K S. This will have to be done in 2 or 3 steps. Return soup to heat, add cubed chicken, and bring to just under a boil. Serve hot, garnished with spoonfuls of cooked rice.

QUICK ONION SOUP
(YIELD: ENOUGH TO SERVE 6)

6   Medium onions, peeled
4   Tablespoons butter
3   Tablespoons all-purpose flour
8   Cups beef consommé
2   Tablespoons brandy
6   Garlic Crusts (see page 303)
2   Cups grated C K S Swiss cheese

I   Slice C K S onions and sauté in butter until transparent, stirring occasionally.

II   Stir in flour and blend well; add consommé and bring soup to a boil, stirring constantly. Boil for 1 minute. Stir in brandy.

III   Set 1 garlic crust in each of 6 soup bowls. Sprinkle each with a tablespoon of grated cheese. Ladle the hot soup over the bread and cheese. Serve immediately, with additional grated cheese in a separate bowl for guests to add as they like.

ALMOND SOUP BRASILIA

(YIELD: ENOUGH TO SERVE 6)

1¾   *Cups blanched almonds*
  4   *Large onions, peeled and cut in quarters*
  3   *Tablespoons butter*
  8   *Cups beef broth*
     Cayenne pepper
12   *Garlic Crusts (see page 303)*
1½   *Cups grated C K S Swiss cheese*

    I   Chop C S or grate K almonds and set aside. Chop C S or grind K S the onions; this will have to be done a few handfuls at a time.

    II   Heat butter in a large saucepan, add onions, and sauté until just starting to turn gold. Add broth, almonds, and cayenne pepper to taste, then simmer the soup, covered, for 15 minutes.

    III   To serve, place 2 garlic crusts in each soup bowl, sprinkle with grated cheese, then ladle the hot soup over all.

ZUPPA REGINA

(YIELD: ENOUGH TO SERVE 6)

3½   *Cups each beef broth and chicken broth*
 ¾   *Cup blanched almonds*
  3   *Slices bread, trimmed*
     Meat from one whole roasted or boiled chicken,
     cut in 1-inch pieces
  1   *Hard-cooked egg yolk*
     Croutons (see page 303)
     Grated C K S Parmesan cheese

    I   Mix beef and chicken broth together in a large soup kettle, and bring to a boil.

ll Meanwhile, place almonds in container C Ⓚ S and whirl for 4 seconds. Pour ½ cup of hot broth over bread, then add to nuts in container along with chicken meat and egg yolk. Process by turning machine quickly on and off 2 or 3 times, stopping once to scrape down container sides.

lll Place meat mixture in bottom of a large soup tureen. Add 1 cup boiling hot broth. Arrange croutons over meat mixture, then ladle in remaining steaming-hot broth. Serve immediately with grated cheese on the side.

Ⓚ KitchenAid users: grind the almonds and chicken meat together, then stir in broth-soaked bread and mashed egg yolk.

WON TON SOUP

(YIELD: ENOUGH TO SERVE 6)

> 8 *Cups chicken broth*
> *Won Tons (see page 366)*
> 2 *Scallions, with 3 inches green top, cut in 1-inch pieces*
> *Soy sauce*

l Bring broth to a boil in a large soup kettle. Use your food processor to prepare won tons. Add them a few at a time to simmering broth. Remove each batch as they rise to the surface and set them aside. Repeat this process until all the won tons are cooked.

ll Return won tons to the soup kettle to heat through. Meanwhile, finely hand-chop the scallions. To serve, divide won tons among soup bowls and ladle soup over. Garnish with scallions and serve hot, with soy sauce on the side.

GAZPACHO

Gazpacho is the most obliging of summer soups. Classically it includes very finely chopped tomato, cucumber, green pepper, onion, and garlic, all nestling in a broth made with fresh puréed tomato juice and rich beef bouillon. Your food processor makes it possible to whirl this Spanish classic together in seconds. When properly prepared (finely chopped and *not* smoothly blended) the texture is so interesting that those small bowls of garden vegetables so frequently served with the soup become superfluous. If, however, you feel the dish is more attractive or tasty when presented in this manner, it is preferable to hand-chop these added attractions for maximum eye appeal.

    8   *Large ripe tomatoes, peeled and seeded*
    2   *Medium cucumbers, peeled, seeded, and cut in 1-inch*
         pieces
    2   *Large green peppers with seeds and pith removed,*
         cut in 1-inch pieces
         Enough sweet onion to make 1 cup finely chopped
    4   *Cloves garlic, peeled*
   ⅓   *Cup olive oil*
    1   *Cup rich beef bouillon (or undiluted canned bouillon)*
 1½   *Tablespoons lemon juice*
         Fresh herbs, salt, and freshly ground black pepper
         to taste

    I   In two steps finely chop about two-thirds of the tomatoes. Set aside in a large bowl.

    II   Finely chop cucumbers, peppers, and onion separately in given order, adding each vegetable with its juices to the large bowl as it is processed.

    III   Purée remaining tomatoes, garlic, and olive oil. Pour this over the chopped vegetables along with the bouillon and lemon juice.

    IV   Mince the herbs, add to the soup, and mix well. Refrigerate for several hours or overnight. Before serving season to taste and, if necessary, add a bit of extra bouillon to thin the soup to preferred consistency.

SUMMER VEGETABLE SOUP WITH FRESH VEGETABLE GARNITURE

(YIELD: ENOUGH TO SERVE 6)

4 Large onions, peeled and cut in eighths
4 Carrots, scraped and cut in 1-inch pieces
7 Ribs celery with leaves, with all strings removed, cut in 1-inch pieces
8 Cups Easy Tomato Juice (see page 242)
1 Leftover ham bone (optional)
3 Tablespoons tomato paste
¼ Cup granulated sugar
2 Tablespoons each lemon juice and Worcestershire sauce
1½ Teaspoons each coarsely crushed peppercorns, rosemary, and caraway seeds
¼ Teaspoon ground cloves
Salt
6 Scallions with 3 inches green top, cut in ½-inch pieces
2 Green peppers, seeded and cut in 1-inch pieces
3 Tablespoons each minced fresh dill leaves and fennel, with all tough stems removed
2 Large tomatoes
1 Cup grated C K S Swiss cheese
½ Cup sour cream

I Chop C S or grind K S onions, carrots, and celery, 2 handfuls at a time.

II Place these vegetables in a large soup kettle. Add tomato juice, ham bone, tomato paste, sugar, lemon juice, Worcestershire sauce, peppercorns, rosemary, caraway seeds, cloves, and salt to taste. Cover kettle and bring ingredients to a boil; then lower heat and simmer soup 1 hour, skimming off froth as necessary. Add more tomato juice or water if necessary to maintain the level of the liquid.

III Chop by machine C S or by hand K scallions and peppers. Peel, seed, and chop tomatoes by hand. Place chopped scallions, peppers, dill, fennel, and tomatoes individually in small bowls.

IV Remove and discard ham bone. Stir additional sugar and lemon juice into the soup, if desired, until it is as sweet and tart as you like. Pour into soup bowls and top each portion with a sprinkle of cheese and a dollop of sour cream. Arrange the fresh vegetables and herbs around the soup for guests to add as they like.

NEAR EASTERN LENTIL SOUP

(YIELD: ENOUGH TO SERVE 6)

> 1½   *Cups red lentils*
> 3   *Large cloves garlic, peeled*
> ¼   *Teaspoon turmeric*
> 6   *Cups water*
> 1   *Large onion, peeled and cut in quarters*
> 2   *Teaspoons vegetable oil*
>   *Salt and freshly ground black pepper*
>   *Heavy cream*

I Put lentils, garlic, and turmeric in a large soup kettle, add 6 cups water, and simmer over very low heat, covered, for 1½ hours.

II Chop C S or grind K S onions. Sauté in oil until lightly browned.

III In several steps, purée lentil mixture in container C S or by using special attachment K. Return purée to soup kettle and add sautéed onions and salt and pepper to taste.

IV Simmer soup over very low heat until heated through. Thin with heavy cream to consistency you prefer. Reheat if necessary and serve hot.

SOUPE NORMANDE

(YIELD: ENOUGH TO SERVE 6)

    1   Pound dried pea beans, dried baby lima beans, or
        flageolet beans
    2   Tablespoons salt
    4   Medium carrots, scraped
    2   Medium onions, peeled
 1½   Ribs celery, with all strings removed
    5   Tablespoons butter
    1   Medium leek, white part only
    2   Tablespoons all-purpose flour
        Freshly ground black pepper
 3 to 5 Tablespoons heavy cream
    ½   Cup fresh chervil leaves, with all stems removed

I   Place beans in a heavy soup kettle and add enough water to bring the liquid level 3 to 4 inches above the beans. Bring mixture slowly to a boil, add salt, and simmer about 1 to 1½ hours or until beans are soft.

II   Drain beans, reserving cooking liquid. Set beans aside and return liquid to soup kettle. Cook over low heat until liquid is reduced to 7 cups.

III   Meanwhile, slice C K S carrots and onions, and chop C K̄ S the celery. Sauté the vegetables in butter over very low heat for 10 minutes, stirring occasionally.

IV   Chop C K̄ S leek, add to sautéed vegetables and cook for 5 minutes more.

V   Sprinkle flour over vegetables, stir in, then remove mixture from heat and add to cooking liquid in kettle. Season to taste with pepper and cook over low heat, covered, for 20 minutes or until vegetables are tender.

VI   Purée beans, sautéed vegetables, and cooking liquid together in container C S or special attachment K. This will have to be done in several steps.

VII   Reheat puréed soup and stir in heavy cream until the soup is the consistency you prefer, then remove from heat.

VIII   Chop C K̄ S chervil and stir half of it into soup. Ladle

K̄ KitchenAid users: hand-chop celery, leeks, and chervil.

soup into bowls and serve at once, garnished with remaining chervil and freshly ground black pepper.

OATMEAL SOUP GUADALAJARA

(YIELD: ENOUGH TO SERVE 6)

1¼	Cups rolled oats
1	Medium onion, peeled and cut in eighths
3	Large cloves garlic, peeled and cut in half
2	Large tomatoes, peeled, seeded, and cut in quarters
1	Large green pepper, seeded and cut in 1-inch pieces
6	Tablespoons butter
8	Cups chicken broth
½	Teaspoon salt
½	Teaspoon light brown sugar

I In a heavy saucepan, brown the oats over medium heat, stirring constantly so they do not burn. Remove from heat and set aside.

II Place onion and garlic in container C Ⓚ S. Process by turning machine quickly on and off 2 or 3 times, stopping each time to scrape down container sides. Add tomatoes and green pepper and whirl 2 seconds more.

III Melt butter in the same saucepan. Add the oats, chopped vegetables, broth, and salt and sugar. Bring the soup to a boil and boil for 6 minutes over medium heat. Season to taste with salt before serving hot.

Ⓚ KitchenAid users: grind vegetables or chop them by hand.

CABBAGE SOUP ATHENS
(YIELD: ENOUGH TO SERVE 6)

   1   *Large onion, peeled and cut in eighths*
  ⅓   *Cup olive oil*
   6   *Medium tomatoes, peeled, seeded, and cut in quarters*
   1   *Teaspoon granulated sugar*
 7½   *Cups chicken broth*
   1   *Small head cabbage*
   4   *Ounces vermicelli, broken in pieces*
   3   *Tablespoons cream cheese*
      Salt and freshly ground pepper

I Coarsely chop C Ⓚ S onion; then sauté in oil until lightly browned.

II Whirl C Ⓚ S tomatoes for 2 or 3 seconds, stopping if necessary to push down any large pieces. Add to onions along with sugar and broth. Bring to a boil, cover and simmer over very low heat for 1½ hours.

III Pull tough outer leaves away and core cabbage; then slice C K S finely. Add to soup along with vermicelli. Cook, stirring frequently, for 15 minutes or until vermicelli is tender. Work cream cheese into soup with the back of a spoon until well blended. Season to taste with salt and pepper before serving hot.

Ⓚ KitchenAid users: chop vegetables by hand.

FRESH TOMATO SOUP WITH CHEESE AND DILL
(YIELD: ENOUGH TO SERVE 6)

   1   *Large onion, peeled and cut in eighths*
   2   *Cloves garlic, peeled and cut in half*
   3   *Tablespoons butter*
 10   *Large ripe tomatoes, peeled*
   5   *Tablespoons all-purpose flour*
   5   *Cups chicken broth*
  ¼   *Cup fresh dill weed, with all tough stems removed*
  ¾   *Cup sour cream*
      Salt and freshly ground black pepper
   1   *Piece Swiss cheese 1½ inch by 2 inch, grated C K S*

I Place onion and garlic in container C Ⓚ S. Whirl for 2 or 3 seconds, stopping once to scrape down container sides.

II Sauté onions and garlic in butter in a large saucepan until lightly browned. Set 2 whole tomatoes aside. Cut remaining tomatoes in half and shake out seeds. Chop 2 at a time in container C Ⓚ S. Process by quickly turning machine on and off 1 or 2 times.

III Stir half the chopped tomatoes into onions and garlic, then cook over high heat, stirring constantly, for 3 minutes. Remove saucepan from heat.

IV Blend In flour until well incorporated, then mix in broth. Return soup to heat and bring to a boil, stirring constantly.

V Lower heat, add the remaining chopped tomatoes, and simmer for 15 minutes.

VI Purée the soup in several steps C S or using special attachment K. Peel, seed, and chop reserved tomatoes by hand Mince C Ⓚ S dill. Stir in tomatoes, sour cream, and dill and reheat over low flame, but do not boil. Season to taste with salt and pepper before serving hot, garnished with grated cheese.

Ⓚ KitchenAid users: finely grind or hand-mince onions, garlic, tomatoes, and dill.

SLICED ZUCCHINI SOUP

(YIELD: ENOUGH TO SERVE 6)

1	Large onion, peeled and cut in quarters
2	Ribs celery, with all strings removed, cut in 1-inch pieces
1/4	Pound country-cured bacon, cut in 1-inch pieces
2	Tablespoons olive oil
1 1/4	Cups uncooked rice
4	Tomatoes, peeled, seeded, and cut in quarters
1/2	Teaspoon granulated sugar
6 1/2	Cups beef broth
4	Small zucchini
3	Tablespoons minced fresh chives
	Salt and freshly ground black pepper
1 1/2	Cups chopped C S or grated K S Parmesan cheese

I   Coarsely chop onion, celery, and bacon in container C S or put through grinder K.

II   Sauté vegetables and bacon in olive oil until onions turn golden. Add rice and cook, stirring 3 minutes more.

III   Coarsely chop C S tomatoes for 2 or 3 seconds or put through grinder K. Add to onion-rice mixture along with sugar and broth. Cook over medium heat until rice is barely tender.

IV   Thinly slice C K S zucchini and add to soup. Stir in the chives and cook, covered, for 5 or 6 minutes. The zucchini should still have a bit of "crunch." Season the soup to taste with salt and pepper. Serve hot with grated cheese on the side.

EGGPLANT SOUP

(YIELD: ENOUGH TO SERVE 6–8)

2   Small eggplants, peeled
5   Tablespoons butter
1   Large onion, peeled and cut in eighths
1   Large clove garlic, peeled and cut in half
4   Medium tomatoes
2   Bay leaves, crushed
    Pinch marjoram
    A few threads of saffron
8   Cups beef broth
1/3   Cup uncooked rice
    Salt and freshly ground pepper
1/2   Pound veal, cut in 1-inch cubes
1/4   Medium onion, peeled
1/8   Teaspoon nutmeg
    Pinch dried oregano
    Salt and freshly ground pepper
    Flour
    Garlic Crusts (see page 303)
2   Tablespoons minced fresh chives

I   Coarsely slice C K S eggplants; cover with boiling salted water and set aside for 15 minutes.

II   Drain eggplant slices, pat dry, and cook in butter over low heat in a large saucepan, covered, for 30 minutes, stirring occasionally so slices brown evenly.

III Coarsely chop onion and garlic in container C S for 2 or 3 seconds, stopping once to scrape down container sides, then add tomatoes and whirl 1 or 2 seconds more (or put vegetables through grinder K).

IV Stir onions, garlic, and tomatoes into eggplant, add bay leaves, marjoram, and saffron, and cook over low heat for 15 minutes, stirring occasionally. Add the broth and rice, season to taste with salt and pepper and simmer, covered, for 40 minutes longer.

V Meanwhile, chop C S or grind K S together veal and ¼ onion. Add nutmeg, oregano, salt and pepper to taste; mix well and shape into tiny meatballs. Roll in flour and set aside.

VI Purée C K S in several stages if you prefer a smooth soup or, if not, leave as is and bring to a boil. Drop In meatballs and allow to boil gently for 15 minutes. Serve hot, garnished with garlic crusts and minced chives.

SPICY TOMATO-SAUERKRAUT SOUP

(YIELD: ENOUGH TO SERVE 6)

5	Cups Easy Tomato Juice (see page 242)
2½	Cups beef broth
1	Teaspoon granulated sugar
1½	Pounds delicatessen-style sauerkraut
3	Medium onions, peeled and cut in quarters
5	Slices country-cured slab bacon
2	Medium potatoes, peeled
1	Tablespoon tomato paste
1½	Teaspoons paprika
1	Teaspoon each salt and fennel seeds
⅛	Teaspoon powdered cloves
2	Knockwurst
½	Cup cooked ham, cut in 1-inch cubes
2	Tablespoons minced fresh chives or fennel leaves

I Bring tomato juice, broth, and sugar to a boil in a large soup kettle. Rinse and drain sauerkraut, add to kettle, then lower heat, cover, and simmer for 30 minutes.

II   Meanwhile, place onions and bacon slices, a few handfuls at a time, in container C S and process by turning machine quickly on and off 3 or 4 times, stopping once or twice to scrape down container sides (or put through grinder K). Sauté together in a separate pan until onions are soft.

III   Grate C K S potatoes, cover with cold water, and soak for 5 minutes. Drain.

IV   Add onion-bacon mixture, potatoes, tomato paste, and seasonings to soup. Cover and simmer over low heat for 20 minutes.

V   Slice C K S knockwurst. Chop C S or grind K S ham. Add knockwurst and ham to soup and cook 10 minutes longer. Sprinkle with chives or fennel leaves before serving hot.

QUICK AND EASY BORSCHT

(YIELD: ENOUGH TO SERVE 6)

    4   Medium beets, peeled and cut to fit spout
 2½   Cups water
    1   Teaspoon salt
 1½   Cups beef consommé
    1   Cup sour cream (more if desired)
    1   Tablespoon each lemon juice and granulated sugar
    1   Tablespoon minced fresh chives
        Cold boiled potatoes
        Chopped scallions
        Hard-cooked egg quarters

I   Finely grate C K S beets; place in saucepan with water and cook for 20 minutes or until tender. Remove from heat and stir in salt and consommé. Refrigerate until well chilled.

II   Stir ¾ cup of the sour cream (more if desired), lemon juice, and sugar into soup; correct seasonings to taste, adding more lemon juice and sugar if necessary. Serve cold, topping each portion with a dollop of the remaining sour cream and a sprinkling of chives. Garnish each portion with cold boiled potato, chopped scallions, or hard-cooked egg quarters if desired.

OMELETS

Omelets in their infinite variety serve beautifully as the focal point around which to build many a delectable brunch, lunch, or light supper. The trick is to work on a small scale—with omelets just big enough to serve one or two; make a succession of small omelets when serving more. You'll be pleasantly surprised to find how simple they are to prepare once you learn the basic technique.

BASIC OMELET RECIPE
(YIELD: ENOUGH TO MAKE 1 OMELET TO SERVE 2)

> 4   *Eggs*
> 2   *Tablespoons water*
>   *Salt and freshly ground black pepper*
> 1   *Teaspoon butter*

   I   Beat together eggs and liquid by hand, then season to taste with salt and pepper.

   II   Heat butter to sizzling in an omelet pan or skillet over medium flame (Teflon lining is a great help), and pour in egg mixture. Stir rapidly in a circular motion with a fork for 30 seconds, lifting the cooked part of the omelet so that uncooked part can run underneath.

III As soon as eggs are set on the bottom but still smooth and creamy on top, press skillet handle down so that omelet slides partway up the side of the pan in your direction, then flip omelet edge over toward the center of the pan.

IV Quickly tilt pan in the opposite direction, allowing omelet to slide up on the side away from the handle.

V Raise pan handle so that omelet flips over and out onto waiting hot plate.

OMELET VARIATIONS

While omelets are quite delicious "as is," they also make perfect vehicles for an almost limitless number of fillings. Your food processor is ideal for preparing these, since the ingredients for omelet fillings usually are finely chopped or sliced. Try any of the following suggestions, but don't hesitate to concoct your own— almost anything that tastes good to you is suitable. Prepare fillings from scratch, or utilize those bits of leftovers that might otherwise go unused. Mix them with sauces (see pages 265 to 272), or top the omelet with the sauce. Just remember to have all ingredients warm or at room temperature before filling the omelet.

Cheeses: Finely grate C K S Cheddar, Gruyère, Parmesan, or Swiss cheese. Use for filling or omelet garnish.

Herbs: Mince C S any fresh herb after removing the stems, and use alone or with other ingredients.

Meats: Mince C S or grind K S cooked chicken, ham, turkey, or veal.

Purées: Fill or top omelet with Mushroom, Onion, Spinach, or Ripe Tomato Purée (see pages 219 to 222).

Sauces: Bind chopped cooked meats, seafood, or vegetables with Curry Sauce, Mornay Sauce, Mushroom Sauce, etc., or use the latter to top the omelet.

Seafood: Mince C S crabmeat, lobster, or shrimp.

Vegetables: Chop C S or thinly slice C K S almost any vegetable, then sauté before using alone or in a cream sauce.

TOMATO-ZUCCHINI OMELET

(YIELD: ENOUGH FILLING FOR 3 SMALL OMELETS)

Ingredients listed in Basic Omelet Recipe
Plus

1	Medium zucchini, cut in 1-inch pieces
1/2	Cup cooked ham, cut in 1-inch pieces
1/4	Medium onion, peeled and cut in quarters
2	Medium tomatoes
2	Tablespoons butter
1/4	Teaspoon granulated sugar

I Place zucchini, ham, and onion in container C Ⓚ S. Whirl for 5 or 6 seconds, stopping as necessary to scrape down container sides.

II Peel and seed tomatoes, then finely chop by hand.

III Sauté zucchini, ham, and onion in butter for 3 minutes. Lower heat, cover pan, and cook 4 minutes longer. Remove mixture from pan with slotted spoon.

IV Add tomatoes to pan, sprinkle with sugar, and cook over low heat, stirring, until most of moisture evaporates. Remove and stir into ham and vegetables. Keep the mixture warm.

V Prepare omelet mixture and cook according to directions to point where eggs are set but still remain soft and creamy on top.

VI Arrange 2 or 3 tablespoons tomato-zucchini mixture along center of omelet, then flip, fold, and slide from pan onto waiting hot plate.

Ⓚ KitchenAid users: grind together or hand-chop ham and onion; hand-chop zucchini.

SWISS CHEESE AND TOMATO OMELET

(YIELD: ENOUGH FILLING FOR 3 SMALL OMELETS)

Ingredients listed in Basic Omelet Recipe
Plus

1	*Piece Swiss cheese (2 inch × 1 inch), cut in half*
2	*Medium tomatoes*
1½	*Tablespoons butter*
1	*Tablespoon minced fresh chives*
¼	*Teaspoon granulated sugar*

I Finely grate C K S cheese. Set aside.

II Peel, seed, and chop tomatoes by hand. Heat butter, add tomatoes, chives, and sugar, then cook over low heat until most of liquid evaporates. Keep the mixture hot.

III Prepare and partially cook omelet. As soon as eggs are set on bottom but are still soft and creamy on top, arrange 2 or 3 tablespoons of hot filling over center and top with a spoonful of grated cheese. Flip, fold, and slide omelet from pan onto waiting hot plate.

HAM AND MUSHROOM OMELET

(YIELD: ENOUGH FILLING FOR 3 SMALL OMELETS)

Ingredients listed in Basic Omelet Recipe
Plus

½	*Cup cooked ham, cut in 1-inch pieces*
½	*Pound fresh mushrooms*
1	*Tablespoon fresh thyme leaves, with all tough stems removed*
1	*Tablespoon butter*
1	*Cup thick Basic White Sauce (see page 271)*

I Place ham, mushrooms, and thyme leaves in container C K S. Whirl for 5 or 6 seconds, stopping once to scrape down container sides.

II Sauté ham and mushroom mixture in butter, stirring frequently, until mushrooms turn golden, then remove from heat and stir in as much sauce as necessary to bind mixture. Keep the mixture warm.

    III Prepare and cook omelet mixture until eggs are set on bottom but still creamy on top. Arrange 2 or 3 tablespoons ham-mushroom mixture along center of omelet, then flip, fold, and slide omelet from pan onto waiting hot plate.

Ⓚ KitchenAid users: chop these ingredients by hand.

MUSHROOM OMELET WITH TOMATO SAUCE

(YIELD: ENOUGH FILLING FOR 3 SMALL OMELETS)

Ingredients listed in Basic Omelet Recipe
Plus

> ½ *Pound fresh mushrooms*
> 2 *Shallots, peeled and cut in quarters*
> 2 *Tablespoons butter*
>   *Lemon juice*
> 3 *Tablespoons sour cream (optional)*
> 2 *Cups Tomato Sauce II (see page 266)*

    I Place mushrooms and shallots in container C Ⓚ S. Process by turning machine quickly on and off 3 or 4 times, stopping once to scrape down container sides.

    II Sauté mushrooms and shallots in butter until golden, then sprinkle with lemon juice and cook over low heat until most of liquid evaporates. Keep the mixture warm.

    III Prepare and cook omelet mixture until eggs are set on bottom but still creamy on top. Arrange 2 or 3 tablespoons mushroom mixture along center of omelet and top with 1 table-spoon sour cream. Flip, fold, and slide omelet from pan onto waiting hot plate. Top with hot tomato sauce and serve at once.

Ⓚ KitchenAid users: hand-chop these.

SOUFFLÉS

BASIC SOUFFLÉ RECIPE

Fold in almost any minced meat or puréed vegetable or fruit—the elegant soufflé will become doubly inviting.

(YIELD: ENOUGH TO SERVE 4 TO 6)

> 3 Tablespoons butter
> 3 Tablespoons all-purpose flour
> 1 Cup cold milk
>   Salt
> ¾ Cup of any of the Additional Ingredients listed below
> 4 Egg yolks
> 5 Egg whites

    I In a heavy pan set directly over medium heat, melt butter and blend in flour. Stir in milk, season to taste with salt, and cook, stirring constantly, until sauce thickens slightly.

    II Fold in your choice of ingredients, then beat in the egg yolks, one at a time, until all have been incorporated. Allow mixture to cool.

    III Preheat oven to 350 degrees F.

    IV Beat Ⓒ K S egg whites until stiff but not dry. Fold gently into mixture and turn at once into buttered soufflé dish or other deep baking dish.

Ⓒ Cuisinart users: whip egg whites separately.

V Bake for 30 minutes or until top of soufflé is puffy and lightly browned. For a less crusty soufflé, set dish in a pan of hot, not boiling water while it bakes.

ADDITIONAL INGREDIENTS FOR SOUFFLÉS

Cheese: Grate C K S 1½ cups Cheddar, Gruyère, or Swiss cheese.

Meat, Poultry, or Seafood: Mince C S or grind K S 1½ cups cooked ham, chicken, turkey, fish, crabmeat, lobster, or shrimp.

Vegetables: Purée C Ⓚ S 1½ cups cooked artichoke hearts, asparagus, broccoli, zucchini, or mixed vegetables, or fold in 1½ cups Mushroom, Spinach, or Ripe Tomato Purée (see pages 219 to 222).

Ⓚ KitchenAid users: hand-mince these or force through a sieve.

ZUCCHINI-MUSHROOM SOUFFLÉ

Ingredients listed in Basic Soufflé Recipe
Plus

> 1   *Medium zucchini, peeled and cut in 1-inch slices*
> 1   *Tablespoon butter*
> ¼   *Cup Mushroom Purée (see page 219)*

I Finely grate C K S zucchini, squeeze dry, then sauté in butter until very soft.

II Combine with purée and fold into Basic Recipe. Proceed to beat in egg yolks and fold in egg whites and bake as directed.

SEAFOOD SOUFFLÉ

Ingredients listed in Basic Soufflé Recipe
Plus

> ¾   *Cup cooked crabmeat, lobster, or shrimp*

I   Finely chop C S or grind K S seafood. Set aside.

II   As soon as soufflé sauce thickens slightly, remove from heat and stir in seafood mixture. Proceed to beat in egg yolks and fold in egg whites. Bake as directed.

TOMATO-CHEESE SOUFFLÉ

Ingredients listed in Basic Soufflé Recipe
Plus

> 1   *Piece Swiss cheese (2 inches × 1 inch)*
> 1   *Tablespoon minced fresh dill*
> ¾   *Cup Ripe Tomato Purée (see page 222)*

I   Finely grate C K S cheese. Mince dill by hand. Mix together cheese, dill, and tomato purée. Set aside.

II   Prepare sauce for soufflé and remove from heat when slightly thickened. Stir in cheese-tomato mixture, then proceed to beat in egg yolks and fold in egg whites. Bake as directed.

HAM AND TOMATO SOUFFLÉ

Ingredients listed in Basic Soufflé Recipe
Plus

> ¾   *Cup cooked ham, cut in 1-inch pieces*
> 1   *Tablespoon minced fresh chives*
> ¼   *Cup Ripe Tomato Purée (see page 222)*

I   Finely chop C S or grind K S ham. Mince chives by hand. Mix together ham, chives, and tomato purée. Set aside.

II   As soon as sauce for soufflé thickens slightly, remove from heat and fold in ham mixture. Proceed as directed in Basic Recipe.

CRÊPES

SUGGESTIONS FOR FILLING & SERVING CRÊPES

Crêpes are equally at home as the perfect introduction to a meal, its highlight the main course, or as a superb finish. Mini-sized crêpes perform beautifully as appetizing—and unusual—hot hors d'oeuvres (see page 81). Use any of the fillings found on pages 147 to 148, or transform your leftovers into delectable stuffings for these adaptable pancakes. Simply combine yesterday's minced bits and pieces of meat, seafood, or vegetables with just enough Basic White Sauce (see page 271), Curry Sauce (see page 272), Béchamel Sauce (see page 272), or Mornay Sauce (see page 272) to bind them together, then top with extra sauce and slide under the broiler until piping hot. If you don't feel like bothering with sauces, try sautéing thinly sliced C K S vegetables, asparagus, or mushrooms, for example, in a little butter, add a cup of heavy cream and bring to a boil, then sprinkle over 2 pinches of flour and allow the mixture to cook down until thick.

Crêpes bring a meal to a satisfying close when you fill them with ice cream or spoonfuls of finely chopped C S fresh fruits and nuts and top with Chocolate Praline Sauce (see page 273), whipped K S cream, or sour cream. Fresh fruits and berries prepared as described in Fruit Turnovers (see page 316) also serve

admirably as fillings for crêpes. Dust the tops of the crêpes lightly
with confectioners' sugar after rolling them up.

CRÊPES · FRENCH PANCAKES

These delicate pancakes are without doubt the easiest to make and most
versatile to serve of all the classic French recipes. Your food processor whips
them up in seconds, then turns its skills to preparing delicious fillings.

(YIELD: ENOUGH TO SERVE 6)

> 4 *Extra-large eggs*
> ¾ *Cup each milk and water*
> ¼ *Teaspoon salt*
> 3 *Tablespoons vegetable or peanut oil*
> 1 *Cup plus 2 tablespoons all-purpose flour*
> 3 *Tablespoons butter or oil*

I   Place eggs in container C or bowl K S. Whirl until well
beaten, then add milk, water, salt, vegetable oil and flour and whirl
for 8 to 10 seconds or until well blended. Refrigerate batter for 2
hours.

II   Rub the inside of a 6-inch skillet or crêpe pan with
½ teaspoon of the butter (or oil). Set pan over low heat for 1
minute, then remove and wipe pan with paper towels. Add another
½ teaspoon butter and repeat the process. This seasons the
skillet so the crêpes won't stick.

III   Stir the cold crêpe batter to make sure it is smooth.
Add ¼ teaspoon butter to seasoned pan, tilting pan back and forth
to coat bottom and sides evenly. The crêpes should be very thin
yet hold together; have 2 to 3 tablespoons ready in your ladle to
add as soon as butter is hot enough, and let experience—and the
size of your pan—show you exactly how much batter will be
required each time.

IV   Test to see whether pan is hot enough by flicking a
few drops of water into it; if the water sizzles, add your measured
crêpe batter and rotate pan quickly around and from side to side
so the mixture spreads all over the bottom surface.

V   As soon as bubbles appear throughout the batter,
loosen one edge of the crêpe with a spatula. If the bottom is light

brown, turn the crêpe over immediately to lightly brown the other side. Slide the crêpe from the pan and set aside on a plate.

VI Prepare subsequent crêpes in the same manner, using about ⅛ teaspoon butter for each until the crêpes no longer stick to the pan. Stack these one on top of the other as they come from the pan. Reheat the crêpes, if necessary, on the middle rack of a warm oven. Crêpes are practically indestructible. Make them well ahead of serving time, then cover and refrigerate and reheat by the method just described when ready to be filled. Crêpes also freeze well. Stack them with sheets of waxed paper between them, wrap the package in freezer foil and freeze at 0 degrees F.

CRÊPES AUX DUXELLES · FRENCH PANCAKES WITH MUSHROOM FILLING

> 1 *Recipe Crêpes (see page 146)*
> 2 *Recipes Duxelles (see page 242)*
> 1 *Cup thick Béchamel Sauce (see page 272)*
> *Heavy cream*
> *Brandy*

I Prepare crêpes, duxelles, and béchamel sauce as directed.

II Mix several tablespoons sauce with the duxelles and fill the crêpes as directed on page 146.

III Thin the remaining sauce to desired consistency with a little heavy cream and a few drops of brandy, then heat and serve spooned over the crêpes.

CRÊPES AUX FRUITS DE MER · FRENCH PANCAKES WITH SEAFOOD

Combine finely chopped C Ⓚ S cooked crabmeat or shrimp, or a mixture of the two, with enough Béchamel Sauce (see page 272) or Curry Sauce (see page 272) to make a rather dry mixture. Spoon the filling over the centers of the prepared crêpes; then roll up and arrange side by side in lightly buttered baking dish. Sprinkle generously with grated C K S Parmesan or Swiss cheese and place for a few minutes under the broiler until the cheese is delicately browned. Serve at once.

Ⓚ KitchenAid users: hand-chop the seafood.

FRENCH PANCAKES WITH CHICKEN AND MUSHROOMS

Sauté finely chopped C Ⓚ S mushrooms in a little butter, combine with finely chopped C Ⓚ S chicken, and sprinkle with a few drops of sherry. Spread mixture over center of prepared crêpes, roll up, and serve hot.

Ⓚ KitchenAid users: hand-chop mushrooms and chicken.

FRENCH PANCAKES WITH HAM

Mix together finely chopped C S or ground K cooked ham with 1 tablespoon minced shallot sautéed in a little butter. Bind with enough Béchamel Sauce (see page 272) to make a rather dry mixture; then spread over center of crêpes. Roll up and serve hot.

FRENCH PANCAKES WITH HAM AND MUSHROOMS

Sauté finely chopped C S mushrooms along with 1 tablespoon minced shallot. Mix with finely chopped C S or ground K cooked ham and bind with Béchamel Sauce (see page 272). Spread mixture over center of prepared crêpes, roll up, and serve hot.

CRÊPES AUX EPINARDS · FRENCH PANCAKES WITH SPINACH

Prepare crêpes (or reheat briefly on a rack in a 300 degree F. oven if prepared in advance) and fill with hot Spinach Purée (see page 221). Roll up, sprinkle with grated C K S Swiss cheese and place under broiler until cheese is delicately browned. Serve hot.

ENTRÉES

ESCARGOTS À LA BOURGUIGNONNE

(YIELD: ENOUGH TO SERVE 6)

Snail Butter (see page 106)
36 *Snails*

I Place a small quantity snail butter in each of 36 snail shells. Add 1 snail to each shell, then cover the snails with the remaining butter, sealing the openings.

II Set shells in a large, flat flameproof casserole, or use the small pans specially indented for holding snail shells, and broil until the butter is hot and bubbling. Serve at once.

FONDUE DE GRUYÈRE · SWISS FONDUE

(YIELD: ENOUGH TO SERVE 6 TO 8)

    1   Pound Swiss cheese, cut in 1-inch pieces
    3   Tablespoons all-purpose flour
   ½   Clove garlic, peeled
    2   Cups dry white wine
    3   Tablespoons kirsch
        Pinch ground nutmeg
        Salt and white pepper
    1   Loaf slightly stale French or Italian bread, cut into
        bite-size pieces

I Finely chop C or grate K S cheese. Mix with the flour until cheese is well coated.

II Rub the inside of an earthenware casserole or pan of a chafing dish with the cut side of the garlic. Add wine and heat just to boiling, then add floured cheese, 1 or 2 handfuls at a time, and cook over very low heat, stirring constantly with a wooden spoon and allowing each batch of cheese to melt before adding the next.

III When all the cheese has melted and the fondue is creamy and bubbling, transfer to a chafing dish if necessary and stir in the kirsch, nutmeg, and salt and white pepper to taste. Serve with bread cubes, each cut with a little crust. Spear the bread cubes with fondue forks and dip into the hot fondue.

HACHIS DE VOLAILLE · CHICKEN HASH

This most delicate of all the hash recipes is enhanced by a border of your favorite vegetable purée. Be sure to choose a purée with enough substance to stand in a decorative border.

(YIELD: ENOUGH TO SERVE 6)

    3   Cups boiled white meat chicken, cut in 1-inch pieces
  1½   Cups light cream
    2   Tablespoons butter
    2   Tablespoons all-purpose flour
    2   Cups milk
        Salt and freshly ground black pepper

1   Egg
2   Tablespoons whipped K S cream
2   Cups vegetable purée (see pages 217 to 223)

I   Coursely chop C or hand-chop K S chicken. Place in a saucepan with 1 cup of the cream; cook, stirring occasionally, until liquid reduces by one-half, then turn mixture into an oven-proof serving casserole.

II   Melt butter and stir in flour. Cook just long enough for mixture to turn faintly golden. Stir in the milk and continue to cook, stirring constantly, until the sauce thickens, then reduce to 1 cup.

III   Preheat oven to 450 degrees F.

IV   Remove sauce from heat and stir in remaining ½ cup cream. Stir 1 cup of the sauce into hash mixture and season to taste with salt and pepper. Beat the egg lightly and stir into the remaining ½ cup of sauce along with the whipped cream; spread this mixture over the top of the hash.

V   Spoon pureé into a pastry bag with a fluted nozzle and pipe through around the outer edges of the hash to form a decorative border. Bake until nicely glazed on top or, if you prefer, you may glaze the dish under the broiler. Serve hot.

CHICKEN MOUSSE

Beautifully white and incredibly delicate in taste, this fine-textured mousse may be served either hot as an entrée or cold as an hors d'oeuvre. Any one of a variety of sauces may be brought forth with it to subtly alter its flavor.

(YIELD: ONE 1-QUART MOUSSE)

2   Pounds uncooked boned, skinned chicken breasts
    trimmed of all gristle and tendons
2   Cups cold light cream
4   Tablespoons cold cream cheese
¼   Teaspoon salt
⅛   Teaspoon each white pepper and cayenne pepper
1   Clove garlic, peeled and crushed
    White from one extra-large egg
    Sauce Aurore (page 272), Tomato Cream Sauce
    (page 269), or Curry Sauce (page 272)

I Cut meat into ½-inch cubes.

II Purée C ⬚K S half the chicken cubes to a near liquid state. Stop motor at least once to scrape down container walls. Place puréed chicken in bowl and set in the freezer.

III Repeat Step II, using the remaining chicken cubes. As you place the second bowl of chicken purée in the freezer, remove the first bowl.

IV Scoop the chilled chicken purée into the container C S. Start the machine and begin to add 1 cup cold light cream a few drops at a time. As soon as the cream has been worked into the meat, add the cold cream cheese 1 teaspoon at a time. When the ingredients are well mixed, scrape the mixture back into the bowl and return to the freezer, removing the second bowl of chicken purée at the same time.

V Repeat Step IV, using the second bowl of purée and the remaining cup cold light cream.

VI Place **all** the chicken purée in the container C S and add the salt, white pepper, cayenne pepper, and garlic; start the motor and add the egg white a bit at a time through the spout until all ingredients are well blended. Place the mixture in a bowl and chill in the freezer for 20 minutes, stirring several times.

VII Meanwhile, preheat oven to 350 degrees F.

VIII Butter a 1½-quart savarin mold, scrape the chilled chicken into it, and smooth the top. Set the mold in a larger pan filled with hot water to a depth of one inch.

IX Bake 1½ to 1¾ hours. Test for doneness by inserting a knife in the thickest part of the mousse. When the knife comes out clean, the mousse is ready to serve with the sauce of your choice.

⬚K KitchenAid users: your colander and sieve attachment will not perform this task. If you have a blender, you may put it to work here; if not, that old standby the mortar and pestle will serve well.

QUENELLES LYONNAISE

Although this haute cuisine classic is time-consuming and a bit tedious, it is rendered considerably less difficult when the quenelles themselves are prepared in advance in your marvelous food processor. In any case, the taste and texture of these little fish dumplings are so heavenly that they are more than worth the effort.

¾ Pound fillets (pike, sole, halibut, or flounder), cut in 1-inch pieces
⅔ Cup each milk and water
18 Tablespoons butter, cut in pieces
1½ Teaspoons salt
2¼ Cups flour
6 Eggs
½ Teaspoon white pepper
   A pinch or two nutmeg
1 Egg white

To Prepare in Cuisinart Processor:

I Whirl the fish pieces to a smooth purée (about 45 seconds), stopping twice to scrape fish from beneath the blades and down from the sides of the container. Pike purée will need to be pressed through a sieve. Transfer to a bowl and refrigerate.

II In a saucepan bring to a boil, stirring constantly, the milk and water, 4 tablespoons butter and ½ teaspoon salt. Add flour all at one time and stir over low flame until flour is well incorporated. Place this panade or paste in container and whirl until smooth (about 40 seconds). With machine running, add 4 eggs one at a time, mixing well after each has been added. Whirl until very smooth. Spread on a plate, cover, and refrigerate.

III Place half the panade, half the fish purée, ½ teaspoon salt, and 1 egg in the container and process until well mixed. Add 6 tablespoons butter and whirl again until the butter is well incorporated. Transfer to a bowl and refrigerate.

IV Add remaining panade and fish purée, 1 egg and 1 egg white, ½ teaspoon each salt and pepper, and nutmeg to container and whirl until smooth and well mixed. Add remaining butter and process until butter is well incorporated.

V Whirl this mixture and the refrigerated batch until well mixed. Cover and refrigerate for at least 6 hours or freeze until needed. The frozen mixture should be defrosted in the refrigerator for 24 hours.

VI Shape into smooth, oval dumplings with 2 tablespoons dipped in hot water. Dip the mixture up with one spoon, and with the other push it into shallow simmering water deep enough to cover the dumplings. An alternate method of shaping is to roll sausage-shaped quenelles on a lightly floured board to the size and shape you prefer. Poach the quenelles in the *simmering* water about 6 at a time (they should not touch) until they rise to the surface of the water and roll over, or turn them carefully with a slotted spoon. Continue the poaching about 8 to 10 minutes or until the quenelles are firm to the touch on both sides. NEVER cover the pan or allow the water to boil while the quenelles are cooking. Remove with a slotted spoon, drain well on a fine cloth. If not using immediately, cool, cover well, and refrigerate or freeze.

VII To serve, place in a pan (preferably one that is attractive enough to bring to table) in which the quenelles will fit without overlapping, cover with a rich cream sauce flavored with Duxelles (see page 242), with Sauce Nantua, or with Sauce Américaine, place on an asbestos pad, and barely simmer for about 20 minutes. Shake the pan every few minutes to prevent the quenelles from sticking. Bring to table immediately and serve hot.

To Prepare in KitchenAid:
Run fish through fine blade of grinder and strain. Season and work in additional ingredients over ice-water-bath attachment to keep mixture well chilled.

To Prepare in Starmix:
Use blender attachment and proceed as directed for Cuisinart machine but cool the panade slightly before placing in blender and stop frequently while mixing to stir ingredients up from the bottom and down from the sides.

SUKIYAKI

(YIELD: ENOUGH TO SERVE 6)

1½	*Pounds uncooked boneless sirloin, partially frozen*
4	*Medium onions, peeled*
4	*Ribs celery, with all strings removed*
⅓	*Pound fresh mushrooms, or canned Japanese mushrooms*
4	*Cups fresh spinach leaves*

10   Scallions, with 3 inches green top
1½   Cakes soybean curd
1   Small piece beef suet
1   8-Ounce can sliced bamboo shoots, drained
1   Cup beef consommé
⅔   Cup Japanese soy sauce
1½   Tablespoons sugar
½   Cup harusame (Japanese clear noodles)

I   Thinly slice C K S meat, onions, celery, and mushrooms. By hand, cut spinach leaves in 1-inch pieces, scallions in 2-inch diagonal slices and bean curd in ¾-inch cubes.

II   Rub a large, heavy skillet or electric frying pan with the suet and set over medium heat. Add onions, celery, mushrooms, spinach, scallions, and bamboo shoots. Sauté for 1 or 2 minutes, then add the consommé, soy sauce, and sugar and bring to a boil, stirring once or twice, for 3 or 4 minutes. Cook Harusame separately.

III   Arrange noodles and meat over the vegetables and simmer over low heat for 2 to 3 minutes more, or until vegetables are tender but still have a bit of crunch; then stir the meat, bean curd, and noodles into the vegetable mixture and cook for 2 or 3 minutes longer. Serve immediately with hot, boiled rice.

STIR-FRIED BEEF
(YIELD: ENOUGH TO SERVE 6 TO 8)

1   Pound flank steak or other lean beef, partially frozen
2   Tablespoons each soy sauce and sherry
1   Tablespoon cornstarch
1   Tablespoon granulated sugar
2   Pounds vegetables (see Vegetable Combinations for Stir-Fried Beef below)
3   Slices fresh ginger root
⅓   Cup vegetable oil
1   Teaspoon salt
1   Cup beef broth

I   Remove all gristle and cut partially frozen meat, across the grain, into pieces sized to fit spout. Thinly slice C* and arrange in a flat shallow bowl. Combine soy sauce, sherry, cornstarch and sugar; sprinkle over meat and mix in lightly with your fingers to coat all surfaces. Allow to stand for one hour.

II Meanwhile, prepare vegetables. Peel and slice ginger root, following the pattern of the vertically running fibers; then mince by hand or machine.

III Heat a wok or large skillet until hot enough for a drop of water to sizzle and bounce over its surface. Add half the oil, then add the beef slices and stir-fry rapidly for a minute or two; cook only until the meat loses its red color.

IV Remove meat from pan and add the remaining oil, salt, and ginger root. Stir-fry for a few seconds, add the vegetables, and continue to stir-fry until these are hot through and are coated with oil.

V Add broth to pan; cover and cook over medium heat until the vegetables are nearly tender. Return beef to pan and stir-fry for 1 minute more. Serve hot over rice.

* KitchenAid and Starmix users: hand-slice for best results.

VEGETABLE COMBINATIONS FOR STIR-FRIED BEEF

There are two tricks to insuring that stir-fried vegetables will arrive at the table crisp and crunchy and at the height of their color and flavor. One involves preparing the vegetables; the other, cooking them.

To retain original freshness, each vegetable should be cut into pieces of equal shape and thickness just prior to cooking them. Your food processor simplifies matters here because not only does it possess a talent for even slicing and shredding but it will do either job in seconds.

The trick in cooking stir-fried vegetables is to shorten the time needed for stir-frying. This is easily accomplished if you parboil or blanch them beforehand. To parboil, cook green vegetables in boiling water only long enough for them to turn bright green; cook nongreen vegetables until they are beginning to be tender but are still crisp. Blanch vegetables by dipping them quickly in boiling water, then drain and rinse with cold water. Dry all vegetables well before adding them to the oil in the wok or skillet.

Since vegetables usually need less heat and more cooking time than does meat, add them to the wok after cooking and removing the meat. Add hard vegetables first if you haven't parboiled or blanched them beforehand; they need more cooking than do their tender counterparts. Slide your vegetables by handfuls into the hot oil, stirring as you go and coating each piece with oil. Proper stir-fry technique is quick but gentle; take care not to crush the vegetables or crowd them together. Add stock if your recipe calls for it, and then cover and cook until the vegetables take on a bright color or are tender but still have a bit of "crunch." Remember, overcooking makes ingredients soggy and limp, a definite "no-no" in Chinese—or for that matter, any—cooking. Almost any combination of vegetables will do for stir-frying. Use your imagination or whatever you have on hand to create interesting contrasts in color and texture. Your food processor will prepare most of the following:

Asparagus: Thickly slice C K S stalks on the diagonal; leave tips whole. Parboil or blanch stalks only.
Broccoli: Separate tops into small florets. Cut thinner stalks in half. Thinly slice C K S stalks on the diagonal and parboil.
Cabbage: Thinly slice C K S and parboil.
Chinese Cabbage: Thinly slice C K S; blanch.
Carrots: Scrape and thinly slice C K S on the diagonal. Parboil.
Cauliflower: Separate into small florets, thinly slice C K S stems diagonally. Parboil.
Celery: Trim leaves and ends and remove all strings. Thickly slice C K S on the diagonal, then blanch.
Ginko Nuts: A Chinese delicacy available in cans. Drain well.
Green Beans: Trim ends and thickly slice C K S on the diagonal. Parboil.
Lettuce: Thickly slice C K S.
Mushrooms: Trim tough stem ends, then slice C K S large specimens vertically, but leave small mushrooms whole.
Onions: Peel and thinly slice C K S.
Peas: Shell and blanch.
Peppers: Seed, then thickly slice C K S into strips or cut by hand in 1-inch squares.
Potatoes: Peel and dice. Parboil.
Snow Peas: Available frozen at most grocery stores, fresh at

Chinese stores. To use, rinse or thaw and separate, then pat dry on paper towels.

Spinach: Wash thoroughly and shake dry. Remove tough stems before using whole or tearing into pieces.

Summer Squash or Zucchini: Peel and thickly slice C K S.

Tree Ears: Another Chinese delicacy and one of my favorites because of their interesting chewy texture. Soak in warm water and rinse well before using.

CHICKEN VELVET

This elegant Chinese dish once took hours to prepare. The chicken breast had to be minced, ground in a mortar and pestle, blended, then run twice through a food grinder before it was combined with beaten egg whites and, finally, cooked. Now you can spin it up in minutes in your Cuisinart* processor.

Prepared as small pancakes or in an unusual omelet-like form, this dish ranks among the most intriguing in Chinese cuisine.

(YIELD: ENOUGH TO SERVE 4 TO 6)

2 Small (or 1 large) chicken breasts, boned and skinned
2 Tablespoons sherry
1 Teaspoon plus 1 tablespoon cornstarch
3/4 Teaspoon salt
5 Egg whites
1/2 Cup cold water
5 Tablespoons to 3/4 cup oil
1 1/2 Cups chicken consommé or 1 can undiluted canned chicken broth
3 Thin slices smoked ham
1 Recipe Stir-Fried Vegetables (see above)
Hot rice (optional)

I Cut chicken into 1-inch cubes and remove *all* gristle and tendons. Whirl 30 to 40 seconds, stopping several times to

* The Starmix processor may be used to prepare this dish, but it is less efficient than the Cuisinart machine. KitchenAid users may finely grind the chicken twice, then pound to a purée in a mortar and pestle.

scrape down sides of container and stir the meat up from underneath the blades. The chicken should be perfectly puréed. If there are *any* individual pieces in evidence, continue the process until smooth. Turn the machine on and add through the spout 1 tablespoon sherry, one drop at a time; then add 1 teaspoon cornstarch, ¾ teaspoon salt, and 1 egg white in the same manner.

II Turn the machine off, scrape down the sides of the container, and stir the mixture up from under the blades. Replace top, turn machine on, and add ¼ cup water a few drops at a time. (Don't add the water too quickly or the mixture will separate.)

III Beat the remaining egg whites until they form soft peaks (these must not be stiff and dry) and fold them into the puréed chicken.

IV There are several methods of cooking this marvelous dish. The easiest by far, but not necessarily the most interesting, is to drop the chicken mixture by teaspoons into 365° F. oil, brown slightly, and then remove and drain in a sieve. Serve as directed in Steps VI and VII.

V To prepare in another way, heat to warm but not hot 3 tablespoons oil in a heavy 10-inch skillet. Add chicken mixture and cook over low flame for 1 minute; then lift the pan from the heat and stir the oil rapidly into the chicken. Return to low heat and cook 1 minute more. Heat 2 tablespoons oil in another 10-inch skillet, turn the omelet into this second pan, and heat 2 minutes more. Serve as directed in Steps VI and VII.

VI Heat the consommé or broth and remaining sherry. Meanwhile mix the remaining cornstarch with ¼ cup cold water. Stir the cornstarch mixture into the consommé and bring to a boil, stirring constantly until sauce is thick and clear. Keep warm. Coarsely chop smoked ham.

VII Serve the Chicken Velvet with the hot sauce poured over and sprinkled with the chopped ham. Stir-fried vegetables and hot rice expand this to an exotic and satisfying meal.

BASIC DEEP-FRIED PORKBALLS

(YIELD: ENOUGH TO SERVE 6)

1½ *Pounds fairly lean pork, cut in 1-inch cubes*
2 *Slices fresh ginger root, peeled*
2 *Tablespoons cornstarch*
2 *Tablespoons water*
¾ *Teaspoon salt*
1 *Tablespoon soy sauce*
2 *Eggs*
Vegetable oil for frying
Cornstarch

I   Remove all gristle and finely chop C pork, 2 or 3 handfuls at a time, together with ginger root, or put through the fine blade of a grinder K S.

II   Combine cornstarch and water, mix well, then stir in salt and soy sauce. Beat 1 egg lightly. Blend cornstarch mixture and egg thoroughly into meat mixture.

III   Heat oil in a deep heavy saucepan or electric fryer. Lightly beat the remaining egg. Form 1-inch balls from meat mixture, dip in cornstarch and then in egg, and add, a few at a time, to sizzling oil, turning frequently to brown evenly. As soon as porkballs float on the surface of the oil, remove from pan and set aside before adding the next batch.

IV   To serve, heat the oil again and refry porkballs for 1 minute, checking to make sure that pork is completely cooked through by cutting one ball open. The interior should be gray with no pinkness at all. Drain porkballs briefly on paper towels before serving hot with rice.

DEEP-FRIED PORKBALLS—VARIATION I

Chop C or grind K S 1 large clove peeled garlic along with pork cubes and ginger slices. Add 1 tablespoon sherry to cornstarch, water, salt, and soy sauce, and mix well, then combine with meat mixture and proceed as directed.

DEEP-FRIED PORKBALLS—VARIATION II

Soak ⅓ cup dried black mushrooms in water, then drain and add, along with ⅓ cup drained water chestnuts, to the meat when chopping C or grinding K S. Proceed as directed in basic recipe.

LION'S HEAD

(YIELD: ENOUGH TO SERVE 6)

Deep-Fried Porkballs—Variation II (see above)
1½ *Tablespoons sherry*
Dash freshly ground black pepper
Vegetable oil for deep-frying
1 *Head mustard cabbage*
2 *Tablespoons vegetable oil*
1½ *Cups beef broth or chicken broth*
1½ *Tablespoons cornstarch*
¼ *Cup water*

I Prepare mixture for porkballs as directed but substitute the sherry for the water and season with the pepper. Take care not to overwork the mixture; mix just long enough to blend ingredients well.

II Heat oil to a depth of several inches in an electric deep fryer or other deep saucepan. Dip your hands in cold water, divide meat mixture into 6 portions, and shape each portion into a large ball; set in a wire basket and deep-fry until all the porkballs are golden. Drain briefly on paper towels.

III Meanwhile, cut cabbage into 6 sections. Heat 2 tablespoons oil, add cabbage, and stir-fry for 2 minutes or until cabbage is slightly wilted. Remove from heat and line the sides and bottom of a heavy saucepan with the vegetable.

IV Heat broth in a small saucepan. Arrange porkballs over cabbage, pour hot broth over all, and simmer, covered, for 1½ hours or until porkballs are cooked through.

V To serve, arrange cabbage on serving platter and top with porkballs. Mix together cornstarch and water and add to cooking liquid, stirring constantly until sauce thickens. Pour sauce over porkballs. Serve hot.

PORKBALLS WITH CAULIFLOWER

(YIELD: ENOUGH TO SERVE 6)

> 1 Recipe Deep-Fried Porkballs (see page 160)
> 1 Head cauliflower
> 1 Slice fresh ginger root, peeled
> 3 Tablespoons peanut oil
> ½ Teaspoon salt
> 1½ Cups beef broth or chicken broth
> 2 Tablespoons each cornstarch and soy sauce
> 1½ Teaspoons granulated sugar
> ½ Cup water

I Prepare and fry porkballs as directed. Meanwhile, break cauliflower into small florets; mince ginger root by hand.

II Heat half the oil in a large, heavy skillet. Add salt and ginger and stir-fry for 1 minute.

III Add remaining oil to pan. Add cauliflower and stir-fry for 2 minutes. Add porkballs and broth and bring mixture to a boil; reduce heat to low, cover pan, and simmer until cauliflower is tender but still a bit crunchy.

IV Combine remaining ingredients, mix well, stir into porkball mixture, and continue to stir until sauce thickens. Serve immediately.

OSSO BUCO

(YIELD: ENOUGH TO SERVE 6)

This delectable Italian classic now takes only 15 minutes of actual work time.

> 3 Medium carrots, scraped and cut in 1-inch pieces
> 2 Large ribs celery, with all strings removed, cut in 1-inch pieces
> 1 Tablespoon butter
> 3 Tablespoons vegetable oil

6   3-inch pieces veal shank with a good deal of
    surrounding meat
1/8 Teaspoon each dried rosemary and sage leaves
1   Cup Ripe Tomato Purée (see page 222)
1   Cup chicken broth
1   Cup dry white wine
1/4 Cup fresh parsley leaves, with all tough stems
    removed
2   Cloves garlic, peeled and cut in half
1   1-inch strip lemon zest (the thin outer skin of the
    fruit, with none of the bitter white underskin included)
    Hot, cooked rice
2   Teaspoons cornstarch
1/2 Cup water
    Salt and freshly ground black pepper

I   Place carrots in container C and whirl for 2 seconds,
then add celery and whirl for 2 seconds more; or coarsely grate
K S carrots and celery.

II   Heat butter and oil in a large, heavy saucepan or
Dutch oven and brown veal pieces on all sides. Set shanks upright
so marrow will not cook out. Add carrots, celery, rosemary, and
sage; cover and simmer for 10 minutes.

III   Mix together purée, broth, and wine. Add to meat and
vegetables, then cover and simmer over *very* low heat for 2 to 2½
hours, adding more broth or water from time to time to keep
vegetables covered. Meat should be *very* tender.

IV   Just before serving, finely chop C S together parsley,
garlic, and lemon zest or mince by hand K. Transfer meat to a
serving platter, surround with hot, cooked rice, and keep warm.
Mix cornstarch into water and add to vegetables, stirring constantly until sauce is thick and clear. Remove from heat and stir
in parsley-garlic mixture. Season to taste with salt and pepper
before serving hot over rice.

FOOD PROCESSOR BRACIOLA
(YIELD: ENOUGH TO SERVE 6)

3	Cloves garlic, peeled and cut in half
2	Tablespoons fresh parsley leaves, with all tough stems removed
1½	Pounds lean chuck, cut in 1-inch cubes
3	Slices white bread, with crusts trimmed
½	Cup water
1	Large egg
	Salt and freshly ground black pepper
8	Slices prosciutto
1	Medium onion, peeled and cut in quarters
1	Piece (2 inches × 1½ inches × ½ inch) Romano cheese, cut in ½-inch pieces
6	Tablespoons raisins
¼	Cup pine nuts
3	Tablespoons olive oil
1	35-Ounce can Italian plum tomatoes
1½	Cups dry red wine
2	Tablespoons granulated sugar
½	Teaspoon each dried basil and fennel seed
	Salt and freshly ground black pepper
	Cooked green noodles

I   Finely chop C S together garlic and parsley or mince by hand K. Set aside.

II   Coarsely chop C S or grind K S beef, 2 or 3 handfuls at a time. Return meat to container C S or bowl K. Soak the bread in the water and add to meat; mix well by turning machine on and off 5 or 6 times.

III   Add egg, reserved garlic-parsley mixture, and salt and pepper to taste to container or bowl; then turn machine quickly on and off 5 or 6 more times or until all ingredients are well mixed.

IV   Turn meat mixture out on a 15-inch piece of wet plastic wrap and smooth into a ½-inch-thick rectangle. Arrange prosciutto in layers over meat.

V   Finely chop C S together onion and cheese, or grate K cheese and mince onion by hand. Combine with raisins and pine nuts; spread mixture over prosciutto.

VI Start at one narrow end of the rectangle and roll meat up jelly-roll fashion; carefully slide plastic wrap from the roll. Wet your fingertips and seal all the seams, then cover roll securely with wax paper and chill for at least 3 hours or overnight.

VII Heat oil in a large skillet and carefully brown meat on all sides, turning gently each time so the roll does not break apart. Transfer the roll to a large Dutch oven.

VIII Purée C K S tomatoes and add to the skillet along with the wine, sugar, basil, fennel seed, and salt and pepper to taste. Simmer the mixture, stirring occasionally, for 15 minutes, then pour over the meat roll.

IX Simmer the braciola over low heat, covered, for 1 hour. Remove meat from pan and keep warm. Cook the sauce until it is reduced to one-half its original quantity, then correct seasonings to taste. To serve, place braciola on a serving dish, surround with hot green noodles, and pour the sauce over all.

PIZZA

(YIELD: ENOUGH FOR 6 6-INCH PIZZAS OR 12 3-INCH PIZZAS)

1	Recipe Pizza Dough (see page 368)
10	Medium-size ripe tomatoes, peeled and seeded
1	Clove garlic, peeled
6	Tablespoons olive oil
1	Teaspoon granulated sugar
1/2	Teaspoon salt
3/4	Pound Fontina cheese
	Anchovy fillets (optional), cut in pieces
	Dried oregano

I Prepare dough according to recipe directions and set aside to double in bulk.

II Meanwhile, chop tomatoes and mince garlic by hand, then combine with 3 tablespoons olive oil, sugar, and salt in a saucepan. Cook over low heat, stirring occasionally, until most of liquid has evaporated, about 30 minutes.

III Roll dough out as directed. Grate C K S cheese. Spread each circle with tomato mixture and top with cheese and anchovy bits, if desired. Season to taste with oregano and sprinkle with remaining 3 tablespoons oil before baking as directed in Pizza Dough recipe.

PIZZA RETTANGOLARE

This rectangular variation of the usual round pizza provides an unusual background for sautéed garden vegetables.

(YIELD: ENOUGH TO SERVE 6)

Follow the recipe for Pizza (see page 165), but roll out the dough in a large rectangular shape and fit it into an oiled rectangular baking sheet, pressing the edges tightly against the sides of the pan. Prepare the tomato mixture as described in Step II of the pizza recipe and spread it over the dough. Top sauce with anchovy bits if desired, season with oregano to taste, and sprinkle top with 3 tablespoons oil. Bake in an oven preheated to 425 degrees F. for 20 minutes. (No cheese is added at this point).

Meanwhile, peel and slice C K S 1 small eggplant. Sprinkle with salt and weight down for 10 minutes. Seed and slice C K S 2 medium green peppers; sauté in 2 tablespoons vegetable oil until tender, then set them aside. Squeeze excess moisture from eggplant slices and sauté with 3 tablespoons oil in the same pan until lightly browned. Arrange green pepper slices neatly on one side of the pizza, the eggplant slices on the other, and mozzarella cheese slices in a row down the center. Return pizza to oven to bake 5 to 10 minutes longer or until nicely browned. Serve immediately.

PATLIJAN DOLMASI · TURKISH STUFFED EGGPLANT

(YIELD: ENOUGH TO SERVE 6)

   6 *Small eggplants*
      Salt
   2 *Medium onions, peeled and cut in eighths*
  10 *Medium fresh mushrooms, cut in half*

6 Tablespoons vegetable oil
1½ Cups cooked lamb, cut in 1-inch pieces
1 Tablespoon each *fresh mint and thyme leaves, with all tough stems removed*
¾ Cup currants
½ Cup pine nuts
3 Tablespoons raw rice
2 Tablespoons tomato sauce or catsup
Salt and freshly ground black pepper
Beef broth
1 Cup yogurt or sour cream
1½ Tablespoons tomato paste

I Cut one end from each eggplant and scoop out the pulp without breaking the shells. Sprinkle hollowed-out shells and pulp with salt and arrange in a colander, then weight down with a bowl and allow to drain for 30 minutes.

II Finely chop onions and mushrooms together in container C S or by hand. Rinse eggplant pulp and shells and blot dry with paper towels. Heat oil in a large skillet and sauté onions, mushrooms, and eggplant pulp for 10 minutes, adding more oil if necessary to keep vegetables from sticking.

III Meanwhile, finely chop C S or grind K S together lamb and fresh herbs; add to the sautéed vegetables and cook until lightly browned, breaking up any large pieces of meat with a fork. Add the currants, pine nuts, rice, and tomato sauce. Season to taste with salt and pepper and cook over low heat, stirring frequently, for 5 minutes.

IV Preheat oven to 350 degrees F. Spoon lamb and vegetable mixture into eggplant shells and set the shells cut sides up in a deep, rectangular baking dish. Pour in enough broth to bring the liquid level halfway up the sides of the eggplants; cover and bake for 1 hour or until soft.

V Set shells on a serving dish. Combine the yogurt with 1 cup of the liquid left in the casserole and mix in the tomato paste. Season the sauce to taste with salt and pepper and spoon over the eggplant. Serve warm or cold.

KIBBE

This Middle Eastern favorite practically makes itself when you put your food processor to work.

(YIELD: ENOUGH TO SERVE 6)

> 1 Cup bulghur*
> 2 Cups lean lamb, cut in 1-inch cubes
> 2 Medium onions, peeled and cut in quarters
>   Salt
> 1 Cup lamb, with some fat included, cut in 1-inch cubes
> 2 Tablespoons butter
> 1/4 Cup pine nuts
>   Dash or two each ground nutmeg and allspice

I   Rinse bulghur under running water, then set it in a bowl with water to cover, to soak for 1 hour.

II   Finely chop C S or grind K S lean lamb and 1 onion together. Season to taste with salt and set aside.

III   Finely chop C S or grind K S together fatty lamb and remaining onion. Sauté this mixture in 2 tablespoons butter with the pine nuts, stirring frequently, until the meat is nicely browned and broken into fine pieces. Remove from heat and season with the spices.

IV   Meanwhile, preheat oven to 375 degrees F.

V   Drain bulghur thoroughly and combine with the lean lamb/onion mixture, adding a bit of ice water if necessary to make mixture easier to handle.

VI   Spread half the lamb-bulghur mixture over the bottom of a buttered baking dish. Top this with the lamb/pine nut mixture and cover with the remaining lamb-bulghur mixture. Cut diagonally twice to form into diamond shapes.

VII   Dot generously with butter and bake until golden brown on top, about 45 minutes. Serve hot.

* This cracked wheat is available at most specialty or health-food stores.

SEEKH KABOBS

These highly spiced kabobs make a compatible accompaniment to any veg-etable or egg curry, although they are also special enough to go it alone. In this case, double the recipe.

(YIELD: ENOUGH TO SERVE 6)

1   *Pound uncooked lamb, cut in 1-inch cubes*
1   *Medium onion, peeled and cut in quarters*
2   *Cloves garlic, peeled and cut in half*
1   *Small piece fresh ginger root, scraped*
2   *Tablespoons each fresh coriander, watercress, or parsley leaves, with all tough stems removed*
1   *Tablespoon split-pea flour**
2   *Tablespoons lemon juice*
1   *Teaspoon salt*
1/2   *Teaspoon each ground cinnamon, ground cloves, and chili powder*
1/4   *Teaspoon freshly ground black pepper*
2   *Tablespoons plain yogurt*

I   Trim any gristle from meat and chop C S or grind K to consistency you prefer. Set aside.

II   Whirl onion and garlic** for 2 or 3 seconds, then scrape down sides of container. Add ginger root and herbs and whirl for 2 seconds more.

III   Combine ground lamb, chopped onion mixture, flour, lemon juice, and spices in a large bowl. Use your fingers to knead mixture for a few minutes, then roll out on a pastry board until smooth.

IV   Divide mixture into 6 equal portions and pat into finger-shaped rolls, or wrap equal portions of mixture around skewers.

V   Broil, turning frequently and basting with the yogurt, until brown on all sides. Serve hot.

---

* If you have split peas on hand you can make this flour simply by reducing some of them to a powder in a grain mill K, or you may substitute all-purpose flour if you wish.
** KitchenAid users may choose to grind onions and garlic along with the meat or mince them by hand with the herbs and ginger root.

MEATBALLS TANGIER

Shape these tiny meatballs, fry until brown, and serve on cocktail picks with Devilish Hot Dip or Mustard Dip as a dipping sauce, or prepare with this intriguing fruit sauce.

(YIELD: ENOUGH TO SERVE 6)

2	*Slices bread, cut in ½-inch pieces*
6	*Tablespoons milk*
3	*Pounds lean chuck, cut in 1-inch cubes*
2	*Tablespoons raisins*
½	*Teaspoon each allspice, ground thyme, and salt*
3	*Tablespoons vegetable oil*
18	*Pitted prunes*
18	*Dried apricots*
1¼	*Cups each Ripe Tomato Purée (see page 222) and orange juice*
6	*Tablespoons honey*
2	*Tablespoons soy sauce*
1½	*Teaspoons ground cinnamon*
1	*Teaspoon allspice*
6	*Cups hot, cooked rice*

I Mix bread and milk and squeeze excess moisture from bread.

II Trim gristle from meat and chop C S or grind K S with raisins, then mix in bread paste and ½ teaspoon each allspice, thyme, and salt.

III Shape into 1-inch meatballs and fry in the oil until brown on the outside, still rare within.

IV Preheat oven to 325 degrees F.

V Set meatballs in ovenproof baking dish along with any pan scrapings. Tuck prunes and apricots in among meatballs.

VI Stir together purée, juice, honey, soy sauce, cinnamon, and allspice. Pour over meatballs, cover with aluminum foil and bake for 30 minutes. Remove foil and bake 30 minutes longer. Serve hot over rice.

MEATBALL AND SAUERKRAUT GOULASH

(YIELD: ENOUGH TO SERVE 6)

> 1 Cup soft bread crumbs
> Milk
> 1½ Pounds each *lean chuck and pork, cut in 1-inch cubes*
> 1 Large can sauerkraut
> ½ Teaspoon ground sage
> ¼ Teaspoon each *caraway seeds, salt, and freshly ground black pepper*
> ¼ Cup vegetable oil
> 4 Medium onions, peeled and cut in 1-inch pieces
> 2 Medium green peppers, blanched in boiling water for 2 minutes, then drained, seeded and cut in 1-inch pieces
> 1 Tablespoon Hungarian sweet paprika
> 4 Medium tomatoes
> 1 Tablespoon granulated sugar
> ½ Cup beef broth or water
> 1 Bay leaf
> Hot cooked noodles
> 1 Cup sour cream

I Mix bread crumbs and enough milk to thoroughly soak, then squeeze dry.

II Cut away any gristle and chop C S or grind K S meats. Set meat aside.

III Drain ½ cup sauerkraut well, reserving the rest, and mince C Ⓚ S by turning machine quickly on and off 1 or 2 times.

IV Mix together bread paste, meats, minced sauerkraut, sage, caraway seeds, salt and pepper only long enough to incorporate ingredients.

V Shape mixture into meatballs and sauté in oil until brown on all sides.

VI Meanwhile, chop C Ⓚ S the onions and then the peppers; add to browned meatballs along with paprika, then cook until onions are transparent.

VII Rinse reserved sauerkraut under running water and drain thoroughly. Peel, seed, and chop tomatoes by hand.

VIII Add sauerkraut, tomatoes, sugar, broth, and bay leaf to meatballs and vegetables; cover and simmer over low heat for 40 minutes. Adjust seasonings to taste. Just before serving over hot noodles, stir the sour cream into the sauerkraut mixture.

Ⓚ KitchenAid users: mince sauerkraut and chop vegetables by hand.

DANISH FISH PUDDING

Delicious hot or cold.

(YIELD: ENOUGH TO SERVE 6)

> 1½   *Pounds salmon or haddock, boned and skinned*
> 3   *Eggs*
> ½   *Teaspoon salt*
> 2   *Tablespoons fresh dill, with all stems removed*
> ⅛   *Teaspoon white pepper*
> 1   *Cup heavy cream*
> ¼   *Cup fine bread crumbs*
>   *Hollandaise Sauce (see page 256) or*
>   *Sauce Américaine (see page 268) or*
>   *Tomato Cream Sauce (see page 269)*

I Cut fish in 1-inch pieces and pick over carefully to remove bones. Place in container C Ⓚ S, blend 5 seconds, and while the motor is still running, add eggs and seasonings through the spout. Stop machine and scrape down container's sides.

II Preheat oven to 300 degrees F.

III Start motor once again and pour in the cream in a thin steady stream. Stop the motor once or twice to scrape bottom of container. Whirl 5 seconds after last of cream has been added. The mousse should have the consistency of whipped cream that will hold a soft peak.

IV Butter a 1-quart ring mold and dust with bread crumbs, shaking out the excess. Spoon the mousse into the mold and cover with aluminum foil.

V Set mold in a large pan and pour water to a depth of 1 inch around the mold.

VI   Bake 1½ to 1¾ hours. Test for doneness by inserting a knife in the thickest part of the pudding. If the knife comes out clean, the pudding is ready to serve.

VII   Unmold and serve hot with Hollandaise Sauce or Sauce Américaine, or cold with chilled Tomato Cream Sauce.

Ⓚ KitchenAid users: purée in a blender.

BUBBLE AND SQUEAK

Bubble and Squeak, a British favorite, is so called because of the squeaking sound the dish makes as it bubbles and bakes.

(YIELD: ENOUGH TO SERVE 6)

1	*Pound loose pork sausage meat*
1	*Medium head cabbage, with tough outer leaves and core removed*
4	*Cups Basic White Sauce (see page 271)*
	Salt and freshly ground pepper
2 or 3	*Drops Tabasco sauce*
	Dash garlic powder
3	*Slices stale bread, cut in quarters*

I   Crumble sausage meat and fry to a golden brown.

II   Coarsely slice C K S cabbage, then cook in water to cover until tender.

III   Meanwhile, prepare white sauce as directed. Season to taste with salt and pepper and stir in Tabasco and garlic powder.

IV   Preheat oven to 250 degrees F.

V   Drain sausage and place in large casserole. Drain cabbage, coarsely chop by hand, and mix with sausage. Stir in white sauce.

VI   Whirl bread slices in container C S for 15 seconds or until finely chopped, or finely grind K. Sprinkle over top of casserole and bake until sauce is hot and bubbly. Serve hot.

CHILI CON CARNE

(YIELD: ENOUGH TO SERVE 6)

2	Pounds lean beef, cut in 1-inch cubes
1½	Tablespoons vegetable oil
2	Medium onions, peeled and cut in quarters
2	Large cloves garlic, peeled and cut in half
8	Medium tomatoes, peeled, seeded and cut in quarters
4	Cups canned kidney beans
3	Tablespoons chili powder
2	Teaspoons granulated sugar
1½	Teaspoons each salt, ground cumin, and oregano
2	Cups cooked macaroni or rice

I   Coarsely chop C S or grind K S meat. Heat oil in heavy saucepan or Dutch oven and brown meat on all sides.

II   Meanwhile, finely chop C S or hand-chop K garlic and onions. Coarsely chop tomatoes by hand. Drain kidney beans, reserving both beans and liquid. Add vegetables, chili powder, sugar, spices, and bean liquid to meat.

III   Bring chili to just under a boil, then lower heat and simmer, covered, for 2 hours. If the chili becomes too thick, add a little water. Stir in reserved kidney beans during the last 15 minutes of cooking. To serve, place 1 or 2 spoonfuls of cooked macaroni or rice in each bowl, then ladle hot chili over. Serve small bowls of chopped scallions, avocados, grated cheese, and crumbled tostadas on the side.

AMERICAN MEAT LOAF

(YIELD: ENOUGH TO SERVE 8)

3½	Pounds lean beef
4	Medium onions, peeled and cut in quarters
1	Medium green pepper, trimmed, seeded and cut in 1-inch pieces
1	Large rib celery, trimmed and cut in 1-inch pieces
2	Tablespoons vegetable oil

5 Slices bread
1 Cup beef broth
½ Cup catsup
¼ Cup mild mustard
1 Teaspoon salt
½ Teaspoon each *dried sage and thyme leaves*
¼ Teaspoon *freshly ground black pepper*

I Preheat oven to 350 degrees F.

II Cut beef into 1-inch pieces, removing any gristle or membranes. Chop C S or grind K S meat. Place chopped meat in large bowl.

III Finely chop C S or grind K onions, pepper and celery. Set aside.

IV Sauté vegetables in oil until tender. Meanwhile, cut bread in ½-inch cubes and cover with broth.

V Squeeze out excess broth and add moistened bread to meat. Stir in sautéed vegetables, catsup, mustard and spices.

VI Press meat mixture into loaf pan. Decorate the top attractively with alternate stripes of catsup and mustard. Bake for 1 hour. Pour off any grease before cutting into slices and serving hot.

STEAK TARTARE

(YIELD: ENOUGH TO SERVE 6)

3   *Pounds sirloin or porterhouse steak*
2   *Large sweet onions, peeled*
6   *Egg yolks*
18 *Flat anchovy fillets, cut in pieces*
12 *Large pimento-stuffed olives, thinly sliced C K S*
    Capers

I Discard gristle and fat from steak and cut meat into 1-inch cubes. In several steps chop C S for 7 seconds or grind K S. Set meat aside.

II Cut onion in 1-inch pieces, place in container C Ⓚ S, a few handfuls at a time, and chop coarsely.

III Arrange layer of onions on each serving plate. Divide chopped steak into equal portions and set in center of onions. Top each serving with an egg yolk, anchovy bits, olive slices, and capers. Serve cold with salt and freshly ground black pepper on the side.

Ⓚ KitchenAid users: hand-chop onions.

MEATBALLS AND SPAGHETTI
(YIELD: ENOUGH TO SERVE 6)

1	Cup stale bread (preferably Italian or French), broken in 1-inch pieces
¼	Cup milk
2½	Pounds lean chuck, cut in 1-inch cubes
1	Tablespoon each fresh sage and thyme leaves, with tough stems removed
1	Tablespoon tomato paste
2	Tablespoons prepared mustard
3	Tablespoons vegetable oil
5	Cups Ripe Tomato Purée (see page 222)
1	Cup water
½	Teaspoon fennel seeds
⅛	Teaspoon each ground cloves and oregano
1	Tablespoon granulated sugar
¼	Cup wine
1	Package (16 ounces) spaghetti

I Coarsely chop bread in container C S or grind K. Mix in as much milk as necessary to make a thick paste. Set aside in a fine strainer to drain off excess milk.

II Cut away any gristle and chop C S or grind K S meat and fresh herbs.

III Mix together C* meat, moistened bread, tomato paste, and mustard.

* Cuisinart users: use your plastic blade and mix in container if desired.

IV Shape meat mixture into meatballs and fry in hot oil until brown on all sides.

V Add purée, water, fennel seeds, cloves, oregano, sugar, and wine. Bring mixture to a boil; lower heat, cover, and simmer, stirring occasionally, for 30 minutes.

VI Meanwhile, prepare spaghetti according to package directions. Serve meatballs and sauce over hot, well-drained spaghetti, accompanied by a side dish of grated C K S Parmesan cheese, if desired.

RED FLANNEL HASH

(YIELD: ENOUGH TO SERVE 4)

1½   Cups cooked corned beef, cut in 1-inch cubes
1   Small onion, peeled and cut in quarters
3   Medium beets, cooked, peeled, and cut in half
3   Medium potatoes, cooked and peeled
2   Tablespoons heavy cream
3   Tablespoons butter

I Finely chop C or grind K S together corned beef and onion. Coarsely chop C S or grate K beets. Chop potatoes coarsely by hand. Combine meat and vegetables and stir in cream.

II Melt butter in a skillet over medium heat, add hash and cook on each side for 15 minutes or until crusty brown, turning once. To serve, turn a serving plate upside down over skillet, then flip over quickly so hash slips out in one piece. Cut into 4 wedges. Serve hot.

CORNED BEEF HASH

To prepare corned beef hash for 4, omit beets from above recipe, finely chop 1¾ cups cubed corned beef with the onion and coarsely chop by hand 4 medium cooked and peeled potatoes. Mix meat and vegetables with 3 tablespoons heavy cream; cook and serve as directed in Red Flannel Hash.

WELSH RABBIT WITH GRILLED TOMATOES

(YIELD: ENOUGH TO SERVE 6)

1½   *Pounds Cheddar cheese*
1   *Tablespoon butter*
1   *Cup flat beer, at room temperature*
1   *Tablespoon dry mustard*
2   *Teaspoons Worcestershire sauce*
24   *Toast Points (see page 304)*
6   *Medium tomatoes*
12   *Strips country-cured bacon*
¼   *Cup bread crumbs*
  Butter

I   Grate C K S cheese. Heat butter in a large skillet and add cheese a handful at a time, stirring constantly with a wooden spoon. As the cheese melts, add ¾ cup of the beer a little at a time, continuing to stir until the mixture is free from lumps.

II   Mix together mustard and Worcestershire sauce with as much of the remaining beer as necessary to make a smooth paste; blend into cheese mixture. Keep the sauce warm.

III   Meanwhile, cut the stem ends from tomatoes, cut them in half and shake out the seeds. Drain cut side down for 5 minutes. Fry bacon until crisp and brown.

IV   Top tomatoes with bread crumbs and bits of butter, then broil for 5 minutes about 5 inches from flame, or until the tops turn golden brown. To serve, arrange 4 toast points on each plate. Top with 1 tomato and crisscross with bacon slices. Cover with cheese rabbit and serve hot.

CROQUETTES

Your food processor is practically custom-made for preparing croquettes, one of the nicest ways to enhance and recycle left-overs. Merely finely chop or grind your cooked meat, fish, or poultry; then combine it with a thick, well-seasoned white or Béchamel sauce and chill well. Shape into balls, cones, cylinders, or ovals, then prepare "à l'anglaise"—dust with flour, dip in beaten egg, and coat with fine bread crumbs—and you'll have croquettes ready for frying.

Just remember to make your crumb mixture from stale white bread trimmed of its crust so the croquette coating will turn delicately and evenly golden as it fries, and to have the frying oil or fat at 390 degrees F. before adding the croquettes.

CROQUETTES DE VOLAILLE · CHICKEN CROQUETTES
(YIELD: ENOUGH TO SERVE 6)

  6 *Fresh mushrooms*
  1 *Tablespoon butter*
  2 *Cups cooked chicken, cut in 1-inch pieces*
  2 *Egg yolks*
  1 *Cup thick, hot Béchamel Sauce (see page 272)*
     Vegetable oil for frying
  2 *Eggs*
  1 *Tablespoon water*
     All-purpose flour
1½ *Cups bread crumbs*

I Cut mushrooms in half and sauté in butter until lightly golden.

II Finely chop C or grind K S together chicken and mushrooms.

III Beat the egg yolks together lightly and mix in a little hot Béchamel sauce, then stir this mixture back into remaining sauce and cook over very low heat, stirring constantly, until mixture rolls away from the sides of the pan. Remove from heat and stir in chicken-mushroom mixture. Cool to room temperature, then spread on a plate. Refrigerate until well chilled.

IV Form mixture into desired croquette shape and refrigerate again until well chilled.

V Heat oil for deep frying in a heavy skillet or deep fryer. Beat 2 eggs lightly with 1 tablespoon water. Dust croquettes with flour, dip in the egg mixture and then in bread crumbs, and fry in the hot oil to a crisp golden brown on both sides, turning once. Drain briefly on paper towels before serving hot.

CROQUETTES DE HOMARD · LOBSTER (SEAFOOD OR FISH) CROQUETTES

Substitute 2 cups of picked-over lobster (or other cooked seafood or fish) for the chicken in the recipe for Chicken Croquettes.

CROQUETTES DE FROMAGE · CHEESE CROQUETTES

(YIELD: ENOUGH TO SERVE 6)

2 Cups Béchamel Sauce (see page 272)
1 Piece Swiss cheese (1-inch-thick wedge,
   2 inches long)
2 Egg yolks
   Vegetable oil for frying
2 Eggs
1 Tablespoon water
   All-purpose flour
1½ Cups bread crumbs

I Prepare sauce as directed. Chop C or grate K S cheese, then add to sauce and cook, stirring constantly, until cheese melts and mixture is smooth.

II Beat the egg yolks lightly, add a little hot cheese sauce, and stir well; return mixture to the remaining sauce and cook briefly over very low heat, stirring constantly, until egg yolks are well blended.

III Remove mixture from heat, cool slightly, and spread in a buttered shallow pan. Refrigerate until very cold, roll into desired croquette shape, and chill further.

IV Heat oil for deep-frying in a heavy skillet or deep fryer. Beat 2 eggs lightly with 1 tablespoon water. Dust croquettes with flour, dip in egg mixture and then in bread crumbs, and fry in the hot oil until crisp and golden brown on both sides, turning once. Drain briefly on paper towels before serving hot.

HAM AND EGG CROQUETTES

(YIELD: ABOUT 16 SMALL CROQUETTES)

> 2   Cups cooked ham, cut in 1-inch pieces
> 2   Hard-cooked eggs, cut in quarters
> 2   Medium onions, peeled and cut in 1-inch pieces
> 6   Pimento-stuffed green olives
> ½   Cup Basic White Sauce (see page 271) at room temperature
>   Generous pinch each dry mustard and freshly ground black pepper
>   Vegetable oil for frying
> 2   Eggs
> 1   Tablespoon water
>   All-purpose flour
> 1½   Cups bread crumbs

I   Mince C S ham, hard-cooked eggs, onion, and olives by quickly turning machine on and off 5 or 6 times, or finely grind K.

II   Add white sauce, dry mustard, pepper, and 1 egg to minced ingredients and mix well. Spread mixture on a plate. Refrigerate until well chilled.

III   Shape into small patties; then refrigerate again until well chilled.

IV   Heat oil in heavy skillet. Beat remaining egg with 1 tablespoon water. Dust patties with flour, dip in beaten egg and then in bread crumbs, and fry in the hot oil to a golden brown on both sides, turning once. Drain briefly on paper towels before serving hot.

SAUSAGES

TIPS ON SAUSAGE-MAKING

• Preparing your sausages with a ratio of 2 parts meat to 1 part fat is your guarantee of best flavor.

• Partially freezing your meat beforehand, or having it at the coldest temperature possible when chopping or grinding, will help the blades of your food processor cut more cleanly.

• Working or kneading the spices into the meat mixture will help distribute them more evenly.

• Refrigerating the prepared sausage mixture for 12 to 24 hours prior to stuffing it into casings or shaping into patties or rolls will allow time for the flavor to develop.

• Using natural casings? Rinse the amount you'll need at one time under running water to penetrate the entire length. Set on paper towels until ready to use. Leftover natural casings will generally keep for up to two years if they're well refrigerated and salted.

• Using the special sausage-stuffing attachment that comes with your food processor or other kitchen equipment makes filling the casings quick and easy. Otherwise the meat mixture can be forced through a funnel into casings with the handle of a wooden spoon well soaked in ice water.

CHAIR À SAUCISSES · PORK SAUSAGE

(YIELD: ABOUT 3 POUNDS)

2 Pounds *lean pork tenderloin, partially frozen*
1 Pound fresh *pork fat, partially frozen*
3 *Ice cubes*
¾ Tablespoon *salt*
⅓ Teaspoon *freshly ground black pepper*
¼ Teaspoon each *ground allspice, sage, and thyme*
1 *Bay leaf, crumbled*
Natural sausage casings (optional)

I Cut pork and pork fat into 1-inch pieces and coarsely chop C S, adding 1 ice cube along with 2 or 3 handfuls of meat and fat at a time; or cut the meat and fat into long strips, mix with the ice cubes, and then put through the food grinder K S once.

II Combine pork and pork fat with the seasonings, kneading or working spices in with your fingers to distribute them evenly.

III Shape into patties or stuff into natural sausage casings (see Tips on Sausage-Making, page 183). Refrigerate or cook immediately.

ITALIAN-STYLE SAUSAGES

(YIELD: ABOUT 3 POUNDS)

1¾ Pounds *lean pork, partially frozen*
¼ Pound *lean beef, partially frozen*
1 Pound fresh *pork fat, partially frozen*
8 Large *cloves garlic, peeled and cut in half*
3 *Bay leaves*
3 *Ice cubes*
¾ Tablespoon *whole black peppercorns*
1½ Teaspoons each *salt, crushed red pepper, and fennel seed*
⅛ Teaspoon *ground nutmeg*
Natural sausage casings (optional)

I Cut meats and pork fat into 1-inch pieces. Coarsely chop C, 2 or 3 handfuls (along with some of the garlic and bay leaves and 1 ice cube) at a time; or cut K S meats and fat into long strips, mix with the garlic, bay leaves, and ice cubes, and put the mixture through the food grinder once.

II Add remaining seasonings to the meat mixture, and work them in well with your fingers to distribute them evenly.

III Shape into patties or stuff into casings (see Tips on Sausage-Making, page 183). Unless you plan to cook sausages immediately, store them in your refrigerator.

SAUSAGES WITH SOYBEANS

If you're cutting down on cholesterol (or your grocery bill), here's a sausage with an interesting texture and a fine nutty flavor.

(YIELD: ABOUT 4½ POUNDS)

⅔	Cup water
1	Cup dried soybeans
1½	Pounds lean pork tenderloin, partially frozen
½	Pound smoked pork butt, partially frozen
1	Pound fresh pork fat, partially frozen
3	Ice cubes
1	Teaspoon salt
⅛	Teaspoon each ground nutmeg and allspice
	Natural sausage casings (optional)

I Bring water and soybeans just to a boil, then drain, coarsely chop C S or grind K S, and set aside to cool.

II Cut pork and fat into 1-inch pieces and coarsely chop C S, 2 or 3 handfuls (with 1 ice cube) at a time; or cut into long strips, mix with the ice cubes, and put through food grinder K S once.

III Mix together meats, fat, soybeans, and spices, and knead the mixture well to distribute ingredients evenly.

IV Shape into patties or stuff into casings (see Tips on Sausage-Making, page 183). Cook immediately, or refrigerate.

SAUSAGES WITH OATMEAL

Another tasty sausage for the cholesterol-conscious breakfaster.

(YIELD: ABOUT 4½ POUNDS)

1½	Cups rolled oats
¾	Cup water
1½	Pounds lean pork tenderloin, partially frozen
½	Pound veal, partially frozen
1	Pound fresh pork fat, partially frozen
3	Ice cubes
2	Teaspoons salt
⅛	Teaspoon each ground allspice, ginger, and sage
¾	Teaspoon caraway seeds (optional)
	Natural sausage casings (optional)

I   Bring oats and water just to a boil in a small saucepan, then drain immediately and cool in the refrigerator for 15 minutes.

II   Cut pork, veal, and pork fat into 1-inch pieces and coarsely chop C, 2 or 3 handfuls and 1 ice cube at a time; or cut meats and fat into long strips, mix with ice cubes and put once through food grinder K S.

III   Combine meats, fat, oats, and seasonings, kneading or working the mixture thoroughly with your fingers.

IV   Shape into patties or stuff into natural sausage casings (see Tips on Sausage-Making, page 183). Refrigerate the sausages or cook them immediately.

SCRAPPLE

(YIELD: ONE LOAF OR ENOUGH TO SERVE 6 TO 8)

1½	Pounds cooked ham, cut in 1-inch cubes
1	Medium onion, peeled and cut in eighths
4	Cups beef broth or chicken broth
½	Teaspoon powdered sage
¼	Teaspoon each salt and freshly ground black pepper (this makes a very peppery loaf—reduce pepper by half if you prefer bland scrapple)

²⁄₃ *Cup corn meal*
½ *Cup hot water*
   Vegetable oil for frying

I Mince C S the ham and onion by quickly flicking the switch on and off 4 or 5 times, stopping twice to scrape sides of container; or finely grind K.

II Bring the ham and onion to a boil with the stock and spices.

III Moisten the corn meal with the hot water and stir it into the boiling mixture. Press out any lumps with the back of a spoon. Cook, stirring constantly, for 10 minutes or until thick, then lower heat to medium and cook until very thick and fairly dry (about one hour), stirring frequently to prevent scorching.

IV Spoon mixture into a loaf pan and chill thoroughly. To serve, cut into thin slices and brown on both sides in a generous amount of oil or butter.

STUFFINGS & DUMPLINGS

TIPS ON STUFFING POULTRY

The recipes for poultry stuffing listed below give quantities designed for loosely packed cavities to allow room for expansion while roasting is underway. While you may fill your bird as densely or loosely as you prefer, there are two rules concerning the preparation of stuffing that ought never to be broken:

1. Once the stuffing has been prepared, it should be brought to room temperature before using it to fill the bird.

2. To prevent spoilage, always stuff your bird just prior to placing in preheated oven.

CHESTNUT AND MUSHROOM STUFFING

(YIELD: ABOUT 6 CUPS)

½ *Pound fresh mushrooms*
½ *Pound sausage meat*
1 *Shallot, peeled and cut in half*
1 *Tablespoon fresh parsley leaves, with all tough stems removed*
2 *Tablespoons butter*
2 *Cups Chestnut Purée (see page 218)*
1½ *Cups soft dry bread crumbs*
16 *Roasted or boiled whole chestnuts, peeled*
Salt and freshly ground black pepper

I   Finely chop C S or grind K S together mushrooms, sausage, shallot, and parsley.

II   Melt butter in large skillet and sauté the chopped vegetables and sausage, stirring frequently until meat is lightly browned.

III   Remove mixture from heat and pour off fat, reserving 3 tablespoons.

IV   Return drained vegetables and meat to heat, stir in chestnut purée, then simmer mixture over low heat for 5 minutes.

V   Stir in bread crumbs, whole chestnuts, and reserved 3 tablespoons fat, season the stuffing with salt and pepper to taste, and cook, stirring occasionally, for 2 minutes.

MINCED MEAT STUFFING
(YIELD: ABOUT 10 CUPS)

$^1/_2$ Pound each *ham, pork, and veal, cut in 1-inch cubes*
1 Large onion, peeled and cut in eighths
3 Small ribs celery, with all strings removed, cut in 1-inch pieces
8 Medium mushrooms, cut in quarters
3 Tablespoons butter
2 Teaspoons salt
$^1/_2$ Teaspoon each *ground nutmeg, powdered sage, dried thyme, and freshly ground black pepper*
6 Cups soft dry bread crumbs
3 Eggs
$^3/_4$ Cup dry sherry

I   Remove all gristle from meats and chop C S or grind K S together, 2 or 3 handfuls at a time. Place in a bowl and mix well.

II   Separately finely chop onion, celery and mushrooms in container C S, stopping once or twice to scrape down container sides. KitchenAid users may coarsely grind the vegetables.

III   Heat butter in a large skillet and sauté the vegetables for 3 minutes. Add the well-mixed meats, then cook for 5 minutes longer, stirring constantly and breaking up any lumps with a fork.

IV   Remove meat mixture from heat, sprinkle with spices, and stir in bread crumbs. Add the eggs one at a time and then the sherry. Mix well after each addition.

PECAN-CRANBERRY STUFFING
(YIELD: ABOUT 6 CUPS)

2 Cups cranberries
5 Tablespoons granulated sugar
2 Tablespoons water
1 Cup pecans
1 Small onion, peeled and cut in quarters
9 Slices stale bread, broken in pieces
3 Tablespoons butter

½   Cup currants
½   Teaspoon each *salt and marjoram*
½   Teaspoon *marjoram*

   I   Pick over cranberries and discard any soft berries or stems. Coarsely chop C S or grind K berries, place them in a saucepan with the sugar and water, and simmer for 5 minutes, stirring frequently.

   II   Meanwhile, coarsely chop C S or grate K pecans. Coarsely chop C S or grind K onion.

   III   Whirl bread in container C S or grind K; there should be enough to make 3 cups of crumbs.

   IV   Melt butter in a large skillet. Add onions and sauté for 2 minutes; add the nuts and sauté for 2 minutes more, stirring occasionally.

   V   Remove sautéed mixture from heat. Stir in berries, bread crumbs, currants, and seasonings. Toss well.

CORNBREAD AND SWEET POTATO STUFFING

(YIELD: ABOUT 6 CUPS)

1   *Medium sweet potato*
¾   *Cup pecans*
1   *Large onion, peeled and cut in eighths*
3   *Ribs celery, with all strings removed, cut in 1-inch pieces*
6   *Slices stale bread, broken in pieces*
3   *Stale cornbread squares*
2   *Tablespoons butter*
1   *Teaspoon poultry seasoning*
½   *Teaspoon salt*
⅓   *Cup hot water*
1   *Egg*

   I   Boil sweet potato in its jacket until very tender.

   II   Meanwhile, coarsely chop C S or grind K pecans, then set aside. Chop C S or grind K S onion and celery. Set aside.

Whirl bread slices and corn squares in container C S or grind K; there should be about 3 cups in all. Set aside.

III Heat butter in a skillet. Add pecans, onions, celery, and seasonings, then sauté until onions are golden. Remove from heat and set aside.

IV Drain sweet potato, and purée in container C S, or, using special attachment K.

V Sprinkle bread crumbs with hot water. Mix in puréed potato and vegetable-nut mixture. Beat egg lightly and stir into stuffing.

BIRD STUFFING WITH A DIFFERENCE

. . . And the difference is the introduction of those two favorite Far Eastern ingredients, water chestnuts and miso paste.

(YIELD: ABOUT 4 CUPS)

4	*Large ribs celery with leaves, with all strings removed*
3/4	*Pound fresh mushrooms*
1	*8-Ounce can water chestnuts, drained*
2	*Medium onions, peeled and cut in quarters*
4	*Tablespoons vegetable oil*
1 1/4	*Cups blanched almonds*
1 1/4	*Cups chicken broth*
1	*Teaspoon miso paste (optional)*
1 1/4	*Teaspoons cornstarch*

I Wash celery well and pat dry, then remove and chop leaves by hand. Slice C K S celery ribs.

II Slice C K S mushrooms and water chestnuts. Coarsely chop C S or grind K S onions.

III Sauté celery leaves, celery, mushrooms, water chestnuts, and onions in the oil, stirring occasionally, until onion is transparent.

IV Meanwhile, grate C K S almonds. Set aside.

V Mix broth with the miso paste and cornstarch and pour over vegetables. Bring mixture to a boil, stirring constantly, until the sauce thickens and clears. Stir in the nuts. Bring to room temperature before using.

SWISS CHEESE AND DILL DUMPLINGS

(YIELD: ABOUT 16)

> 1 *Piece* cold *Swiss cheese about 2 inches* × *2 inches* × *2 inches (or enough to equal 1 cup)*
> 6 *Tablespoons cold butter, cut into pieces*
> ¼ *Cup all-purpose flour*
> 1 *Tablespoon fresh dill leaves, with all tough stems removed*
> 2 *Egg yolks*

To Make Dumpling Batter in the Cuisinart:

I Cut cheese into 1-inch pieces, then place in container. Whirl for 6 seconds; add butter, flour, and dill and whirl for 3 or 4 seconds more.

II Add eggs and process by turning machine quickly on and off 2 or 3 times or until well mixed.

To Make Dumpling Batter in the KitchenAid or Starmix:

I Finely grate cheese. Chop dill by hand.

II Cream all ingredients together in your machine's bowl or by hand.

To Shape the Dumpling Batter:

I Dust your hands with flour and shape dough into walnut-sized balls.

II Drop into boiling soup. After the dumplings rise to the surface, boil for 1 moment more. Serve immediately.

CRUNCHY ALMOND BALLS

Use these to dress up any soup.

(YIELD: ABOUT 1 DOZEN)

> 1 Cup blanched almonds
> 3–4 Slices stale bread, cut in pieces (enough to make
> ⅔ cup crumbs)
> ½ Teaspoon salt
> 3 Egg whites
> 4 Tablespoons vegetable oil

I Finely chop C S or grate K together nuts and stale bread slices. Mix in salt.

II Beat egg whites until frothy by machine K S or by hand C. Set 2 or 3 tablespoons aside. Fold remaining egg whites into almond–bread crumb mixture.

III Heat 2 tablespoons oil in a medium-sized skillet. Shape almond mixture into very small balls. Dip half the balls in the reserved egg whites and fry in the oil to a golden brown on all sides, then set aside to drain on a paper towel.

IV Add the remaining 2 tablespoons cooking oil to the skillet, dip the remaining almond balls in the reserved egg whites and fry, brown, and drain as directed in Step III. If necessary to reheat, place almond balls in a medium-hot oven for a few minutes.

OUTDOOR COOKING

HOW TO PREPARE AND COOK HAMBURGERS

Your food processor makes it easy to prepare fresh, high-quality meats for that most authentically American of meat dishes, the ubiquitous hamburger.

Trim your boneless beef—chuck, round, or sirloin—of all gristle or coarse membranes. These may be separated far more easily if you cut the fat away with them, then trim and discard the gristle line and retain the fat. Each pound of meat you chop or grind should contain about 30 percent fat. Once you've discovered what proportion of fat to lean best suits your taste, you'll automatically include the right amount.

If you're chopping your trimmed meat in the Cuisinart or Starmix, cut it into 1-inch cubes and whirl it, two or three handfuls at a time, about 6 or 7 seconds for coarse or 10 seconds for finely chopped meat. KitchenAid or Starmix users who have the separate grinding attachment should cut the meat into long strips and feed it into the machine's hopper.

To prepare the meat for cooking, shape it into round flat patties with as little handling as possible, then cook in a bit of hot butter in a heavy skillet until brown on one side, turning once to finish cooking on the other side. Your hamburgers will be close to perfection, however, if you cook them without any added fat. All you need do is sprinkle the hot skillet with salt, put in the hamburgers and sear on one side, then flip over, lower the heat and cook to the preferred degree of doneness. With either cooking method, season to taste with salt and freshly ground black pepper before serving.

BEEFBURGERS AU POIVRE

(YIELD: ENOUGH TO SERVE 6)

3	Pounds round steak, cut in 1-inch pieces
3	Tablespoons whole peppercorns
5	Tablespoons butter
1/4	Cup Worcestershire sauce
2	Teaspoons lemon juice
12	drops Tabasco sauce
	Salt
1/2	Cup cognac
3	Tablespoons minced fresh chives

I   Chop C or grind K S round steak to suit your taste. Form into 12 beefburgers.

II   Crush peppercorns S or hand-crush C K. Spread on flat dish or pastry board, then press both sides of each beefburger into the pepper, making sure that sides are well coated. Refrigerate beefburgers for 30 minutes.

III   Pan-fry or grill beefburgers. Meanwhile, melt butter in a skillet and stir in Worcestershire sauce, lemon juice, and Tabasco.

IV   As soon as beefburgers reach desired degree of doneness, remove to serving plates and sprinkle with salt to taste.

V   Stir cognac into butter mixture and set aflame, then pour flaming sauce over beefburgers. Serve at once, garnished with minced chives.

FILLED HAMBURGERS

(YIELD: ENOUGH TO SERVE 6)

> 3 Pounds boneless chuck, cut in 1-inch cubes (see
> How to Prepare and Cook Hamburgers, page 195)
> 1 Medium onion, peeled and cut in quarters
> 1 Teaspoon all-purpose flour
> 1 Egg
> Freshly ground black pepper

I Trim away all gristle and coarsely chop C or grind K S together meat and onions, 2 or 3 handfuls at a time.

II Mix together meat, onion, flour, egg, and pepper to taste. Spread to a thickness of ¾ inch on a large sheet of wax paper, then use a 3-inch cookie cutter to cut mixture into 12 patties.

III Place any of the fillings listed on pages 197 and 198 by teaspoons on 6 of the patties; top each with one of the remaining patties. Panfry, broil, or charcoal grill as desired.

BEEFBURGER FILLINGS

SAVORY FILLING

> 1-Ounce jar gherkins or pimento-stuffed green
> olives, drained

I Whirl in container C S for 1 or 2 seconds, or finely grind K.

PINEAPPLE-HAM FILLING

> ¾ Cup cooked ham, cut in 1-inch pieces
> 1 8-Ounce can pineapple chunks, drained

I Chop C (turning machine rapidly on and off 4 or 5 times) or grind K S ham and pineapple together.

CHEDDAR CHEESE AND SCALLION FILLING

1   Piece Cheddar cheese (1½ inch × 1½ inch) cut in ½-inch pieces

2   Scallions, with 3 inches green top, cut in ½-inch pieces

1   Teaspoon prepared mustard

I   Place cheese and scallion pieces in container C Ⓚ S. Finely chop by quickly turning machine on and off 3 or 4 times, stopping once to scrape down sides.

II   Combine cheese and scallions with mustard and mix well.

Ⓚ KitchenAid users: grate cheese and hand-mince scallions.

HORSERADISH–CREAM CHEESE FILLING

6   Ounces cold cream cheese, cut in pieces

1   1-Inch piece fresh horseradish, scraped and cut in ½-inch pieces, or 1 tablespoon well-drained prepared horseradish

I   Whirl C Ⓚ S together cream cheese and horseradish for 4 or 5 seconds, stopping once to scrape down container sides.

Ⓚ KitchenAid users: finely grate horseradish.

LAMB-BURGER FILLINGS

A lamb-burger is actually a hamburger with lamb substituted for the beef. These may be grilled or fried either filled or unfilled. To prepare fillings, simply whirl ingredients together C, stopping once or twice to scrape down sides of container, or run solid ingredients through a grinder K S, and then mix all ingredients well.

PINE NUT FILLING

- ¾ Cup pine nuts
- ½ Cup raisins
- 2 Cloves garlic, peeled and cut in half
- ⅛ Teaspoon each *allspice and nutmeg*

MINTED CREAM CHEESE FILLING

- ¼ Cup mint leaves, with all tough stems removed
- 8 Ounces cold *cream cheese, cut in pieces*
- 2 Tablespoons undiluted frozen orange juice
  Salt and freshly ground pepper

CURRIED CREAM CHEESE FILLING

- 8 Ounces cold *cream cheese, cut in pieces*
- ½ Teaspoon curry powder

CHEESE AND APPLE FILLING

- 1 Piece Monterey jack cheese (1½ inch × 1½ inch), cut in ½-inch pieces
- 1 Medium onion, peeled and cut in eighths
- 1 Medium apple, peeled, cored, and cut in eighths
- ¼ Teaspoon curry powder

DILL AND ONION FILLING

> 3 Tablespoons fresh dill leaves, with all tough stems removed
> 1 Large onion, peeled and cut in eighths

CHICKEN-BURGERS

Set on hamburger rolls and garnished with lettuce, tomato, grilled bacon, and mayonnaise, these delightful patties give a nice change of pace from the ubiquitous beefburger. When grilling out-of-doors, prefry so the burgers will hold together over the open fire.

(YIELD: ENOUGH TO SERVE 6)

> 6 Chicken breasts, skinned, boned, cut in 1-inch pieces
> 3 Large onions, peeled and cut in eighths
> ½ Teaspoon ground thyme
> Salt and freshly ground black pepper
> Butter

I Coarsely chop C the chicken and then the onions 2 handfuls at a time, turning the machine on and off quickly 3 or 4 times after each addition; or grind K S together, using the coarse blade.

II Work the thyme, salt and pepper into the chicken, mix the onions with the meat, and shape into patties. Fry in butter for 2 minutes on each side, turning once, then chill prefried burgers until serving time. Grill indoors or outdoors, basting with butter. Serve hot.

BURGER BASTING SAUCES

Sauce 1 Whirl C S 4 large cloves garlic, peeled and cut in half, with ½ cup vegetable oil in container for 7 seconds.

Sauce 2 Combine ½ cup melted butter with 2 tablespoons *each* Worcestershire sauce and lemon juice.

Sauce 3 Combine equal amounts of vegetable oil, catsup, and prepared mustard.

Sauce 4 Combine equal amounts of soy sauce, prepared mustard, and molasses.

SANDWICHES

SANDWICH FILLINGS

Any of the fillings listed below are delightful whether used for lunch-box treats, for distinctive sandwiches in a wide variety of shapes and sizes, for teatime, or as picnic-basket pick-me-ups. All you need is loaf or two of trimmed and well-chilled *uncut* bread, some softened butter, and your choice of fillings.

To make Pinwheel Sandwiches, cut the bread lengthwise in thin slices with butter, top with a filling, and cover with a plain unspread slice, then start at one narrow end and roll the slices together in jelly-roll fashion. Wrap in a damp cloth and chill well before cutting the rolls vertically. For an interesting effect, arrange a row of olive halves or tiny gherkins over the filling at one end; start at that end when rolling up and your pinwheels will have an attractive and tasty center.

For Checkerboard Sandwiches, slice loaves of dark and white bread horizontally. Arrange two white slices over two dark slices, spreading butter and filling over the first three but leaving the top slice bare. Wrap in wet towels and press down slightly—the fillings should be firm enough so the layers don't slip. Chill well, then cut thinly into vertical slices.

Ribbon Sandwiches are a variation on the checkerboard motif.

Prepare your bread and cover with butter and filling in the same way, but alternate white and dark bread slices, leaving the top slice uncovered. Wrap, chill, and cut as directed.

Create Sandwich Rolls by cutting white or dark loaves in thin vertical slices. Spread each slice with softened butter and cover with filling, then roll up and secure with a toothpick. Chill well and remove picks before serving.

To prepare Cornucopias, cut your bread into thin vertical slices and spread with butter. Secure each slice at one end with a toothpick, allowing the other end to flair outward. Set on a well-greased baking sheet; bake in a 350 degrees F. oven until lightly toasted. Cool, then remove toothpicks before piping filling into them through a pastry bag.

Mosaic Sandwiches are made with the aid of heart-shaped or round cookie cutters. You'll need two of each, one considerably smaller than the other. Cut white or dark bread vertically and use the larger cookie cutter to make hearts or circles from all the slices. Spread half the bread shapes with butter and top with filling; then, using the small cookie cutter, cut out the centers of the remaining heart-shaped or circular slices and set the thin outer pieces over each of the spread shapes so that the filling shows through.

Sandwich Loaves are designed to be cut into thick slices and eaten with a fork. Serve them for a tempting lunch or late-night snack accompanied by a salad and a light dessert. To prepare, trim uncut white or dark bread of all crusts and chill well. Cut lengthwise in thin slices and spread with softened butter, reserving one slice unspread. Use different, but complementary, fillings on each slice, then stack slices to re-create the loaf, topping with the reserved plain slice. Make sure you use fillings firm enough to keep the loaf intact when you press down. Cut two 8-ounce packages of cream cheese into pieces and whirl in your food processor until light and fluffy; thin with as much heavy cream as necessary to reach a nice spreading consistency. Frost the stacked loaf with this mixture and decorate with radish roses, olive slices, carrot strips, or fresh herbs arranged in an attractive pattern.

It is possible to produce a bouquet of interesting and delectable sandwich fillings by merely whirling C S together ingredients until fairly finely chopped and/or well mixed. KitchenAid users should grind solid ingredients and mix well with remaining ingredients. In all cases, keep sandwich fillings well chilled.

AVOCADO FILLING

(YIELD: ABOUT 2 CUPS)

2 Ripe avocados, peeled and pitted
6 Tablespoons Roquefort cheese
3 Tablespoons cream cheese
2 Tablespoons lemon juice

CARROT-RAISIN FILLING

(YIELD: ABOUT 1½ TO 2 CUPS)

3 Medium carrots, scraped and cut in 1-inch strips
½ Cup raisins
3 Tablespoons Foolproof Mayonnaise (see page 252)

CHICKEN-CARROT-RAISIN FILLING

3 Medium carrots, scraped and cut in 1-inch strips
⅓ Cup raisins
¾ Cup cubed cooked chicken
4 Tablespoons Foolproof Mayonnaise (see page 252)

CELERY KNOB FILLING

(YIELD: ABOUT 1½ CUPS)

1 Scallion, white part only, cut in ½-inch pieces
1 Cup Celery-Knob Purée (see page 218)
1 Tablespoon capers
2 Tablespoons cream cheese

CHICKEN FILLING

(YIELD: ABOUT 1½ TO 2 CUPS)

- 1 Cup cooked chicken, cut in cubes
- 1 Large rib celery, with all strings removed, cut in 1-inch pieces
- ¼ Medium onion, peeled and cut in 1-inch pieces
- 3 Tablespoons Foolproof Mayonnaise (see page 252)

CHICKEN-ALMOND FILLING

(YIELD: ABOUT 1½ TO 2 CUPS)

Add ¼ cup toasted almonds and 1 tablespoon chutney to Chicken Filling.

CHICKEN AND CHESTNUT FILLING

(YIELD: ABOUT 1½ TO 2 CUPS)

- 1½ Cups cooked white chicken meat, cut in cubes
- ¾ Cup cooked chestnut halves, or ½ cup Chestnut Purée (see page 218)
- ½ Rib celery, with all strings removed
  Salt and freshly ground black pepper
- 3 Tablespoons Foolproof Mayonnaise (see page 252)

CHUTNEY-NUT FILLING

(YIELD: ABOUT 1½ TO 2 CUPS)

- ¾ Cup chutney
- ¾ Cup walnuts
- 12 Ounces cream cheese, cut in pieces
- 1 Tablespoon heavy cream

CRABMEAT FILLING

(YIELD: ABOUT 1½ TO 2 CUPS)

1½ Cups cooked crabmeat, picked over
2 Scallions, with 3 inches green top, cut in ½-inch pieces
½ Rib celery, with all strings removed, cut in 1-inch pieces
1 Tablespoon fresh thyme leaves, with all stems removed
4 Tablespoons Foolproof Mayonnaise (see page 252)
  Salt and freshly ground pepper

CREAM CHEESE AND OLIVE FILLING

(YIELD: ABOUT 2½ CUPS)

¼ Sweet onion, peeled and cut in 1-inch pieces
12 Ounces cream cheese, cut in pieces
1½ Cups pimento-stuffed olives, cut in half

FRUIT AND NUT FILLING

(YIELD: ABOUT 1½ TO 2 CUPS)

½ Cup pitted dates
½ Cup walnuts
½ Cup raisins
12 Ounces cream cheese, cut in pieces
1 Tablespoon heavy cream

HAM FILLING

(YIELD: ABOUT 1½ TO 2 CUPS)

1½ Cups cooked ham, cut in 1-inch cubes
½ Rib celery, with all strings removed
½ Teaspoon Dijon mustard
4 Tablespoons Foolproof Mayonnaise (see page 252)

LOBSTER FILLING

(YIELD: ABOUT 1½ TO 2 CUPS)

1½	Cups cooked picked-over lobster (with roe if possible) cut in 1-inch pieces
1	Rib celery, with all strings removed, cut in 1-inch pieces
2½	Tablespoons tomato catsup
1	Tablespoon lemon juice
¾	Teaspoon Worcestershire sauce
3	Tablespoons Foolproof Mayonnaise (see page 252)
	Salt and cayenne pepper

FRESH MUSHROOM FILLING

(YIELD: ABOUT 1½ TO 2 CUPS)

1	Cup fresh mushrooms, cut in equal-size pieces
¼	Small onion, peeled and cut in 1-inch pieces
4	Ounces cream cheese, cut in pieces
2	Tablespoons sour cream
6	Drops Tabasco sauce
	Salt and freshly ground black pepper

NUTTY APRICOT FILLING

(YIELD: ABOUT 1½ TO 2 CUPS)

½	Cup filberts
½	Cup dried apricots, cut in quarters
12	Ounces cream cheese, cut in pieces
1	Tablespoon heavy cream

SALMON FILLING
(YIELD: ABOUT 2½ CUPS)

- 2 Cups cooked salmon, picked over to remove skin and bones
- 2 Tablespoons dill leaves, with all thick stems removed
- 3 Tablespoons Foolproof Mayonnaise (see page 252)
  Salt and freshly ground black pepper

SHRIMP FILLING
(YIELD: ABOUT 1½ TO 2 CUPS)

- 12 to 16 Cooked, peeled and cleaned shrimp, cut in half
- 1 Hard-cooked egg, cut in quarters
- 1 Tablespoon fresh dill leaves, with all stems removed
- 4 Tablespoons Foolproof Mayonnaise (see page 252)
  Salt and freshly ground black pepper

SMOKED SALMON FILLING
(YIELD: ABOUT 1½ TO 2 CUPS)

- ¼ Pound smoked salmon, cut in 1-inch pieces
- 12 Ounces cream cheese, cut in pieces
- ¼ Bermuda onion, cut in 1-inch pieces
- 2 Tablespoons capers
- 1 Tablespoon heavy cream (optional)

SWEET ORANGE FILLING
(YIELD: ABOUT 1½ TO 2 CUPS)

- ¼ Cup orange marmalade (use a good grade with as much rind as possible)
- 12 Ounces cream cheese, cut in pieces
- 1 Tablespoon heavy cream
- ¾ Cup pitted dates, coarsely chopped

TONGUE FILLING

(YIELD: ABOUT 1½ TO 2 CUPS)

1½   Cups cooked smoked tongue, cut into 1-inch cubes
2   Small sweet gherkins
1   Tablespoon minced fresh chives
1½   Teaspoons mustard
3   Tablespoons Foolproof Mayonnaise (see page 252)

TUNA FILLING

(YIELD: ABOUT 1½ TO 2 CUPS)

1   6½ Ounce can good grade tuna fish
1   Rib celery, with all strings removed, cut in 1-inch pieces
¼   Medium onion, cut in 1-inch pieces
6   Pitted ripe olives, halved
3   Small sweet gherkins, cut in quarters
2   Sprigs watercress or parsley, with all stems removed
1½   Teaspoons lemon juice
3   Tablespoons Foolproof Mayonnaise (see page 252)
1   Hard-cooked egg, cut in quarters

WATERCRESS FILLING

(YIELD: ABOUT 1½ TO 2 CUPS)

1½   Cups watercress leaves, with all stems removed
8   Ounces cream cheese, cut in pieces
3   Tablespoons sour cream
   Salt and freshly ground black pepper

ARTICHOKE FILLING

(YIELD: ABOUT 1½ CUPS)

12   *Small cooked artichoke hearts*
1   *Clove garlic, peeled and cut in half*
2   *Teaspoons lemon juice*
    Salt and freshly ground black pepper
6   *Tablespoons butter, cut in pieces*
2   *Tablespoons Foolproof Mayonnaise (see page 252)*

I   Place artichoke hearts, garlic, and lemon juice in container C Ⓚ S. Season to taste with salt and pepper. Process for 5 or 6 seconds, stopping as necessary to scrape down container sides.

II   Add butter and whirl for 5 or 6 seconds more. Add mayonnaise through top while machine is running.

III   Keep chilled.

Ⓚ KitchenAid users: hand-mince artichoke hearts and garlic, then mix by hand.

CUCUMBER FILLING

(YIELD: ABOUT 1½ TO 2 CUPS)

1   *Large cucumber, peeled and seeded*
    Salt
¼   *Small onion, peeled and cut in eighths*
1   *Tablespoon dill leaves, with all stems removed*
    Freshly ground black pepper
2   *Tablespoons Foolproof Mayonnaise (see page 252)*

I   Cut cucumber in 1-inch pieces and finely chop C Ⓚ S. Scrape into fine sieve, salt to taste, and allow to drain for 10 minutes.

II   Whirl onion and dill together for 1 or 2 seconds. Add drained cucumber, pepper to taste, and mayonnaise. Turn machine quickly on and off twice to blend ingredients. If mixture seems a bit too moist, drain in a sieve for a moment or two and stir in an additional tablespoon of mayonnaise.

III   Keep chilled.

Ⓚ KitchenAid users: finely grate cucumber, hand-mince onion and dill, and mix by hand.

TOMATO FILLING

(YIELD: ABOUT 1½ TO 2 CUPS)

> 3   *Medium tomatoes, peeled and seeded*
> 12   *Ounces cream cheese, cut in pieces*
> 6   *Fresh basil leaves, with all stems removed*
>   *Salt and freshly ground black pepper*
> 2   *Tablespoons sour cream*

I   Chop tomatoes coarsely by hand and drain on paper towels.

II   Place cream cheese and basil in container C S or bowl K. Season to taste with salt and pepper, and whirl for 5 or 6 seconds or until well blended, stopping once or twice to scrape down sides of container or bowl.

III   Add tomatoes and sour cream. Hand-mix or process to spreading consistency by quickly turning machine on and off 2 or 3 times.

IV   Keep chilled.

VEGEMATO SANDWICH FILLING

(YIELD: ABOUT 3 CUPS)

> 1   *Large cucumber, peeled and seeded*
> 5   *Scallions, with 3 inches green top*
> 1   *Cup tightly packed watercress leaves, with all stems removed*
> 5   *Hard-cooked eggs*
> 1¼   *Cups Foolproof Mayonnaise (see page 252)*
> 3   *Tablespoons cream cheese*
> 2   *Teaspoons prepared mild mustard*
>   *Salt and freshly ground black pepper*

I   Cut cucumber in ½-inch slices. Place in container C Ⓚ S and turn quickly on and off 2 or 3 times. Remove, drain well, and squeeze dry.

Ⓚ KitchenAid users: finely grind cucumbers, scallions and watercress and drain well. Hand-chop eggs. Mix all ingredients.

II Cut scallions in ½-inch pieces. Place in container C S along with watercress, hard-cooked eggs, 1 cup mayonnaise, cream cheese, and mustard. Season with salt and pepper, then whirl for 6 seconds, stopping the machine once or twice as necessary to scrape down sides.

III Combine cucumbers and vegetable mixture. Stir in additional mayonnaise if desired. Chill well before serving.

OPEN-FACED SANDWICHES

SLICED CHICKEN AND CUCUMBER SANDWICHES

Spread thinly sliced white bread with Nut Butter (see page 105) and cover with thinly sliced white-meat chicken. Top with thinly sliced C K S, well drained, fresh cucumbers and sprinkle with Basic Vinaigrette/French Dressing (see page 257).

CUCUMBER SANDWICHES

Spread thin slices of rye bread with Paprika Butter (see page 107). Arrange seeded, thinly sliced, well drained C K S cucumbers on top and sprinkle with minced C S fresh dill.

EGG SALAD SANDWICHES

Spread thinly sliced white bread with Egg Salad (see page 247). Serve cold, sprinkled with minced C S fresh parsley, chives, and halved cherry tomatoes.

ONION SANDWICHES

Spread slices of rye bread or pumpernickel with Watercress Butter (see page 106). Top with thinly sliced C K S onions. Season to taste with salt and freshly ground black pepper.

SARDINE SANDWICHES

Spread thin slices of rye bread with Mustard Butter (see page 105) and arrange well-drained sardines on top. Cover with very thinly sliced C K S Bermuda onion and garnish with hard-cooked egg quarters and lemon wedges.

SMOKED SALMON SANDWICHES GRAND HOTEL

Spread thin slices of pumpernickel bread with Tomato Filling (see page 211). Top with slices of smoked salmon, and garnish each sandwich with ¼ teaspoon of black caviar and a sprinkle of hard-cooked egg yolk pressed through a fine sieve.

SMOKED SALMON, TOMATO, AND ONION

Spread thinly sliced bread with Tomato Filling (see page 211). Arrange over this slices of smoked salmon, then top with thinly sliced C K S sweet onion and thin slices of hand-sliced tomato.* Garnish with chopped chives and/or freshly ground black pepper.

* Unless your tomatoes are the golf-ball variety unfortunately all too available at supermarkets, you will have to slice them by hand.

STEAK TARTARE SANDWICHES

(YIELD: ENOUGH TO SERVE 6)

I Cut 1 large sweet onion into eighths, chop C S, and set aside.

II Remove gristle and fat from 3 pounds prime sirloin or porterhouse steak and cut in 1-inch cubes, then chop C S for 7 seconds or finely grind K S.

III Mix chopped onions, meat and 2 uncooked egg yolks lightly with a fork.

IV Spread meat mixture on thinly sliced pumpernickel lightly covered with Dijon mustard, and garnish with anchovy fillets, capers and thin slices of pimento-stuffed olives.

V Serve cold, seasoned to taste with salt and freshly ground black pepper.

GRILLED STEAK TARTARE SANDWICHES

To serve hot, simply top each sandwich with a second slice of bread. Heat 4 tablespoons vegetable oil in a skillet, then fry each sandwich on both sides only long enough to brown the bread. The bread should be hot and the tartare mixture cold. Serve immediately.

HOT SANDWICHES

FALAFEL

(YIELD: ENOUGH TO SERVE 6 TO 8)

3   *Cups dried chickpeas*
1   *Tablespoon plus 1 teaspoon salt*
1   *Large clove garlic, peeled and cut in half*
3   *Tablespoons all-purpose flour (more, if necessary)*
2   *Eggs*
1   *Tablespoon ground cumin seed*
1   *Teaspoon each baking powder, oregano, and thyme*
½   *Teaspoon cayenne pepper*
    Vegetable oil
    Pita or Sahara bread

Green salad
Tahini Dressing (see page 264)

I Place chickpeas in large bowl, add water to cover, and mix in 1 tablespoon salt. Cover and allow to stand overnight.

II Drain chickpeas well; then, in several steps, finely chop C S or grind K along with the garlic and 1 teaspoon salt.

III MIx chickpeas, flour, eggs, cumin, baking powder, oregano, thyme, and pepper.

IV Pour oil into a skillet to a depth of 1½ inches and heat to 390 degrees F. Form the chickpea mixture into 1-inch balls by rolling between your palms. Test for firmness by dropping a ball into the hot oil. If it falls apart, work a bit more flour into the chickpea mixture.

V Fry chickpea balls until crusty brown. Remove, drain briefly on paper towels, and keep warm.

VI To assemble the falafel, cut each pita in half and open a pocket in each half. Warm briefly, then place a spoonful of green salad in the bottom of each. Add 3 or 4 fried chickpea balls and another spoonful of salad, and top each with 1 or 2 spoonfuls of Tahini Dressing. Serve warm.

CROQUE-MONSIEUR

This crusty, sautéed sandwich comes in many versions. Try one of the variations below, or make up your own—all are exceedingly delicious.

(YIELD: ENOUGH TO SERVE 6)

> 8 *Ounces mozzarella cheese*
> 12 *Slices white bread*
> ½ *Cup clarified butter, softened*
>   *Dijon mustard*
> 6 *Thin slices cooked ham*
> 4 *Eggs*

I Thinly slice C K S cheese. Trim crusts from bread and spread one side of each slice with a thin coating of butter and mustard.

II Arrange cheese slices over 6 slices bread, top with ham and another layer of cheese, then cover with the remaining bread slices.

III Beat the eggs lightly; dip the assembled sandwiches in the egg and sauté in the remaining butter until crisp and golden on each side, turning once. Serve hot as is, or cut in small squares and use as a hot appetizer.

Variation Substitute thinly sliced chicken for the ham and thinly sliced C K S Swiss cheese for the mozzarella. Add thin slices C K S of avocado to the filling and omit the mustard. Proceed as directed.

GRILLED CHEESE AND ONION

Toast slices of white bread on one side. Spread butter over untoasted side, cover with thinly sliced C K S onions, and top with grated C K S Cheddar or Swiss cheese. Return to broiler just long enough to melt the cheese.

VEGETABLES

VEGETABLE PURÉES

PURÉE DE CAROTTES · CARROT PURÉE
(YIELD: ABOUT 1½ CUPS)

 6 Medium carrots, scraped and cut in 1-inch pieces
 2 Tablespoons uncooked rice
1½ Cups water
 2 Teaspoons granulated sugar
 ¼ Teaspoon salt
  Pinch each ground nutmeg and freshly ground
  black pepper
1½ Tablespoons butter
 ¼ Cup heavy cream

 I Chop C S or grate K carrots.

 II Cover and cook carrots, rice, water, sugar, salt, nutmeg, and pepper in a heavy saucepan until the water cooks away (about 30 minutes).

 III Purée C K S the carrot-rice mixture with the butter and cream.

 IV Stir over low heat until the purée has a thick, smooth consistency.

PURÉE DE CÉLERI-RAVE · CELERY-KNOB PURÉE

(YIELD: ABOUT 1½ CUPS)

> 1½ Cups peeled and quartered small, young celery knobs
> ¾ Cup mashed potatoes
> 1½ Tablespoons butter
> Heavy cream
> Salt
> Freshly ground black pepper

I Cook celery knobs in salted, boiling water until tender (about 20 minutes.)

II Drain well, then stir over low heat until excess moisture has cooked away.

III Purée C K S celery and potatoes.

IV Stir over low heat for one minute. Beat in butter and enough cream to achieve a nice texture. Season to taste with salt and pepper. Serve hot.

PURÉE DE CHÂTAIGNES · CHESTNUT PURÉE

(YIELD: ABOUT 1½ CUPS)

> 2 Dozen chestnuts (châtaignes or marrons)
> 1 Tablespoon vegetable oil
> Chicken broth, water, or milk
> 1 Tablespoon butter
> Hot milk

I Heat the oven to 500 degrees F.

II Cut an X on the flat side of each nut and toss with the oil in a flat pan. Roast for about 5 minutes or until the cut shells begin to curl away from the nutmeats.

III Keep the chestnuts hot as you peel them so that the shells and dull-brown underskins slip off more easily.

IV If the purée is to be served as a vegetable, bring the nuts to a boil in broth or water to cover, then lower the heat and simmer for 30 minutes. For a sweet or dessert purée, simmer the nuts in milk to cover for the same length of time. Allow the nuts to cool in the cooking liquid.

V Chop the nuts coarsely, then purée C K S. Add butter, replace the lid and continue to purée, pouring hot milk through the spout a bit at a time until the mixture reaches a smooth, rather firm consistency.

VI If the purée is to be served hot, reheat over very low flame, stirring constantly so that it does not scorch.

PURÉE DE CHAMPIGNONS · MUSHROOM PURÉE
(YIELD: ABOUT 1½ CUPS)

> 1 *Pound Mushrooms*
> 4 *Tablespoons butter*
> 1¾ *Cups thick Béchamel Sauce (see page 272)*

I Finely chop mushrooms C S.

II Sauté chopped mushrooms in butter until liquid evaporates.

III Stir in the béchamel sauce and continue to stir over low heat until the purée is very thick and well mixed. Serve hot.

PURÉE SOUBISE · ONION PURÉE
(YIELD: ABOUT 2 CUPS)

> 7 *Large onions, peeled and cut in eighths*
> 3 *Tablespoons butter*
> ⅓ *Cup uncooked rice*
> 1 *Cup boiling water*
> ½ *Teaspoon salt*
> 1½ *Cups thick Béchamel Sauce (see page 272)*

I Coarsely chop onions C S.

II Sauté in butter until translucent. Do not brown.

III Add rice, water, and salt; then cover the pan and simmer until the water cooks away (about 30 to 40 minutes).

IV Purée C S the onion-rice mixture with the béchamel sauce.

V Cook over low heat, stirring constantly, until thick and smooth (about 8 minutes). Serve hot.

PURÉE DE POIS FRAIS · PURÉE OF FRESH PEAS
(YIELD: ABOUT 2 CUPS)

> 4 *Pounds unshelled peas*
> 8 *Tablespoons (1 stick) butter*
> *Salt*
> *Granulated sugar*

I Shell peas and boil in salted water for 10 to 15 minutes, or until tender.

II Drain well, then purée C K S.

III Simmer purée and butter over low heat, stirring constantly, until thick. Season to taste with salt and a bit of sugar.

PURÉE D'OSEILLE · SORREL PURÉE
(YIELD: ABOUT 1½ CUPS)

> 2½ *Pounds sorrel*
> 2 *Tablespoons butter*
> *Salt*

I Simmer well-washed sorrel 15 minutes in the water that clings to the leaves. Stir occasionally.

II Drain well and purée C K S.

III Reheat with the butter. Add salt to taste and serve hot.

PURÉE D'ÉPINARDS · SPINACH PURÉE

(YIELD: ABOUT 1½ CUPS)

3 Pounds well-washed spinach leaves, with tough
stems removed
½ Cup Béchamel Sauce (see page 272)
Pinch granulated sugar
Salt
Nutmeg

I Bring salted water to boil in a large saucepan, add spinach, then cook only long enough for water to return to boil. Remove from heat and drain spinach.

II Squeeze spinach dry and purée C K S.

III Stir in the béchamel sauce and mix well. Add sugar, salt, and nutmeg to taste. Serve hot.

PURÉE DE NAVETS · TURNIP PURÉE

(YIELD: ABOUT 1½ CUPS)

8 Small turnips, peeled
2 Tablespoons butter
Heavy cream
Salt
Freshly ground black pepper

I Cut turnips into cubes and boil in salted water until tender (about 25 minutes).

II Drain well, then purée C K S.

III Simmer purée over low heat, stirring constantly, until all excess moisture has cooked away.

IV Add butter and enough cream for the purée to reach a smooth, firm consistency. Season to taste with salt and pepper and serve hot.

RIPE TOMATO PURÉE

(YIELD: ABOUT 2 CUPS)

16 to 20   *Fully ripe tomatoes, cut in quarters*
1   *Tablespoon butter or olive oil*
½   *Teaspoon granulated sugar*

I   Scrape seeds from tomatoes and purée the fruit. Purée C K S.

II   Heat the butter or oil in a heavy stainless steel pan. Strain the tomatoes into the pan and discard the pulp.

III   Sprinkle with sugar, then cook over medium heat until fairly thick (about 1½ hours). Lower the heat and reduce to desired consistency, stirring constantly. Use immediately, or cool quickly, then refrigerate or freeze.

GREEN TOMATO PURÉE

The green tomatoes that crowd your garden at summer's end need not be abandoned. This delicate green purée will accommodate almost any recipe that calls for red purée.

(YIELD: ABOUT 2 CUPS)

16 to 20   *Green tomatoes that have begun to turn white on the bottom*
1   *Tablespoon butter or olive oil*
1   *Teaspoon granulated sugar*
¼   *Cup water*

I   Wash the tomatoes, cut in half around the center and scrape out seeds, then cut into 1-inch pieces. Purée C K S.

II   Heat the butter or oil in a heavy stainless steel pan. Add the tomatoes, sugar, and water, then cook over medium-low heat for about one hour or until fairly thick. Lower the heat and reduce to desired consistency, stirring constantly. Strain.

PUMPKIN PURÉE

(YIELD: ABOUT 3 TO 4 CUPS)

> 1   *Ripe pumpkin, about 3 to 4 pounds*
> *Butter*
> *Pinch* each *salt and ground cloves*

I   Preheat oven to 350 degrees F.

II   Cut the pumpkin in half and cut away the seeds and stringy fibers. Set the cleaned pumpkin in a large roasting pan and add hot water to a depth of ½ inch.

III   Bake for 1½ to 2 hours, or until the pulp is tender.

IV   Scrape out pulp and place in container C S or finely grind K. Season to taste with butter, cloves, and salt, and then purée. Winter squash, which also makes a tasty purée, can be prepared by following this same procedure.

VEGETABLES–PLAIN & FANCY

One of the most appealing aspects of the super-efficient food processor is the way in which it transforms commonplace vegetables into Cinderella-thin slices and absolutely perfect shreds. Since a perfectly sliced or grated vegetable cooks more uniformly, there are no overcooked pieces to become mushy in the bottom of the pan, no thick undercooked pieces to detract from the marvelous overall texture of a flawlessly cooked vegetable.

Try sautéing sliced or chopped beets, cabbage, carrots, rutabaga, turnips, yellow squash, or zucchini in a tablespoon of butter for a few minutes, then cover tightly and cook over low heat, shaking the pan from time to time to prevent sticking, until vegetables are tender.

Grated or shredded vegetables become something special when you sauté them briefly in butter, then add 1 tablespoon of water to the pan, cover it, and cook them over very low heat until tender, shaking the pan occasionally. Add 2 to 3 tablespoons heavy cream, if you like, and continue to cook over very low heat until most of the cream evaporates.

And don't forget the seasonings—a pinch each of salt, sugar, nutmeg, and thyme will considerably enhance most vegetables.

HARICOTS VERTS AMANDINE · GREEN BEANS WITH ALMONDS

(YIELD: ENOUGH TO SERVE 6)

1½ *Pounds green beans*
4 *Tablespoons butter*
¼ *Cup toasted slivered almonds*
   Salt and freshly ground black pepper

I Parboil beans for 5 minutes; drain thoroughly. Trim ends and thinly slice C K S beans; place in a little boiling water, cover tightly, and bring to a second boil. Reduce heat to low and steam until beans are crisp but tender. If you prefer, you may cook them instead in boiling water to cover.

II Drain beans and set aside; add butter to pan and allow to heat briefly. Return beans to pan, add slivered nuts and salt and pepper to taste, then toss lightly until beans are well coated with butter and heated through. Serve hot.

BUTTERED CARROTS

(YIELD: ENOUGH TO SERVE 6)

2 *Pounds carrots, scraped (fresh, young carrots need not be scraped)*
4 *Tablespoons butter*
   Salt and freshly ground black pepper

I Thickly slice C K S carrots.

II Melt butter in a large, heavy skillet over very low heat. Add carrots and cover tightly, then cook for 10 to 15 minutes or until tender. Shake the skillet from time to time to coat the slices evenly with butter, taking care not to overcook or brown the vegetable.

III Remove from the heat and season to taste with salt and pepper.

HERBED CARROTS

Buttered carrots are even more flavorful when seasoned with fresh herbs. Chop C S or hand-mince K 2 tablespoons fresh dill, mint, or parsley leaves (with all tough stems removed), and add to the carrots along with the salt and pepper. Toss gently and serve hot.

CAROTTES VICHY
(YIELD: ENOUGH TO SERVE 6)

    10 Medium carrots, scraped
    ⅔   Cup chicken broth
     2 Tablespoons butter
     1 Tablespoon granulated sugar
        Pinch salt
     2 Tablespoons chopped fresh parsley

I Slice C K S carrots.

II Simmer, covered, in the broth, butter, sugar, and salt until broth cooks away.

III Uncover and shake the pan over medium-low heat until carrot slices are glazed. Sprinkle with parsley before serving hot.

CARROT PUDDING

(YIELD: ENOUGH TO SERVE 6 TO 8)

> 2 Pounds carrots, scraped
> 2 Medium onions, peeled and cut in eighths
> 4 Cups chicken broth
> 1½ Teaspoons salt
> 6 Eggs
> 1 Cup Matzo Meal (see page 303)

I Slice C K S carrots. Coarsely chop C S or hand-mince K onion. Place both vegetables in a saucepan with the broth, cover and bring to a boil, then simmer over low heat until tender.

II Preheat oven to 375 degrees F.

III Drain onions and carrots, reserving cooking liquid. Place vegetables in container C S or bowl K, add salt, and whirl until vegetables are puréed, stopping once or twice to scrape down container sides.

IV Add the eggs and matzo meal, whirl for 2 or 3 seconds more, and then gradually add a bit of the reserved cooking liquid to bring mixture to a nice thick consistency.

V Pour into a well-buttered 5-cup ring mold. Bake for 45 minutes or until firm. Unmold on a serving platter and heap a cooked green vegetable or vegetable purée into the center. Serve hot.

FRENCH-FRIED POTATOES

(YIELD: ENOUGH TO SERVE 6)

> 6 to 8 Medium potatoes
> Vegetable oil for deep-frying
> Salt

I Peel potatoes, dropping each into cold water to prevent discoloration.

II Heat oil to 370 degrees F. in an electric deep fryer or other deep pan (see How to Deep-Fry, at end of charts).

III Dry each potato thoroughly before cutting as directed for the Cuisinart machine or the Starmix (see Introduction). Then fry, a few at a time, in the hot oil until crisp and brown. Drain briefly on paper towels before seasoning to taste with salt. Serve hot.

POMMES DE TERRE ANNA

This classic dish presents potato slices attractively arranged and baked in butter.

(YIELD: ENOUGH TO SERVE 6)

> 6 *large potatoes, peeled*
> 6 *Tablespoons butter*
> *Salt and freshly ground black pepper*

I Preheat oven to 425 degrees F.

II Thinly slice potatoes C K S.

III Rinse slices, dry well, and arrange one-third of them in a generously buttered round mold or small rounded glass baking dish so that the slices overlap attractively. Sprinkle with salt and pepper to taste and dot with 2 tablespoons butter.

IV Repeat Step III until all potato slices have been arranged in the dish.

V Cover the dish with aluminum foil and bake 50 minutes or until slices are tender.

VI Carefully pour off any excess butter. Turn potatoes onto a hot ovenproof serving plate without disturbing their attractive pattern. Serve very hot.

POMMES DE TERRE CRECY

Add alternate layers of parboiled sliced carrots to Pommes de Terre Anna for a colorful—and tasty—variation.

TARTE AUX POMMES DE TERRE ET AU FROMAGE · POTATO AND CHEESE PIE

(YIELD: ENOUGH TO SERVE 6)

¼   Pound Cheddar cheese, cut in 1-inch cubes
2   Medium onions, peeled and cut in quarters
2   Tablespoons butter
1½   Cups cottage cheese
3   Small garlic cloves, peeled and cut in half
¼   Cup sour cream
3   Cups hot mashed potatoes
1   Tablespoon plus 1 teaspoon all-purpose flour
¾   Teaspoon salt
⅛   Teaspoon nutmeg
½   Recipe Pie Pastry (see page 357)

I   Finely grate C K S cheese and set aside. Coarsely chop C Ⓚ S onions; sauté in butter until soft, then set aside.

II   Place cottage cheese, garlic, and sour cream in container C S or bowl K. Mix for 5 seconds.

III   Add potatoes, sprinkle with flour, salt and nutmeg, then mix again by turning machine quickly on and off 3 or 4 times.

IV   Preheat oven to 350 degrees F. Roll out pastry and line a 9-inch pie plate.

V   Fill pastry shell with potato-cheese mixture, arrange sautéed onions over the top and sprinkle with grated Cheddar. Bake 75 minutes or until center of pie is fairly firm and the crust is golden brown. Serve at room temperature or chilled.

Ⓚ KitchenAid users: hand-chop onions and garlic.

ESCALLOPED POTATOES

(YIELD: ENOUGH TO SERVE 6)

3   Medium potatoes, peeled
1   Large onion, peeled
2   Tablespoons all-purpose flour
½   Teaspoon salt

3   Tablespoons butter
      Generous pinch dried sage leaves
1⅓ Cups milk
      Paprika

I Preheat oven to 350 degrees F.

II Slice C K S potatoes and set aside. Slice C K S onion.

III Arrange enough potato slices in a deep, well-buttered casserole to form a layer about 1 inch thick. Sprinkle with 1 tablespoon flour and ⅛ teaspoon salt. Dot with 1 tablespoon butter. Arrange half the sliced onion over the potatoes.

IV Repeat Step II finishing with a layer of the potatoes.

V Dot with 1 tablespoon butter and sprinkle with sage. Pour milk over potato and onion slices. There should be enough to fill the casserole about three-quarters full. If not, add more milk. Sprinkle with paprika.

VI Secure a sheet of aluminum foil tightly over the casserole and bake for 2 hours. Remove the foil cover during the last 45 minutes of baking to brown the top. If the top does not brown to your liking, raise heat to 400 degrees F. for 10 minutes. Serve hot.

ESCALLOPED POTATOES AND CABBAGE

Add alternate layers of shredded or grated cabbage (½ head) to Escalloped Potatoes recipe.

OLD-FASHIONED HASH-BROWNED POTATOES

(YIELD: ENOUGH TO SERVE 6)

6   Strips lean country-cured bacon
6   Medium potatoes, peeled
2   Medium onions, peeled
¼   Teaspoon salt
⅛   Teaspoon each *freshly ground black pepper, ground sage, and thyme*

I Sauté bacon in a large, deep skillet over medium heat until crispy brown.

II Meanwhile, grate C K S potatoes and drop them into cold water as they are finished to prevent darkening. Grate C K S onions and reserve juice.

III Drain grated potatoes thoroughly, then blot dry with paper towels. Remove bacon and half the bacon fat from the skillet and reserve both. Spread potatoes over the fat remaining in the skillet and brown lightly on one side.

IV Flatten the potatoes with a spatula; sprinkle with grated onion, onion juice, and seasonings. Continue to cook until potatoes are crisp and brown on the underside, then cut into 6 wedges and carefully remove from skillet.

V Add reserved bacon fat to the skillet, turn wedges over carefully and set uncooked side down in hot fat. Top each wedge with a strip of bacon and cook until underside is crisp and brown. Serve immediately.

POMMES DE TERRE DUCHESSE · DUCHESS POTATOES

(YIELD: ENOUGH TO SERVE 6)

    8 Medium potatoes, peeled
    1 Small egg plus 2 egg yolks
    2 Tablespoons butter
    1 Teaspoon salt
       Dash each ground nutmeg and white pepper

I Cut potatoes in quarters, place in a saucepan with water to cover, and bring to a boil. Cook over medium heat until tender, then drain. Return potatoes to pan and shake over low heat for 2 or 3 minutes or until potatoes are dry.

II Place potatoes in container C S. Process by turning motor quickly on and off about 3 times, removing cover each time to stir potatoes on bottom to the top.

III Add whole egg, egg yolks, butter, and seasonings. Turn machine rapidly on and off 2 to 3 times until ingredients are well blended, stopping to scrape down container sides.

IV Pipe through a pastry tube to form a decorative border and broil until lightly browned, or force into roses or mounds on a buttered cookie sheet and bake until nicely browned in an oven preheated to 325 degrees F.

To store any unused duchess potato mixture, brush surface lightly with vegetable oil, and then press plastic wrap directly down on potato mixture. Refrigerate until needed. To use, reheat in the top of a double boiler over very low heat, stirring constantly.

POTATOES DAUPHINE

Perhaps the most delectable potato dish of all, these golden puffs enhance even the most ordinary meal.

(YIELD: ENOUGH TO SERVE 6)

Vegetable oil for frying
1   *Cup Pâte à Chou (see page 358)*
1   *Cup Duchess Potatoes (see above)*

I Heat 1½ inches oil in a deep skillet.

II Place puff paste and potato mixtures in container C S or bowl K. Process by turning machine quickly on and off 3 times (or until well mixed), removing the cover each time to scrape down the container sides.

III When the oil is *very* hot, drop in mixture by teaspoonfuls and cook until puffed and golden brown. Drain briefly on paper towels before serving hot.

POTATO PUFFS ALSACIENNE

(YIELD: ENOUGH TO SERVE 6)

    1   Large clove garlic, peeled
    5   Sprigs parsley, with all stems removed
    2   Pounds potatoes (about 6 to 8 medium), peeled and
         cooked until tender
    2   Tablespoons all-purpose flour
    2   Eggs
    ½   Cup melted butter
    ¼   Teaspoon salt
    ⅛   Teaspoon each freshly ground black pepper and
         nutmeg

I   Heat oven to 325 degrees F.

II   Place garlic and parsley in container C Ⓚ S. Whirl for 5 seconds or until finely chopped. Stop motor and scrape down container sides.

III   Cut potatoes in 1-inch slices and place in container along with flour, eggs, 2 tablespoons melted butter, and the spices. Turn machine quickly on and off 6 or 7 times or until thoroughly mixed, stopping once or twice to scrape down container sides.

IV   Use a pastry bag with a fluted nozzle (or a tablespoon) to form small decorative mounds of potato mixture on a greased cookie sheet, taking care that these do not touch.

V   Bake 10 minutes, then place under broiler until golden brown. Spoon the remaining hot melted butter over the puffs and serve hot.

Ⓚ KitchenAid users: hand-mince garlic and parsley.

CREAMED POTATO SLICES VICTORIA

(YIELD: ENOUGH TO SERVE 6)

    3   Tablespoons butter
 1¼   Cups heavy cream
    1   Cup milk

8 Medium potatoes, peeled
¾ Teaspoon salt
⅛ Teaspoon freshly ground black pepper

I Melt butter in large, heavy skillet, then add cream and milk. Heat over lowest possible flame. Do not boil.

II Thinly slice C K S potatoes. Rinse and pat dry. Slip the slices singly into the hot cream; they should be well distributed and barely covered by the liquid.

III Sprinkle half the salt and pepper over the potatoes and simmer for 30 minutes, then turn slices carefully, add remaining salt and pepper, and simmer for 30 minutes more.

POTATO PANCAKES

(YIELD: 8 TO 10 PANCAKES)

4 to 5 Medium potatoes, peeled
1 Medium onion, peeled and cut in quarters
¾ Cup Matzo Meal (see page 303)
2 Eggs
2 Teaspoons salt
½ Teaspoon freshly ground black pepper
Vegetable oil for frying

I Finely grate C K S potatoes, placing each finished batch in cold water to prevent discoloration. There should be about 3 cups in all.

II Squeeze grated potatoes between paper towels until all moisture is wrung out. Cuisinart users: mix the potatoes, onion, matzo meal, eggs, salt, and pepper in the container, using the steel knife. When the mixture appears coarsely chopped, remove from machine.

Starmix users: place all ingredients in the blender jug and blend until the onion is coarsely chopped. KitchenAid users: grate or hand-mince onion and use the flat beater to mix all ingredients well.

In all machines, stop 3 or 4 times to stir up the mixture from the bottom.

III Heat vegetable oil to 375 degrees F. In a large skillet. Drop the pancake mixture by tablespoons into the hot fat and fry until golden brown on both sides, turning once. Drain briefly on paper towels before serving hot.

SWEET POTATO AND APPLE CASSEROLE

(YIELD: ENOUGH TO SERVE 6)

3   *Medium sweet potatoes, peeled*
1   *Large apple, peeled and cored*
1   *Teaspoon all-purpose flour*
3   *Tablespoons light brown sugar*
1/4   *Teaspoon salt*
1   *Tablespoon butter*
    Generous pinch ground cinnamon
1   *Cup orange juice*
1/3   *Cup water*

I Preheat oven to 350 degrees F.

II Slice C K S sweet potatoes, cover with cold water and set aside. Slice C K S apple.

III Arrange enough potato slices in a deep, well-buttered casserole dish to form a 1-inch layer. Sprinkle with 1/2 teaspoon flour, 1 tablespoon brown sugar, and 1/8 teaspoon salt. Dot with 1 teaspoon butter. Arrange half the apple slices over the potatoes.

IV Repeat this process, finishing with potato slices, then dot with 1 teaspoon butter and sprinkle with the cinnamon and 1 tablespoon brown sugar.

V Pour orange juice and water over potato and apple slices. Secure a sheet of aluminum foil tightly over top of the casserole and bake for 2 hours, removing the foil during the final 45 minutes of baking to brown the top. Serve hot.

FRIED TURNIP SLICES

(YIELD: ENOUGH TO SERVE 6)

 6 *White turnips, peeled*
 3 *Tablespoons vegetable oil*
 1 *Egg*
 1 *Teaspoon water*
 3 *Tablespoons all-purpose flour*
    Salt

I Thinly slice C K S turnips.

II Partially cook turnip slices in boiling salted water, then drain and pat dry on paper towels.

III Heat oil in a heavy skillet. Beat together egg and water. Dip turnip slices first in flour, then in egg, and fry to a crispy brown in the hot oil. Drain briefly on paper towels before seasoning to taste with salt. Serve hot.

FRIED SWEET POTATO SLICES

Substitute 4 small peeled sweet potatoes for the turnips and proceed as directed in recipe for Fried Turnip Slices (see above).

HEAVENLY SUMMER SQUASH PIE

(YIELD: ENOUGH TO SERVE 4 TO 6)

 ½   *Recipe Pie Pastry (see page 357)*
 3 to 4 *Medium summer squash*
 1   *Cup water*
 3   *Eggs*
 1   *Cup heavy cream*
 ¼   *Cup sherry*
 1   *Teaspoon granulated sugar*
 ½   *Teaspoon salt*
 ⅛   *Teaspoon each ground cinnamon, ginger and nutmeg*
      Pinch each mace and freshly ground black pepper

I Prepare and chill pastry dough.

II Thinly slice C K S squash, place in a saucepan with the water, and cook over medium heat until most of the liquid evaporates.

III Preheat oven to 425 degrees F. Purée squash, add remaining ingredients to container C S or bowl K, and mix well. Roll out pie dough, line a 7½-inch pie plate, and crimp the edges. Spoon puréed mixture into pie shell.

IV Bake for 15 minutes, then reduce oven temperature to 350 degrees F. and bake for 30 minutes more, or until a knife inserted in the center comes out clean. Serve hot.

ONION TART

(YIELD: ENOUGH TO SERVE 6)

6 *Medium onions, peeled*
2½ *Tablespoons butter*
¾ *Cup sour cream*
2 *Eggs*
2 *Tablespoons brandy*
⅛ *Teaspoon salt*
  Pinch each freshly ground black pepper and ground nutmeg
½ *Recipe Pie Pastry (see page 357)*
2 *Strips lean country-cured bacon*

I Preheat oven to 350 degrees F.

II Slice C K S onions and sauté in butter until translucent.

III Mix C K S sour cream, eggs, brandy, and spices.

IV Roll out pie crust and line an 8-inch pie plate.

V Mix together onions and cream mixture and pour into pastry shell. Cut bacon in 1-inch pieces and arrange attractively on top. Bake until filling is firm and bacon is brown (about 40 to 50 minutes). Serve warm.

CABBAGE CURRY

This East Indian dish presents the lowly cabbage in an unusual and particularly tasty way.

(YIELD: ENOUGH TO SERVE 6)

> 2 *Pounds firm cabbage*
> 1 *Medium onion, peeled*
> 1 *Tablespoon butter*
> 2 *Teaspoons salt*
> 1 *Teaspoon ground turmeric*
> ½ *Teaspoon chili powder (optional)*
> 1 *Teaspoon masala**

I Discard soft outer leaves and thinly slice C K S cabbage. Coarsely machine C S or hand-chop K onion.

II Sauté onion in butter until lightly browned, then mix in salt, turmeric, and chili powder. Add cabbage and cook over medium heat, without stirring, for 15 minutes, then stir gently. Continue to cook, partially covered, until the cabbage is cooked through. Stir gently from time to time to keep from sticking.

III Stir in the masala and cook, stirring constantly, for 1 or 2 minutes longer. The curry should be very dry. Serve hot.

* This mixture of finely ground black peppercorns, cardamom, caraway, cinnamon, cloves, and coriander is available at any store that sells Indian specialties, or you may prepare your own (see page 274).

RED-WINE CABBAGE

(YIELD: ENOUGH TO SERVE 8)

      1   Medium head red cabbage, with tough outer leaves
          and core removed
      2   Tart apples, peeled, cored, and cut in eighths
      1   Small onion, peeled and cut in quarters
      3   Strips country-cured bacon, cut in quarters
      1   Tablespoon butter
    ⅓   Cup tarragon vinegar
      2   Tablespoons lemon juice
      1   Cup dry red wine
      1   Cup water
    ½   Cup granulated sugar
    ¼   Teaspoon salt
      4   Whole cloves
      1   Bay leaf
      1   Tablespoon all-purpose flour

I   Thinly slice C K S red cabbage, then rinse well and set aside to drain thoroughly.

II   Place apples, onion, and bacon in container C Ⓚ S. Process by turning machine quickly on and off once or twice.

III   Heat the butter in a large heavy skillet and sauté the apple, onion, and bacon, stirring occasionally until the bacon is fairly crisp.

IV   Stir in the vinegar, lemon juice, wine, water, sugar, and spices. Mix well and bring to a boil. Add the drained cabbage, then cover and simmer the mixture over low heat for 1 hour, stirring every 10 minutes. Add more water if necessary to keep cabbage from sticking. The dish is perfectly suitable for serving at this point, but to mellow it and further enhance its flavor and texture, sprinkle with flour and let stand for several minutes, then stir flour well in and bake in a preheated oven (300 degrees F.) for 45 minutes, stirring occasionally.

Ⓚ KitchenAid users: hand-chop these ingredients.

NUT-FRIED EGGPLANT

Eggplant is delicious fried, but when it is cut into strips, dipped in chopped nuts, and fried, it is exquisite.

(YIELD: ENOUGH TO SERVE 6)

2   Medium eggplants, peeled
1½ Cups walnuts, pecans, or almonds
2   Eggs
2   Teaspoons water
     Vegetable oil for frying

I   Cuisinart and KitchenAid users: cut eggplant into ½-by-2-inch sticks by hand. Starmix owners: use your French fry cutter. Cover eggplant with boiling salted water and allow to stand for 20 minutes.

II   Meanwhile, finely chop C S or grate C K S nuts. Beat eggs together with 2 teaspoons water. Heat enough oil in a heavy skillet to deep fry.

III   Drain eggplant sticks well and pat dry. Dip first in beaten egg and then in nuts and fry to a crisp golden brown in the hot oil. Drain briefly on paper towels before serving hot.

EGGPLANT PARMESAN

(YIELD: ENOUGH TO SERVE 6)

2   Medium eggplants, peeled
     Salt
     Olive oil for frying
     Freshly ground black pepper
1   Piece (2 inches × 2 inches × ½ inch) Parmesan
     cheese cut in ½-inch pieces
6   Slices stale bread, broken in pieces
2   Large cloves garlic, peeled and cut in half
1   Tablespoon fresh parsley leaves, with all tough stems
     removed
3   Cups Tomato Sauce I (see page 265) or
     Ripe Tomato Purée (see page 222)
1   Piece (3 inch × 2 inch × 2½ inch) mozzarella cheese

I Thickly slice C K S eggplant, sprinkle with salt, and weight down; set aside for 15 or 20 minutes. Drain and squeeze out excess moisture between paper towels.

II Sauté eggplant slices in hot oil until lightly browned on both sides, turning once.

III Meanwhile, Cuisinart users should whirl Parmesan cheese for 15 seconds in container, add bread pieces, garlic, and parsley, then whirl for 5 or 6 seconds more. KitchenAid and Starmix users should finely grate cheese and bread, mince garlic and parsley by hand, then mix these ingredients together.

IV Preheat oven to 400 degrees F. Drain sautéed eggplant slices briefly on paper towels and arrange one-third of them in a fairly deep round or square baking dish. Sprinkle with one-third mixture of Parmesan, bread crumbs, garlic, and parsley, and cover with tomato sauce. Thinly slice C K S mozzarella and arrange a few slices over the sauce.

V Continue to build layers of eggplant, bread-crumb mixture, sauce, and mozzarella, ending with the mozzarella. Bake for 15–20 minutes or until top bubbles and turns golden.

BAKED MUSHROOM CAPS WITH ALMOND STUFFING

Serve these either as a vegetable in their own right or as a go-with for plain meat, fish or egg meals.

(YIELD: ENOUGH TO SERVE 6)

> 24   *Medium-to-large fresh mushrooms*
> 2   *Slices stale bread, broken in pieces*
> ⅔   *Cup blanched almonds*
> 1   *Small onion, peeled and cut in quarters*
> 4   *Tablespoons butter*
> ⅓   *Cup tomato catsup*
>   *Milk and water*

I Remove stems, wipe mushrooms with a damp cloth, and set aside.

II Preheat oven to 350 degrees F.

III Whirl bread pieces and almonds in container C K until finely ground. Add mushroom stems and onion and turn on and off quickly 3 times, stopping once to scrape down container sides. KitchenAid users should finely grind together bread, almonds, onion, and mushroom stems.

IV Heat butter and sauté bread crumb–almond mixture over medium heat, stirring frequently, until onion is transparent.

V Stir in the catsup, then remove from heat and mound mixture in reserved mushroom caps.

VI Set stuffed mushrooms in a baking dish, pour in enough milk and water to reach halfway up the sides of the caps, and bake for 35 minutes. Remove from the pan and set on a hot platter. Serve hot, topped with bits of crisp bacon if desired. Decorate with sprigs of parsley tucked here and there between the mushrooms.

CUCUMBERS SWEDISH STYLE
(YIELD: ENOUGH TO SERVE 4 TO 6)

5	*Medium cucumbers, peeled*
	Salt
6	*Strips lean country-cured bacon*
2	*Tablespoons granulated sugar*
2½	*Tablespoons vinegar*
	Generous pinch ground nutmeg
2	*Teaspoons all-purpose flour*
	Freshly ground black pepper

I Slice C K S cucumbers. Spread on a plate, sprinkle with salt, and top with another heavy plate. Let stand 30 minutes. Drain well.

II Meanwhile, coarsely chop bacon and brown in a heavy saucepan.

III Add cucumber slices, sugar, vinegar, and nutmeg to pan. Simmer 10 minutes. Sprinkle with flour, then stir a few minutes more. Pour off excess grease before serving very hot, sprinkled with pepper.

DUXELLES

    ½ Pound very fresh perfect mushrooms
    1 Shallot, peeled and cut in quarters
    2 Tablespoons butter
    ½ Teaspoon salt
    2 Teaspoons minced parsley

I Trim mushrooms and wipe with a damp cloth. Cut in quarters and place in container C S with the shallot. Whirl for 5 or 6 seconds or until finely chopped. KitchenAid users should hand-mince these.

II Heat the butter and cook the vegetables until all the moisture has evaporated. Season to taste with salt and parsley.

PRESERVED HORSERADISH

    Horseradish roots
    Salt
    White vinegar

I Wash and scrape roots, cut in 1-inch pieces, and cover with cold water to prevent discoloring.

II Drain, pat dry, and finely grate C K S horseradish, then place in cooled, sterilized pint jars, filling each about ⅔ full. Add 1 teaspoon salt to each pint and fill to the top with vinegar. Seal jars.

EASY TOMATO JUICE
(YIELD: 1 QUART)

    12 Medium tomatoes, cored and cut in quarters
    ½ Teaspoon granulated sugar
       Salt and lemon juice to taste

I Place half of the tomato quarters in container C S. Process for 30 seconds or until liquified. Strain juice into pitcher.

II Repeat Step I with remaining tomato quarters.

III Stir sugar, lemon juice, and salt to taste into juice. Refrigerate until serving time.

SALADS

SALADS

Salads with their varied ingredients and interesting textures provide a change-of-pace accompaniment to elegant or simple dining. Almost any fresh vegetable partners perfectly with any other, so don't limit yourself to the obvious.

For lettuce, try loose-leafed varieties like butterhead or Bibb, romaine, leaf lettuce, or those flavorful lettuce substitutes escarole and endive, as well as the more compact head varieties. Choose from other leafy greens like spinach, watercress, collards, Swiss chard, or kale, or the young leaves of such root vegetables as beets and turnips. Young tender dandelion leaves or the peppery leaves of nasturtiums are guaranteed to perk up the most run-of-the-mill salad.

But whatever greens you do select, always choose only the freshest and most perfect leaves. Crisp them well in ice water, pat thoroughly dry, then tear into bite-size pieces before arranging in your salad bowl. Top the greens with your favorite garden-fresh vegetables and herbs, sliced, grated, and/or chopped. Mix and match them to suit your taste and toss with Basic Vinaigrette/ French Dressing (see page 257) or any variation thereof.

VEGETABLE MEDLEY

(YIELD: ENOUGH TO SERVE 6)

> 1   *Medium cucumber, peeled*
> 1   *Small yellow summer squash*
> 1   *Small zucchini*
> 3   *Small carrots, scraped*
> 1   *Green and 1 sweet red pepper, blanched in boiling*
>   *water for 2 minutes, then seeded*
> 12 *Scallions, with 3 inches green top*
> 3   *Medium tomatoes*
> 12 *Radishes*
> 2   *Cups salad greens*
>   *Basic Vinaigrette/French Dressing or any variation*
>   *(see pages 256–261)*

I   Slice C K S cucumber, squash, zucchini, carrots, and peppers. Cut scallions in half lengthwise and tomatoes in eighths by hand. Make radish roses by cutting thin, petal-shaped cuts around the sides of each.

II   Arrange cucumber, squash, zucchini, carrot, and pepper slices and scallions attractively on a bed of salad greens. Surround with tomato wedges and radish roses.

III   Chill salad well before serving with sauce in a dish on the side.

LONG, HOT SUMMER SALAD

(YIELD: ENOUGH TO SERVE 6)

> 6   *Tomatoes, peeled*
>   *Basic Vinaigrette/French Dressing or any variation*
>   *(see pages 256 to 261)*
> 2   *Medium cucumbers, peeled*
> 2   *Medium carrots, scraped*
> 2   *Small zucchini*
> 1   *Large sweet onion, peeled*
> 8   *Radishes, trimmed*
> 3   *Cups lettuce leaves*

6 Hard-cooked eggs, cut in quarters
10 Sprigs parsley

I Slice tomatoes by hand and marinate in dressing.

II Thinly slice C K S cucumbers, carrots, zucchini, onion, and radishes. Arrange sliced vegetables over lettuce leaves in a large salad bowl.

III Top vegetables with marinated tomatoes, quartered eggs, and parsley sprigs. Keep chilled until serving time. Toss with dressing just before serving.

SPRINGTIME COLESLAW

(YIELD: ENOUGH TO SERVE 8)

1 Medium head cabbage
2 Medium carrots, scraped and cut in 1-inch pieces
2 Ribs celery, with all strings removed, cut in 1-inch pieces
1 Medium green pepper, seeded and cut in 1-inch pieces
5 Medium scallions, with 3 inches green top, cut in 1-inch pieces
5 Extra-large pimento-stuffed green olives
4 Tablespoons each granulated sugar and lemon juice
¼ Cup each milk and sour cream
1 Cup Foolproof Mayonnaise (see page 252)
¾ Teaspoon salt

I Finely chop C S or grate K cabbage. Scrape into large bowl.

II Mince C S or grind K carrots, celery, green pepper, scallions and olives. Combine with cabbage.

III Mix together C Ⓚ S sugar, lemon juice, milk, sour cream, mayonnaise, and salt. Pour over vegetables and toss well. Refrigerate coleslaw for at least 4 hours. Serve cold.

Ⓚ KitchenAid users: mix dressing by hand or use flat mixing blade in steel bowl.

COLESLAW IN TOMATO SHELLS

Hollow out and drain 6 tomatoes and fill with Springtime Coleslaw (see above).

TZATZIKI · CUCUMBER AND YOGURT SALAD
(YIELD: ENOUGH TO SERVE 6)

2   Cups plain yogurt
2   Medium cucumbers, peeled and seeded
1   Clove garlic, peeled and crushed
1   Tablespoon olive oil
    Juice of ½ lemon
    Salt and freshly ground black pepper.

I Line a fine sieve with cheesecloth and place over a deep bowl. Spoon yogurt into cheesecloth. Set both sieve and bowl in refrigerator and allow yogurt to drain for 2 hours.

II Thinly slice C K S cucumbers. Set 10 slices aside. Drain cucumbers well. Mix together yogurt, cucumber slices, garlic, oil, and lemon juice. Season to taste with salt and serve cold, garnished with coarsely grated black pepper and reserved thinly sliced cucumbers.

CHICKEN OR TURKEY SALAD
(YIELD: ENOUGH TO SERVE 6)

3   Medium ribs celery, with all strings removed, cut in
    1-inch pieces
1   Medium onion, peeled and quartered
½   Cup Foolproof Mayonnaise (see page 252)
3   Cups cooked chicken or turkey, cut in cubes
    Hard-cooked eggs
    Tomatoes
    Pitted ripe olives

I Place celery, onion, and mayonnaise in container C S. Process by turning machine quickly on and off 2 or 3 times.

KitchenAid users: coarsely grind or hand-chop celery, onion, and chicken or turkey.

II Add chicken or turkey and process C S by quickly turning machine on and off 1 or 2 times. The meat should not be too fine.

III Refrigerate until serving time. To serve, heap on an attractive serving plate or into a bowl, surround with egg quarters and tomato wedges, and garnish with sliced ripe olives.

TOMATOES WITH CHICKEN SALAD AND TOMATO CREAM SAUCE

Scoop out and reserve for another use the pulp from 6 large firm ripe tomatoes. Drain tomato shells well and fill with Chicken or Turkey Salad (see above). Top each with a dollop of Tomato Cream Sauce (see page 269). Serve cold.

EGG SALAD
(YIELD: ENOUGH TO SERVE 6)

3 Scallions, with 3 inches green top, cut in ½-inch pieces
½ Rib celery, with all strings removed, cut in 1-inch strips
9 Hard-cooked eggs, cut in quarters
4 Strips crisply cooked country-cured bacon
½ Cup Foolproof Mayonnaise (see page 252)
Salt

I Place scallions, celery, egg quarters, and bacon in container C Ⓚ S; whirl for 2 seconds.

II Add ½ cup mayonnaise or more, if desired. Salt to taste, and process by quickly turning machine on and off 2 or 3 times.

III Scrape into bowl and keep chilled.

Ⓚ KitchenAid users: mince and mix ingredients by hand.

CUCUMBERS (ZUCCHINI) AND TOMATOES VINAIGRETTE

(YIELD: ENOUGH TO SERVE 6)

> 2 Medium cucumbers, peeled*
> Salt
> 6 Large, ripe tomatoes
> 4 Scallions, with 3 inches green top
> Basic Vinaigrette/French Dressing (see page 257)

I Thinly slice C K S cucumbers. Place in a shallow bowl, sprinkle with salt, and weight down with a heavy plate. Refrigerate for 1 hour.

II Slice tomatoes thinly by hand and arrange attractively over the bottom of a large, shallow serving dish.

III Drain cucumber slices thoroughly and arrange over tomatoes.

IV Hand-mince C K S scallions and use to garnish salad. Sprinkle vegetables with dressing and refrigerate until serving time. Serve cold.

* Six small zucchini may be substituted for the cucumber.

TURNIP AND CARROT SALAD

(YIELD: ENOUGH TO SERVE 6)

> 2 White turnips, peeled
> 4 Medium carrots, scraped
> 1 Tablespoon granulated sugar
> 1 Teaspoon salt
> Dash red pepper
> 3 Tablespoons vinegar

I Coarsely grate C K S turnips and carrots.

II Combine sugar, salt, and pepper with the vinegar.

III Pour dressing over grated vegetables and toss lightly. Chill before serving cold.

CONFETTI COTTAGE CHEESE

(YIELD: ENOUGH TO SERVE 6)

    1   Medium carrot, peeled and cut in 1-inch pieces
    3   Scallions, with 3 inches green top, cut in ½-inch
         pieces
    3   Cups cottage cheese
    ½   Cup Foolproof Mayonnaise (see page 252)
    1   Tablespoon lemon juice
         Freshly ground black pepper
    1   Medium tomato, peeled, seeded, coarsely chopped,
         and well drained

I Place carrot pieces in container C Ⓚ S and whirl for 5 or 6 seconds. Add scallions, then whirl 1 second longer.

II Add cottage cheese, mayonnaise, lemon juice, and black pepper to taste. Process for 2 seconds by quickly turning machine on and off twice.

III Turn cottage cheese mixture into bowl and mix in chopped tomato. Chill well before serving cold on a bed of crisp greens.

Ⓚ KitchenAid users: finely grind carrot and scallion together, then mix ingredients in metal bowl. Hand-chop tomato and add as directed.

SOUTH SHORE TOMATO ASPIC

When this zesty, colorful aspic is brought forth as an accompaniment with cocktails it serves 8 . . . as a summer salad it will satisfy 4 to 6 persons.

½   *Cup celery leaves, well washed*
½   *Medium onion, peeled and cut in quarters*
4   *Cups tomato juice*
1   *Tablespoon granulated sugar*
¾   *Teaspoon salt*
6   *Whole peppercorns*
4   *Whole cloves*
1   *Small bay leaf*
3   *Tablespoons unflavored gelatin*
3   *Tablespoons each lemon juice and sour cream*
1   *Cup cooked fish, cut in pieces*
1   *Tender inside rib (6 inches long) celery, cut in 1-inch pieces*
2   *Scallions, with 3 inches green top, cut in ⅛-inch slices*
3   *Tablespoons fresh dill leaves with all stems removed*
     Crackers or Toast Points (see page 304)

I Place celery leaves and onion in container C Ⓚ S. Whirl for 2 or 3 seconds, stopping once to scrape down container sides.

II In a large saucepan, bring celery leaves, onion, 3 cups tomato juice, sugar, and spices to a boil. Reduce heat, cover, and allow to simmer for 15 minutes. Remove from heat and strain into large bowl.

III Combine gelatin with remaining tomato juice. Let stand for 5 minutes to soften, then dissolve in hot tomato juice.

IV Stir lemon juice and sour cream into tomato mixture. Refrigerate until mixture begins to set.

V Meanwhile, pick over fish to remove any bones. Place celery, scallions, and dill in container C Ⓚ S. Whirl for 3 or 4 seconds, stopping once to scrape down sides. Add fish and whirl 1 second more.

VI Fold minced fish mixture into partially set aspic. Rinse a 1-quart mold with cold water and pour in aspic. Refrigerate until thoroughly set. Unmold on a chilled platter and serve with crackers or toast points or arrange on lettuce leaves.

Ⓚ KitchenAid users: hand-chop vegetables and dill and flake fish.

TOMATO-CUCUMBER ASPIC

(YIELD: ENOUGH TO SERVE 6)

4   *Large cucumbers, peeled and seeded*
2   *Cups tomato juice*
1   *Cup white vinegar*
2   *Envelopes unflavored gelatin*
1   *Tablespoon onion juice*
    Salt, freshly ground black pepper, and cayenne pepper
    Foolproof Mayonnaise (see page 252)

I   Finely grate C K S cucumbers. Place in a large saucepan, add 1 cup tomato juice and the vinegar, and bring to boil. Lower heat and simmer until cucumber is tender, then remove from heat.

II   Purée C S cucumbers with their cooking liquid and return mixture to saucepan. KitchenAid users may prepare the aspic without puréeing to achieve a different, but equally delicious result.

III   Soften gelatin in remaining cup tomato juice and add to puréed cucumber along with onion juice, salt, pepper, and cayenne to taste. Stir over very low heat for 3 to 4 minutes.

IV   Oil a ring mold and fill with aspic mixture. Chill until set. To serve, unmold on a serving plate and heap meat, vegetable, or egg salad in center. Decorate with peaks of mayonnaise forced through a pastry tube.

DRESSINGS & SAUCES

FOOLPROOF MAYONNAISE

Since I believe it is not wise to eat uncooked egg whites (see end of charts), I do not recommend the use of whole eggs here. The Cuisinart machine has the disadvantage of requiring a rather large amount of ingredients in the bottom of the container before it will blend properly. This recipe compensates by starting off with the ingredient usually used for saving curdled mayonnaise . .,. prepared mustard. When this is whirled with the egg yolks at the beginning of the process it seems to prevent curdling and allows for a bit more vinegar, lemon juice, or water to be used later on in the preparation to thin the sauce. While this recipe was created especially for the Cuisinart processor, it works equally well when prepared in the Starmix machine. KitchenAid users, see separate recipe below.

> 1 Tablespoon Dijon mustard
> 3 Egg yolks
> ½ Teaspoon salt
>   Lemon juice or wine vinegar
> 1½ to 2 Cups olive oil

    I Whirl mustard, egg yolks, and salt for 30 seconds. While the motor is running add, through the spout, one teaspoon lemon juice or vinegar, then add ½ cup of oil 1 drop at a time. Continue to add oil in a very thin stream until mayonnaise blends to the thickness you like it. Thin by adding 2 teaspoons warm vinegar or lemon juice and whirl 30 seconds longer. Refrigerate.

II Mayonnaise may be thinned a little prior to using by whirling for 10 seconds, then adding a teaspoon of warm vinegar or lemon juice (or more to taste) a few drops at a time while motor is running.

FOOLPROOF MAYONNAISE FOR KITCHENAID FOOD PREPARER

(YIELD: ABOUT 2 CUPS)

>   2 *Egg yolks*
>   1 *Teaspoon* each *granulated sugar and salt*
>   1 *Tablespoon Dijon mustard*
>   1/4 *Teaspoon paprika*
>   2 *Tablespoons vinegar*
>   2 *Cups olive oil or vegetable oil*
>   2 *Tablespoons lemon juice*

I Chill the bowl well before beginning, then set in the egg yolks, sugar, salt, mustard, and paprika. Using the wire whip, turn to Speed 6 and whirl until ingredients are well blended, about 30 seconds.

II Turn the machine slowly again to Speed 6 and gradually add the vinegar, a teaspoon or so at a time. When all the vinegar has been incorporated, turn off the motor and scrape down the sides of the bowl.

III Return the machine gradually to Speed 6 and add 1/4 cup of the oil, 1 drop at a time, then add the remaining oil 1 tablespoon at a time, beating for 10 to 15 seconds after each addition. When all the oil has been thoroughly absorbed, keep the motor running and gradually add the lemon juice, then whirl for 30 seconds longer.

IV Keep chilled. To thin beat in 1 teaspoon of vinegar.

SAUCE RUSSE · RUSSIAN DRESSING

(YIELD: ABOUT 1 CUP)

    1   *Cup Foolproof Mayonnaise (see page 252)*
    1   *Teaspoon each chopped pimentos and fresh chives*
    3   *Tablespoons chili sauce*

I Whirl all ingredients in container C Ⓚ S by quickly turning machine on and off once or twice.

II Keep chilled. Serve with seafood, stuffed eggs, or vegetable salads.

Ⓚ KitchenAid users: beat mayonnaise and chili sauce together; then mince vegetables by hand and stir into sauce.

TARTAR SAUCE

(YIELD: 1½ CUPS)

  ½   *Medium onion, peeled and cut in quarters*
  2   *Large pimento-stuffed green olives*
  1   *Medium sweet gherkin, cut in half*
  1   *Tablespoon fresh parsley leaves, with all stems removed*
  1   *Tablespoon capers*
  1   *Cup cold Foolproof Mayonnaise (see page 252)*

I Finely chop onion, olives, pickle, parsley, and capers in container C S or by hand K. Drain well.

II Stir chopped ingredients into cold mayonnaise just prior to serving.

QUICK AÏOLI (GARLIC MAYONNAISE)

(YIELD: ABOUT 1 CUP)

  2   *Tablespoons bread crumbs*
1½   *Tablespoons lemon juice*

  3   Large cloves garlic (or more to taste), peeled and
      cut in half*
  2   Large egg yolks
½ to ⅔ Cup olive oil
      About 1 tablespoon boiling water

I Place bread crumbs in bowl K or container C S. Turn on machine, quickly add lemon juice and garlic, then drop in egg yolks one at a time. The mixture should be quite stiff.

II Whilo tho bladc is still whirling, gradually add the oil, a few drops at first, then slowly increase amount until oil runs in a thin, steady stream.

III When half the oil has been incorporated, add 1 teaspoon boiling water to thin the mixture a bit, then continue whirling and adding oil gradually until all the oil has been incorporated, adding another teaspoon or so of boiling water if mayonnaise seems too thick.

IV Store in the refrigerator.

* KitchenAid users: crush or chop garlic by hand.

PISTOU
(YIELD: ABOUT 1½ CUPS)

  1   3-ounce piece Parmesan cheese
  2   Strips country-cured bacon
  4   Cloves garlic, peeled and cut in quarters
  ⅓   Cup each fresh, tightly packed basil and parsley
      leaves, with all tough stems removed
  4   Egg yolks
  ⅔   Cup olive oil

I Finely chop C or grate S* cheese; set aside. Blanch bacon in 3 cups boiling water for 3 minutes, then drain well and cut in quarters. Place bacon pieces in container C S and whirl for 5 seconds. Add garlic and herbs, whirl until mixture takes on the

* Starmix users: your nut-grating blade performs best here.
  KitchenAid users: this is one of those recipes that is easiest to prepare in a food processor or blender. If you own either machine, put it to work here.

consistency of a thick paste, then add the egg yolks and whirl until mixture is doubly thick.

II Turn on machine and gradually add cheese through spout. When all the cheese has been incorporated, keep the motor running and add the oil by drops through the spout.

III The result will be a distinctive thick green sauce that will enliven almost any hot soup. Refrigerate.

HOLLANDAISE SAUCE

(YIELD: ABOUT 1½ CUPS)

½ *Pound (2 sticks) sweet butter*
1 *Cup hot water*
6 *Egg yolks*
4 *Teaspoons lemon juice*
Generous pinch each *salt and white pepper*

I Melt butter over medium heat. Meanwhile, pour hot water into container C S or bowl K. Allow to stand 1 minute, then discard water. KitchenAid users: your hot water jacket is helpful here.

II Add egg yolks, lemon juice, and seasonings to warmed container or bowl. Whirl until well mixed.

III As soon as butter is very hot, turn on machine and add it through the spout in a very thin but steady stream. Do not add butter too quickly. When all the butter has been incorporated, turn machine off. Serve at once.

SAUCE VINAIGRETTE · VINAIGRETTE/FRENCH DRESSING

The traditional combination of vinegar, oil, and seasonings known interchangeably as "vinaigrette" and "French" may be subtly transformed by the judicious addition of any number of different ingredients. You may choose to vary the type of vinegar—malt, cider, or tarragon vinegar are equally suitable—or the vinegar itself may be replaced by orange, lemon or grapefruit juice. For the olive oil in the Basic Recipe which follows, you may substitute peanut oil, vegetable, or salad oil (although to my mind olive oil does make a superior sauce). Experiment and see which combinations fit your salads—and your taste.

BASIC VINAIGRETTE/FRENCH DRESSING

In this recipe, as well as in the following variations, KitchenAid users should beat the dressing in the large bowl and hand-chop or mince solid ingredients.

(YIELD: ABOUT 1 CUP)

> ¼ *Cup wine vinegar*
> ¾ *Cup olive oil*
> ⅛ *Teaspoon salt*
> *Generous pinch freshly ground black pepper*

    I Place all ingredients in bowl K or container C S. Whirl only long enough to mix.

    II Pour over salad.

To vary the flavor of the Basic Recipe slightly, add any or all of the following:

> 1 *Hard-cooked egg, finely chopped C S*
> 1 *Small sweet gherkin, finely chopped C S*
> 2 *Teaspoons minced fresh chives*
> ½ *Medium green pepper, finely chopped C S*
> 2 *Teaspoons well-drained capers, chopped C S*

AVOCADO VINAIGRETTE/FRENCH DRESSING

(YIELD: ABOUT 1½ CUPS)

> 1 *Shallot, peeled and sliced*
> 1 *Tablespoon butter*
> 1 *Ripe avocado, peeled, pitted, and quartered*
> 1 *Teaspoon mixed fresh herbs (basil, chervil, chives, parsley, or tarragon in any combination)*
> 1 *Cup Mustard Vinaigrette/French Dressing (see page 261)*

I   Sauté the shallot in the butter until slices are soft and transparent.

II   Place shallot slices, avocado, herbs, and dressing In container C S. Process by turning machine quickly on and off 4 or 5 times—stopping once to scrape down sides—or until ingredients are well blended.

VINAIGRETTE/FRENCH DRESSING WITH ROQUEFORT OR BLUE CHEESE

Add 3 tablespoons crumbled Roquefort or blue cheese to ingredients for Basic Vinaigrette/French Dressing (see page 257). Whirl as directed. Serve with tomatoes and greens or fruit salad.

CHIFFONADE VINAIGRETTE/FRENCH DRESSING

Ingredients for Basic Vinaigrette/French Dressing (see page 257) plus

    2   Small pickled beets, cut in quarters
    4   Medium pimento-stuffed green olives
    ½   Small onion, peeled and cut in quarters
    1   Tablespoon fresh parsley, with all stems removed
    3   Hard-cooked eggs

I   Place all ingredients except the eggs in container C S. Process by quickly turning machine on and off 3 or 4 times, stopping once to scrape down container sides.

II   Mince the eggs by hand and add to dressing.

III   Serve with any greens.

VINAIGRETTE/FRENCH DRESSING WITH CHILI SAUCE

Add 3 tablespoons chili sauce and 2 tablespoons watercress leaves, with all tough stems removed, to ingredients for Basic Vinaigrette/French Dressing (see page 257), then whirl as directed. Serve with cold meat, fish, or vegetable salads.

CREAMY CHIVE VINAIGRETTE/FRENCH DRESSING

Add ⅓ cup sour cream and 1 tablespoon minced fresh chives to ingredients for Basic Vinaigrette/French Dressing (see page 257). Whirl as directed. Serve with fruit salads.

CHUTNEY VINAIGRETTE/FRENCH DRESSING

Add 3 tablespoons *each* chutney and catsup and 1 teaspoon fresh parsley leaves with all tough stems removed to ingredients for Basic Vinaigrette/French Dressing (see page 257). Whirl as directed. Serve with cold meats or chicken salad.

COTTAGE CHEESE VINAIGRETTE/FRENCH DRESSING

Add 3 tablespoons cottage cheese, 1 small sweet gherkin, and 1 tablespoon watercress leaves with all tough stems removed to ingredients for Basic Vinaigrette/French Dressing (see page 257). Whirl as directed. Serve with fresh vegetable salads.

CREAMY VINAIGRETTE/FRENCH DRESSING

Substitute lemon juice for the vinegar called for in Basic Vinaigrette/French Dressing and whirl dressing as directed. Turn on machine and gradually pour in 4 to 6 tablespoons of light cream, 1 tablespoon at a time, or as much as necessary to make the dressing creamy and thick. Serve with chicken, potato, or fruit salads.

CURRY VINAIGRETTE/FRENCH DRESSING

Add 1 teaspoon curry powder and 1 shallot, peeled and cut in quarters, to the ingredients for Basic Vinaigrette/French Dressing (see page 257), then whirl as directed. Serve with mixed greens, fish, or meat salads.

GARLIC VINAIGRETTE/FRENCH DRESSING

Suspend a garlic clove, peeled and cut in half, in your vinegar bottle for 3 or 4 days prior to preparing Basic Vinaigrette/ French Dressing (see page 257). Discard garlic before placing vinegar in bowl K or container C S along with other ingredients. Whirl as directed.

For a more audacious taste of garlic, whirl the garlic clove with the dressing.

VINAIGRETTE AUX FINES HERBES · VINAIGRETTE/FRENCH DRESSING WITH HERBS

Add 2 tablespoons minced fresh chervil, parsley, or tarragon, separately or in combination, to ingredients for Basic Vinaigrette/French Dressing (see page 257). Serve over mixed salad greens or sliced tomatoes or add herbs to the salad after tossing with the dressing.

HORSERADISH VINAIGRETTE/FRENCH DRESSING

Add 1½-inch piece fresh horseradish root, scraped and cut in pieces, 2 teaspoons paprika, and 2 or 3 drops Tabasco sauce to ingredients for Basic Vinaigrette/French Dressing (see page 257). Whirl until horseradish is very finely chopped. Serve with cold meats.

MINT VINAIGRETTE/FRENCH DRESSING

Substitute lemon juice for the vinegar when preparing Basic Vinaigrette/French Dressing and add 2 tablespoons mint leaves, with all tough stems removed, along with the other ingredients. Whirl as directed. Serve with fruit salads.

MUSHROOM VINAIGRETTE/FRENCH DRESSING

Prepare Basic Vinaigrette/French Dressing as directed (see page 257). Stir in ¼ cup thinly sliced C K S fresh mushrooms. Serve with mixed greens.

VINAIGRETTE À LA MOUTARDE · MUSTARD VINAIGRETTE/FRENCH DRESSING

Add 1 teaspoon dry or 2 teaspoons prepared mustard to ingredients for Basic Vinaigrette/French Dressing (see page 257). Whirl as directed. Serve with mixed greens.

TARRAGON VINAIGRETTE/FRENCH DRESSING

Prepare Basic Vinaigrette/French Dressing (see page 257) with tarragon vinegar, or add 1 tablespoon fresh tarragon leaves, with all stems removed, to the ingredients and whirl as directed. Serve with mixed greens.

SAUCE RAVIGOTE

(YIELD: ABOUT 1 CUP)

       1   Small onion, peeled and cut in 1-inch pieces
       1   Tablespoon well-drained capers
       2   Teaspoons fresh chervil leaves, with all tough stems
           removed
       1   Teaspoon each fresh parsley and tarragon leaves,
           with all tough stems removed
      ½   Cup Basic Vinaigrette/French Dressing (see page
           257) or Mustard Vinaigrette/French Dressing (see
           above)
       1   Hard-cooked egg
       1   Teaspoon chopped fresh chives

I Place onion, capers, chervil, parsley, and tarragon in container C S. Whirl for 4 seconds or until the onion is finely chopped, stopping once to scrape down container sides.

II Add dressing and process by quickly turning machine on and off once or twice.

III Force egg through a fine sieve, and stir it, along with the chopped chives, into the dressing.

IV Serve with cold meats and seafood.

THOUSAND ISLAND DRESSING

(YIELD: ABOUT 1½ CUPS)

> 1   *Cup Foolproof Mayonnaise (see page 252)*
> 3   *Tablespoons chili sauce*
> ½   *Rib celery, with all strings removed, cut in 1-inch pieces*
> ½   *Medium green pepper, seeded and cut in 1-inch pieces*
> ½   *Teaspoon paprika*
>   *Salt*
> 1   *Tablespoon* each *cider vinegar and cream*
> 1   *Hard-cooked egg*

I Place mayonnaise, chili sauce, celery, pepper and paprika in container C Ⓚ S. Season with salt to taste and process by quickly turning machine on and off 3 or 4 times, stopping once to scrape down container sides.

II Add vinegar and cream and whirl only long enough to mix ingredients well.

III Finely chop the egg by hand and mix with dressing.

IV Keep chilled.

Ⓚ KitchenAid users: beat mayonnaise, chili sauce, paprika, salt, vinegar, and cream in stainless steel bowl. Hand-mince celery and green pepper and finely chop egg and stir into dressing.

BLUE CHEESE SALAD DRESSING

(YIELD: ABOUT 1½ CUPS)

$\frac{2}{3}$ Cup blue cheese, crumbled
1   Clove garlic, peeled and cut in half
6   Tablespoons lemon juice
1   Tablespoon each fresh chervil and tarragon leaves,
      with all tough stems removed
¼   Teaspoon each salt and freshly ground black pepper
⅛   Teaspoon ground nutmeg
1   Cup heavy cream

I   Whirl C S all ingredients in container until mixture is smooth. KitchenAid users: hand-mince garlic, chervil, and tarragon and mix with flat beater blade.

II   Keep chilled.

GREEN GODDESS SALAD DRESSING

(YIELD: ABOUT 2 CUPS)

½   Small onion, peeled and cut in quarters
¼   Cup tightly packed fresh parsley leaves, with all
      tough stems removed
2   Cloves garlic, peeled and cut in half
4   Anchovy fillets, cut in pieces
2   Scallions, green part only, cut in ¼-inch pieces
1   Cup Foolproof Mayonnaise (see page 252)
½   Cup sour cream
2   Tablespoons each tarragon vinegar and lemon juice
¼   Teaspoon freshly ground black pepper

I   Hand-mince K or finely chop in container C S onion, parsley, garlic, anchovies, and scallions. Add remaining ingredients to steel bowl K or container C S and whirl until well mixed, stopping as necessary to scrape down sides.

II   Keep chilled.

TAHINI DRESSING

(YIELD: ABOUT 1 CUP)

   2   *Cloves garlic, peeled and cut in half**
  ½   *Cup sesame oil (Tahini)*
  ½   *Cup water*
   3   *Tablespoons lemon juice*
   2   *Teaspoons salt*

    I Place all ingredients in container C S or bowl K*; then whirl until well blended.

    II Keep chilled.

* KitchenAid users: hand-mince garlic.

TOMATO-TABASCO SALAD DRESSING

(YIELD: 2 CUPS)

  ½   *Cup wine vinegar*
   1   *Cup olive oil*
  ½   *Medium onion, peeled and cut in quarters*
   1   *Clove garlic, peeled and cut in half*
  ⅔   *Cup Ripe Tomato Purée (see page 222)*
   1   *Teaspoon salt*
   1   *Heaping teaspoon granulated sugar*
   1   *Teaspoon each Tabasco sauce and yellow mustard*
  ½   *Teaspoon freshly ground black pepper*

    I Place all ingredients in container C S or bowl K*. Whirl for 3 or 4 seconds, stopping once to scrape down container sides, or until ingredients are well mixed.

    II Keep chilled. Shake before using.

* KitchenAid users: hand-mince onion and garlic.

TOMATO SAUCE I

(YIELD: 3 CUPS)

  2 *Large onions, peeled and cut in quarters*
  1 *Medium carrot, scraped and cut in 1-inch pieces*
  1 *Rib celery, with all strings removed, cut in 1-inch pieces*
  1 *Clove garlic, peeled and cut in half*
  1 *Tablespoon fresh basil leaves, with all tough stems removed*
  4 *Tablespoons each butter and olive oil*
  4 *Pounds plum tomatoes, peeled and seeded*
1¼ *Cups beef broth*
 ½ *Teaspoon granulated sugar (or more to taste)*
    Salt and freshly ground black pepper

I Coarsely chop onions, carrot, celery, garlic, and basil in container C S. Process by quickly turning machine on and off 4 or 5 times, stopping as necessary to scrape down sides or move larger pieces to bottom. KitchenAid users: grind vegetables and basil.

II Heat butter and oil in a large, heavy soup kettle and sauté vegetable mixture over low heat until soft.

III Meanwhile, coarsely chop tomatoes 4 or 5 at a time by quickly turning the machine on and off several times. Add tomatoes and beef broth to the sautéed vegetables, sprinkle with sugar and salt and pepper to taste, then bring to a boil.

IV Turn the heat *very* low, cover and simmer for 2 to 3 hours, stirring occasionally to keep sauce from sticking. The sauce should be thick and rich.

TOMATO SAUCE II

(YIELD: ABOUT 4 CUPS)

1	Large onion, peeled and cut in eighths
1	Large leek, trimmed and cut in 1-inch pieces
3	Cloves garlic, peeled and cut in half
2	Teaspoons each fresh basil, oregano, and thyme leaves with all tough stems removed
2	1-Inch strips orange zest (thin outer skin of the fruit, with none of the bitter white underskin included)
16	Medium tomatoes
3	Tablespoons olive oil
3	Cups chicken broth
2	Cups dry white wine
1	Teaspoon Tabasco sauce
1	Tablespoon fennel seeds
	Generous pinch saffron
	Salt and freshly ground black pepper

I Place onion, leek, garlic, basil, oregano, thyme, and orange zest in container C S. Whirl for 5 or 6 seconds, stopping once or twice to scrape down container sides. KitchenAid users: finely grind these vegetables and herbs.

II Peel, seed, and chop tomatoes by hand.

III Heat olive oil and sauté onions, leeks, garlic, herbs, and zest until vegetables are soft but not brown. Add tomatoes, cover, and simmer 5 minutes.

IV Remove cover from pan and boil vegetables, stirring occasionally, for 5 minutes more, then purée mixture in container C S or using purée attachment K.

V Return purée to pan and add broth, wine, Tabasco, fennel, saffron, and salt and pepper to taste. Simmer, uncovered, for 45 minutes to 1 hour or until sauce is nicely thickened.

ITALIAN TOMATO MEAT SAUCE

(YIELD: ENOUGH TO SERVE 6)

2 *Pounds round steak, cut in 1-inch pieces*
1 *Medium carrot, scraped and cut in 1-inch pieces*
1 *Large onion, peeled and cut in quarters*
2 *Tablespoons fresh parsley leaves, with all stems removed*
3 *Tablespoons olive oil*
  Flour
1 *Cup red wine*
8 *Medium mushrooms*
5 *Medium tomatoes, peeled and seeded*
2 *Cups beef broth or water*
  Salt and freshly ground black pepper

I Trim gristle from meat and chop C or grind K S. Set aside.

II Place carrot, onion, and parsley in container C S, and turn machine quickly on and off 2 or 3 times, stopping once to scrape down container sides. KitchenAid users: grind these vegetables.

III Heat oil in a large, heavy saucepan and sauté carrots, onion, and parsley until onions are lightly browned. Dust meat lightly with flour; add to pan and cook until lightly browned, stirring frequently with a fork to break up any large pieces.

IV Stir in wine and cook until most of liquid evaporates. Meanwhile, coarsely chop C S or grind K mushrooms and tomatoes.

V Add mushrooms, tomatoes, and broth to meat, season to taste with salt and pepper and cook over low heat for 1½ hours, or until quite thick. Serve with Pasta (see page 365).

SAUCE AMÉRICAINE

(YIELD: ABOUT 2 CUPS)

> 1 Live lobster, about 1½ pounds
> Salt
> 4 Tablespoons butter
> 2 Tablespoons olive oil
> 2 Shallots, peeled and cut in half
> 1 Tablespoon each *fresh chervil and parsley leaves,*
> *with all stems removed*
> 1 Clove garlic, peeled
> 1½ Cups *Ripe Tomato Purée (see page 222)*
> ⅔ Teaspoon all-purpose flour
> 2 Tablespoons brandy

I Have your fishmonger clean and cut the lobster in pieces, reserving the tomalley or liver. Season the lobster pieces with salt and sauté in 2 tablespoons butter and the olive oil until the lobster begins to turn red, about 5 to 7 minutes.

II Finely chop C S shallots and fresh herbs or mince by hand K. Add to the skillet along with the garlic clove and the tomato purée; simmer until the shallots are tender.

III Meanwhile, use a fork to cream together the tomalley, remaining butter, and flour. Remove lobster pieces and garlic from sauce. Discard garlic; remove lobster meat from pieces of shell. Stir tomalley mixture into sauce along with sliced lobster meat and brandy, and cook for 4 or 5 minutes without letting sauce boil.

SWEET-AND-SOUR SAUCE

(YIELD: ABOUT 3 CUPS)

> 2 Medium onions, peeled
> 2 Medium green peppers, trimmed
> ½ Carrot, scraped
> 2 Cloves garlic, peeled and cut in half
> 3 Slices ginger root, peeled
> 3 Tablespoons vegetable oil

    8-Ounce can pineapple chunks
    4-Ounces (½ 8-ounce jar) jar sweet mixed pickles
½ Cup malt vinegar
1 Cup water
3 Tablespoons soy sauce
2 Tablespoons sherry
1 Teaspoon each salt and freshly ground black pepper
½ Cup granulated sugar
3 Tablespoons cornstarch

I Thinly slice C K S onions, peppers, and carrot. Finely chop C S together or hand-chop garlic and ginger root.

II Heat oil in a large skillet over high flame, add garlic and ginger, and stir-fry 1 minute. Stir in sliced vegetables and stir-fry for 3 minutes more.

III Drain pineapple chunks and pickles, reserving juices. Set fruit and pickles aside and add juices, vinegar, ½ cup of water, soy sauce, sherry, salt, and pepper to stir-fried vegetables. Coarsely chop C S or hand chop K reserved pineapple and pickles.

IV Bring mixture to a boil. Mix sugar and cornstarch into remaining ½ cup water. Stir into the boiling mixture along with the pineapple and pickles. Cook over medium heat, stirring constantly, until sauce is thickened and clear.

TOMATO CREAM SAUCE

It is rare to find a sauce as fresh-tasting and as adaptable as this one. Use it chilled to dress up almost any cold meat, fish or egg dish or hot to enhance the most simple dish.

(YIELD: ABOUT 2½ CUPS)

    8 Ounces cream cheese, cut in pieces
¾ Cup Ripe Tomato Purée (see page 222)
2 Large cloves garlic, peeled and cut in half*
2 Tablespoons fresh basil, with stems removed*
⅛ Teaspoon Tabasco sauce (or more to taste)
    Salt
⅓ Cup chilled heavy cream

* KitchenAid users: hand-mince garlic and basil.

I Place all ingredients in container C S or bowl K*. Whirl for 5 or 6 seconds, stopping once or twice as necessary to scrape down container sides.

II Keep chilled until serving time, then use hot or cold.

SALSA PIQUANTE

(YIELD: ABOUT 3½ CUPS)

2 *Medium sweet onions, peeled and cut in eighths*
2 *Small chili peppers, seeded and cut in 1-inch pieces*
6 *Tomatoes, peeled, seeded, and cut in eighths*
¼ *Teaspoon salt*
¼ *Cup vinegar*

I Place onions and peppers in container C Ⓚ S. Turn machine quickly on and off 3 or 4 times or until peppers are finely chopped, stopping once to scrape down container sides. Remove and set aside in a bowl.

II Add tomatoes, a few handfuls at a time, to container and whirl each batch for 1 or 2 seconds.

III Stir tomatoes into onions and peppers, sprinkle with salt, and cover with vinegar. Chill.

Ⓚ KitchenAid users: finely hand-chop onions, chili peppers, and tomatoes.

SAUCE NANTUA

(YIELD: ABOUT 2½ CUPS)

½ *Cup heavy cream*
2 *Cups Béchamel Sauce (see page 272)*
Salt and freshly ground black pepper
3 to 4 *Tablespoons Shrimp Butter (see page 105) or*
Lobster Butter (see page 104)

¼   *Cup cooked shrimp or lobster meat, cut in pieces*
     (optional)

I   Scald heavy cream; mix into béchamel sauce, then strain mixture through a fine sieve into a saucepan. Cook for 5 minutes until well heated, but do not allow mixture to boil.

II   Remove sauce from heat, season to taste with salt and pepper, and stir in shrimp or lobster butter. If desired, finely chop G S seafood and add to sauce

III   Allow to cool slightly, removing any butter that rises to the surface. Serve warm over fish or eggs.

BASIC WHITE SAUCE

(YIELD: ABOUT 2 CUPS)

4   *Tablespoons butter*
4   *Tablespoons all-purpose flour*
½   *Teaspoon salt*
2   *Cups cold milk**
    White pepper

I   In a heavy saucepan, melt butter over medium heat. Add flour and salt and stir with a fork until smooth. Remove pan from heat.

II   Add milk all at once, stirring until mixture is well blended and lump-free.

III   Return pan to medium heat and cook, stirring constantly, until sauce is creamy and thick. Season with white pepper to taste.

* To make a thinner sauce, increase milk to 2½ cups. To make a thicker sauce, reduce amount of milk to 1¼ cups.

MORNAY SAUCE

Add ½ cup grated C K S Swiss cheese and ⅓ cup grated C K S Parmesan cheese to hot Basic White Sauce. Stir over low heat until cheese melts.

BÉCHAMEL SAUCE

When preparing Basic White Sauce, sauté sliced C K S onion in butter until soft, then discard onion and blend in salt and flour as directed. Substitute 1 cup cream for 1 cup of the milk and proceed as directed.

CURRY SAUCE

Melt butter as directed in Basic White Sauce. Add flour, salt, and 1 teaspoon curry powder, then proceed as directed.

SAUCE AURORE
(YIELD: ABOUT 2¼ CUPS)

> 2 Cups hot Béchamel or
>   Mornay Sauce (see above)
> 3 Tablespoons Ripe Tomato Purée (see page 222)
> 1 Tablespoon butter

I Prepare béchamel or Mornay sauce as directed, then stir in the tomato purée and butter.

II Serve with fish mousse or nearly any vegetable soufflé.

COCONUT CREAM

(YIELD: ABOUT 1 CUP)

> 5   *Ounces fresh coconut, cut in 1-inch pieces*
> 1½   *Cups light cream*

I Finely chop C S or grate K coconut. Heat in saucepan with light cream until mixture reaches just below simmering point. Remove from heat and let stand for 30 minutes.

II Line a deep bowl with several layers of cheesecloth and pour the mixture through. Wring out cheesecloth tightly to extract remaining liquid.

III Keep chilled. Serve over fruit or molded desserts.

HARD SAUCE

(YIELD: ABOUT 1 CUP)

> 8   *Tablespoons (1 stick) sweet butter, cut in pieces*
> 1½   *Cups confectioners' sugar*
> 2 to 3 *Tablespoons brandy, rum or whiskey*

I Place butter in container C or bowl K S; whirl until light and fluffy. With motor running, add sugar a little at a time and beat until creamed.

II Add brandy, rum, or whiskey to taste. Whirl until thoroughly blended.

CHOCOLATE PRALINE SAUCE

(YIELD: ABOUT 2½ CUPS)

> 8   *Ounces milk chocolate, cut in pieces*
> 1   *Cup light cream*
> ½   *Cup Hazelnut Praline Powder (see page 326)*
>   *Brandy or rum (optional)*

I Coarsely chop C or grate K S chocolate. Place in saucepan with cream and bring mixture to a boil, then lower heat and simmer sauce, stirring frequently, until thickened.

II Stir in praline and, if desired, a little brandy or rum to taste.

CARAMEL SYRUP

(YIELD: ABOUT ¾ CUP)

2 Cups granulated sugar
1 Cup water

I Bring sugar and water to a boil in a small saucepan over high heat; cook, without stirring, until the mixture caramelizes.

II Remove from heat and cool slightly.

CLARIFIED BUTTER

To clarify butter, slowly heat in a small saucepan. Skim off the froth that rises to the surface. When the butter is completely melted, remove from the heat and let stand for a few minutes. Pour off and use the clear oil that floats on top. Discard the milky sediment on the bottom of the pan.

MASALA

(YIELD: ABOUT ¼ CUP)

¼ Cup each whole cloves and peppercorns (or 2 tablespoons each ground cloves and black pepper)
1 2-inch piece stick cinnamon (or 2 teaspoons ground cinnamon)

2   Tablespoons cardamom seed (or 1 tablespoon
    ground cardamom)
2   Teaspoons caraway seed (optional)

I   Starmix users: place whole cloves, whole peppercorns, cinnamon stick, cardamom and caraway seeds in container
S; whirl until pulverized. Cuisinart and KitchenAid users: combine
just the ground spices and mix well.

II   Store mixture in an airtight container.

CONDIMENTS

INDIA RELISH

(YIELD: 6 HALF-PINTS)

3	Quarts green tomatoes, seeded and cut in quarters
2½	Tablespoons salt
3	Pounds cabbage, cored and cut in 1-inch pieces
4½	Cups cider vinegar
2	Medium green peppers, seeded and cut in 1-inch pieces
2	Medium red peppers, seeded and cut in 1-inch pieces
2	Medium onions, peeled and cut in quarters
3	Cups granulated sugar
2¼	Teaspoons each celery seed and mustard seed
1	Teaspoon cardamom seed
½	Teaspoon each dry mustard and coarsely crushed whole peppercorns
1½	Teaspoons whole cloves
	2-Inch stick cinnamon

l Coarsely chop C S tomatoes, 3 at a time, or grind K. Place in large china or glass bowl, stir in salt, and toss thoroughly. Cover bowl loosely with a clean towel and let stand overnight.

II Rinse tomatoes, drain well, and place in large stainless-steel saucepan. Finely chop C S or grate K cabbage in several steps and add, along with vinegar, to tomatoes. Boil for 25 to 30 minutes.

III Meanwhile, finely chop C S or grind K green and red peppers and onions, 1 or 2 handfuls at a time.

IV Remove saucepan from heat and add peppers, onions, sugar, celery seed, mustard seed, cardamom seed, and dry mustard. Tie peppercorns, cloves, and stick cinnamon in cheesecloth and add to saucepan.

V Simmer mixture over low heat, stirring frequently, until fairly thick, about 1½ hours.

VI Discard spice bag and spoon relish into hot, sterile jars, leaving ½-inch headspace. Seal and set in boiling waterbath canner. As soon as water returns to boil, process relish for 5 minutes, then remove from heat. Check seals before cooling jars in a draft-free spot on towel or rack. Store in a cool, dry place.

HOT DOG RELISH

(YIELD: ABOUT 4 PINTS)

6 *Medium green tomatoes, seeded and cut in quarters*
2 *Large onions, peeled and cut in eighths*
½ *Head cabbage, cored and cut in 1-inch pieces*
6 *Green peppers, seeded and cut in 1-inch pieces*
¼ *Cup salt*
3 *Cups* each *vinegar and granulated sugar*
1 *Cup water*
1 *Tablespoon* each *mustard seed and celery seed*
1 *Teaspoon turmeric*
3 *Sweet red peppers, seeded*

I Coarsely chop C S or grind K tomatoes, onions, cabbage, and peppers, 2 handfuls of each at a time. Sprinkle with salt and let stand overnight, then rinse and drain well.

II In a large stainless steel saucepan, boil vinegar, sugar, water, and spices for 5 minutes. Meanwhile, finely hand-chop red peppers.

III Add all vegetables to vinegar-sugar mixture and simmer for 10 minutes. Remove from heat.

IV Spoon relish into hot, sterile jars. Seal and place in boiling waterbath canner. As soon as water comes back to a boil, process for 5 minutes, then remove from heat. Check seals, adjusting them if necessary, before cooling jars in a draft-free place on towel or rack. Store in a cool, dry storage spot.

PICCALILLI

(YIELD: 4 PINTS)

16 *Medium green tomatoes, seeded and cut in quarters*
2 *Pounds cabbage, cored and cut in 1-inch pieces*
3 *Medium onions, peeled and cut in quarters*
2 *Medium green peppers, seeded and cut in 1-inch pieces*
2 *Medium sweet red peppers, seeded and cut in 1-inch pieces*
1/3 *Cup un-iodized salt*
2 *Cups firmly packed brown sugar*
3 *Cups white vinegar*
2 *Tablespoons whole pickling spices*

I Finely chop C S or grind K all vegetables, 2 or 3 handfuls at a time. Mix in the salt and let stand overnight, then drain and press in a clean, thin white cloth to force out as much liquid as possible.

II Combine sugar and vinegar in a large stainless steel saucepan. Tie the spices in a cheesecloth bag; add to the pot and bring the sugar and vinegar to a boil.

III Add the well-drained vegetables and bring to a boil again, then lower the heat and simmer for 30 minutes or until there is just enough liquid left in the saucepan to keep the vegetables moist.

IV Remove and discard the spice bag. Pour the hot relish into hot, sterile jars, leaving ½ inch of head space. Seal and place in a boiling waterbath canner. As soon as water returns to a boil, process for 5 minutes. Check seals after removing jars from canner, then cool on a towel or rack in a draft-free spot. Store in a cool, dry place.

CHOW-CHOW

(YIELD: ABOUT 4 PINTS)

5	Green tomatoes, any variety, seeded and cut in quarters
2	Green peppers, seeded and cut in 1-inch pieces
1	Sweet red pepper, seeded and cut in 1-inch pieces
½	Small cabbage, cored and cut in 1-inch pieces
4	Small onions, peeled
2	Large cucumbers, peeled
5	Green plum tomatoes
⅓	Cup salt
1½	Quarts water
3	Medium carrots, scraped
1	Cup (about 20) green beans
1	Cup lima beans
2	Cups granulated sugar
1¼	Cups vinegar
2	Tablespoons each mustard seed and turmeric
1	Tablespoon celery seed

I Coarsely chop C S or grind K green tomatoes (not the plum tomatoes), green and red peppers and cabbage, a few handfuls of each at a time. Thickly slice C K S onions, cucumbers, and green plum tomatoes.

II Place these chopped and sliced vegetables in a large glass or ceramic bowl, pour the salt and water over, and mix well. Allow to stand overnight, then drain, rinse and drain again.

III Thickly slice C K S the carrots and slice C or snip S the green beans. Parboil in water along with the lima beans until barely tender. Remove from heat and drain well.

IV Combine the sugar, vinegar, and spices in a large stainless steel saucepan, bring to a boil, and boil for 5 minutes. Add all the vegetables and boil for 10 minutes more.

V Spoon the vegetables into hot, sterile jars and cover with the cooking liquid. Seal and place in a boiling waterbath canner. As soon as the water returns to the boil, process for 10 minutes. Check seals after removing jars from canner and allow to cool on a towel or rack in a draft-free place. Store in a cool, dry spot.

CARROT–GREEN TOMATO RELISH

(YIELD: 3 PINTS)

15	*Green tomatoes, cut in eighths*
5	*Tablespoons salt*
16	*Large carrots, scraped and cut in 1-inch pieces*
4½	*Cups cider vinegar*
3	*Small onions, peeled and cut in quarters*
2	*Medium green peppers, seeded and cut in 1-inch pieces*
1	*Medium sweet red pepper, seeded and cut in 1-inch pieces*
4	*Cups granulated sugar*
2¼	*Teaspoons each celery seed and mustard seed*
1	*Teaspoon each cardamom seed and coarsely crushed whole peppercorns*
¼	*Teaspoon dry mustard*
	¾-Inch stick cinnamon
1½	*Teaspoons whole cloves*

I Chop tomatoes in container C S, a few handfuls at a time, or put them through the coarse blade of your grinder K. Sprinkle with the salt and stir, then cover and let stand overnight.

II Drain tomatoes and place in a large stainless steel kettle.

III Chop C S or grind K carrots, two handfuls at a time. Add to tomatoes along with vinegar; boil mixture over medium heat for 25 to 30 minutes.

IV Meanwhile, chop C S or grind K the onions and peppers. This will have to be done in 2 or 3 steps.

V Add onions, peppers, sugar, celery seed, mustard seed, cardamom seed, peppercorns and dry mustard to kettle. Tie the cinnamon stick and whole cloves in a cheesecloth bag and add to kettle.

VI Reduce heat to low, stir the mixture once or twice, and simmer about 1 hour, stirring occasionally, until relish is fairly thick.

VII Discard spice bag and spoon relish into hot, sterile jars, leaving ¼-inch headspace. Seal and place in boiling water-bath canner. Allow water in canner to return to boil, then process relish for 5 minutes. Remove jars and test seals. Cool in a draft-free place on a rack or towel. Store on a cool, dark storage shelf.

CORN AND PEPPER RELISH

(YIELD: ABOUT 6 PINTS)

12	Medium-size ripe tomatoes, peeled, seeded, and cut in quarters
2	Green peppers, seeded and cut in 1-inch pieces
2	Sweet red peppers, seeded and cut in 1-inch pieces
6	Medium-size green tomatoes, seeded and cut in quarters
2	Large onions, peeled and cut in eighths
1	Large cucumber, peeled and cut in 1-inch pieces
6	Ears fresh young corn
1⅔	Cups vinegar
1½	Cups granulated sugar
1	Tablespoon plus 1 teaspoon salt
2	Teaspoons mustard seed
1	Teaspoon celery seed
½	Teaspoon ground allspice
¼	Teaspoon ground cloves

I Coarsely chop C S or grind K ripe tomatoes, peppers, green tomatoes, onions and cucumber, 2 or 3 handfuls of each at a time.

II Cut corn from cobs, then scrape cobs lightly to extract the milk from the base of each kernel. Reserve both corn and milk.

III Boil vinegar, sugar, and spices for 5 minutes in a large stainless steel saucepan. Add all vegetables and bring to a boil, then lower heat and simmer for 1½ hours.

IV Spoon into hot, sterile jars leaving ¼ inch headspace. Seal jars and set in a boiling waterbath canner; as soon as water returns to a boil, process for 5 minutes, then remove from heat. Check seals before cooling on a towel or rack in a draft-free spot. Store in a cool, dry place.

TOMATO CATSUP

(YIELD: 4 8-OUNCE JARS)

More zesty than a steak sauce! Richer than commercial catsup! It's Own-Made Tomato Catsup . . . the super condiment!

2	*Large onions, peeled and cut in eighths*
2	*Sweet red peppers, seeded and cut in 1-inch pieces*
10	*Pounds (about 15 large) ripe tomatoes, peeled, seeded, and cut in quarters (You may include some slightly imperfect specimens, but cut away all bad spots, please.)*
2	*Cups granulated sugar (more if desired)*
2	*Teaspoons ground cinnamon*
1	*Teaspoon each paprika, salt, and ground allspice*
½	*Teaspoon each celery salt and dry mustard*
¼	*Teaspoon ground cloves*
½	*Cup lemon juice*

I Cuisinart and Starmix users: place onions and peppers a few handfuls at a time in container and whirl for 5 or 6 seconds, stopping once or twice to scrape down container sides, then set aside while you purée tomatoes 3 or 4 at a time. Kitchen-Aid users: put all vegetables through the fine blade of your grinder.

II Mix vegetables together and simmer in a large stainless steel kettle for 40 to 50 minutes or until vegetables are quite soft.

III Purée vegetables in container C S. KitchenAid users: if you own a blender, use it here. In all cases C K S, rub the purée through a strainer. Do not give up too easily on this process, every bit of strained pulp means more flavor and substance for your catsup.

IV Return puréed vegetables to heat and mix in all ingredients except lemon juice. Cook over medium heat, stirring every 10 minutes, for 1½ hours.

V Stir in lemon juice and taste the catsup, add more sugar if you prefer a sweeter sauce, and then cook over medium-low heat, stirring every 5 minutes until the catsup is quite thick (about 1 hour longer). Stir more frequently when the sauce begins to reach the consistency of the commercial variety.

VI The catsup is ready to bottle when no liquid fills the empty spaces when a spoon is drawn across the bottom of the pot. Use a funnel to avoid spilling and spoon hot catsup into sterilized jars. Seal with commercial caps or paraffin and set in a boiling waterbath canner. Process for 10 minutes as soon as water returns to boil. Cool to room temperature after removing from canner and adjust seals if necessary. Store in a cool place, wrapped in brown paper to retain rich catsup color.

APPLE BUTTER

(YIELD: 4 HALF PINTS)

    20   Medium apples, cored and cut in eighths
     2   Quarts water
     6   Cups apple cider
    4½   Cups granulated or light brown sugar
     1   Teaspoon each allspice, ground cinnamon, and
         ground cloves

I Finely chop C S or coarsely grate K apples, 2 or 3 handfuls at a time. Combine with water in a large saucepan and cook over medium heat until soft.

II Purée hot apple mixture in container C S or in special attachment K. When using the Cuisinart or Starmix this will have to be done in several steps, then pressed through a strainer.

III Bring cider to a very low boil, add puréed apples and sugar, and cook for 40 minutes, stirring mixture frequently to prevent scorching.

IV Add the spices and continue to cook over low heat, stirring constantly, until mixture thickens to spreading consistency, then pour into hot, sterile jars and seal.

BREADS

MAKING ANY YEAST BREAD IN YOUR FOOD PROCESSOR

If you've been baking bread without the aid of a food processor, you'll find that mixing and kneading with these machines are incredibly fast procedures and take a bit of getting used to. If you're a baking neophyte, you'll need to familiarize yourself with many aspects of the breadmaking process in addition to learning to work with your machine. But whether you're experienced or inexperienced, you'll find it easier to become accustomed to the workings of your Cuisinart food processor if you start with recipes that yield just one loaf. KitchenAid and Starmix users can bake two loaves as easily as one. As you grow more comfortable with the process, you can adapt any recipe with complete confidence.

MIXING THE INGREDIENTS

The aim in mixing breadmaking ingredients by hand is to produce a dough that is firm and not at all sticky, one that pulls away in a mass from the sides of the mixing bowl. A similar result should be achieved when mixing ingredients in your food processor, except that a properly mixed dough should form a ball around the double-edged steel blade in the Cuisinart or cling to the dough hook and clean the sides of the bowl in both the KitchenAid and Starmix.

The Cuisinart food processor will mix and knead the ingredients for any recipe yielding 1 loaf quite nicely, while the KitchenAid and Starmix bowls will accommodate doughs which incorporate up to 8 cups of flour. Follow the directions in each recipe for your particular processor, checking carefully to see whether slight adjustments in amounts of flour or liquid will be necessary before the dough achieves the desired stiffness. Since it's impossible for every baker to measure flour in the same way, you may find that your dough will require additional liquid before it will form a ball around the Cuisinart blades or cling properly to the KitchenAid or Starmix dough hook, or extra flour to remove its stickiness and prevent it from climbing over the collar of the dough hook as sticky or soft doughs have a tendency to do in the KitchenAid. Keep about ½ cup of the flour called for in a recipe in reserve, to compensate for any measurement discrepancies. In humid weather you may need as much as 1 additional cup of flour before your dough will reach the proper consistency. Add additional liquid or flour to the Cuisinart container or the Starmix bowl with the motor running,* wating until each addition is incorporated before adding the next.

Flours, like flour measurements, also differ. A whole-grain flour, for example, takes a bit longer than its white counterpart to absorb liquids. When your recipe calls for this type of flour, keep 1 to 2 cups in reserve when mixing ingredients. Allow the dough to rest at least 10 minutes, then proceed to mix in the reserved flour. You may also find that doughs containing whole-grain flours will not form a ball around the blades or cling to the dough hook as described, but you can still go on to knead it.

KNEADING THE DOUGH

Kneading is one of the most essential of the breadmaking processes, for through this act of pushing, pulling, folding, and refolding the dough, air bubbles are eliminated, the dough is rendered smooth and flexible, and a fine texture is imparted to the finished bread. Kneading used to be the most physically exhausting part of breadmaking. Your food processor makes this easy.

To knead dough in the Cuisinart, allow the ingredients to form a ball around the double-edged steel blades, adding more liquid if necessary, then lift the dough out and tear it into 5 or 6 pieces. Return these pieces of dough to the container, pressing them

* KitchenAid users: stop machine before adding flour.

down slightly against the blades. Turn on the machine and let the contents whirl until the dough forms a ball around the blades once more. Repeat this procedure 5 or 6 times or until the dough is smooth and elastic.

The KitchenAid kneads all bread doughs beautifully. I have used its dough hook for 6 years and can find no fault with it. My personal preference for using the flat beater for mixing ingredients, which necessitates switching to the dough hook when the dough is ready to be kneaded, seems a minor drawback in light of the superb job this machine does in general, since the dough hook will also mix as well as knead. To knead any bread dough in the KitchenAid, merely substitute 2 minutes of kneading time on the machine for every 8 minutes called for in a normal recipe. In most cases, the dough forms a ball and becomes smooth and elastic without further kneading. If the amount of dough you're mixing is extra large, it may rise up around the top of the hook and become a bit messy, but this need only be wiped off and won't deter the process in any significant way. To solve the problem, simply divide the dough in two pieces and knead each separately.

The Starmix mixes and kneads doughs well with the same dough hook, although those perfectionists who like to see their doughs smooth and satiny may wish to hand knead for about 30 seconds when the machine has finished its job. Kneading time in the Starmix calls for substituting 2 to 4 minutes for each 8 minutes indicated in a normal recipe.

The Starmix, however, has several drawbacks when it comes to kneading. When large quantities of stiff dough are involved, the top of the mixing and kneading bowl must be held on and the motor base restrained. Otherwise it might walk off the counter. The problem can be eliminated if you make only one loaf of bread at a time.

Another disadvantage is that dough may force its way under the dough hook and become dry (especially if you leave the dough hook in place while the dough doubles in bulk), making the hook impossible to remove without brute force. When this happens, I usually submerge both bowl and dough hook in warm water to soak overnight, then pry them apart. No harm has come to my machine, but this is no guarantee that you will be so fortunate. You may, of course, avoid the problem altogether by turning the kneaded dough into another bowl to double in bulk, but in recipes that call for further kneading once the dough rises, this does seem like extra bother.

DOUBLING IN BULK

Recipes for yeast breads always specify that the dough must rise until it reaches a volume almost double its original size, a state more familiarly known to breadmakers as "doubled in bulk." Room temperature and humidity, type of flour and amount and type of yeast, all play a part in determining the amount of time needed for the prepared dough to double in bulk. So does altitude—the higher above sea level you live, the faster the dough will rise.

Doubling in bulk is a vital step in the breadmaking process because unless the dough has a chance to rise properly, the finished loaf will be too dense. The proper way to double in bulk is to set your dough in a deep, oiled bowl, turning it once to grease the top. Cover the bowl lightly with a dish towel or other light cloth, then set it in a warm, draft-free place for the length of time specified in your recipe. The interior of an unlit gas oven, where the pilot light supplies heat, is ideal, but an electric oven will serve just as well if you warm it slightly in advance, then turn off the heat before setting in the dough.

To determine whether your dough has risen sufficiently, press two fingers lightly and quickly into its center to a depth of 1 inch. If the indentations remain after you withdraw your fingers, the dough is ready to be punched down. If the indentations fill in, however, re-cover the dough and allow it to stand for another 15 to 20 minutes, then repeat the test.

PUNCHING DOWN THE DOUGH

As soon as the dough has risen and doubled in bulk, it is ready to be punched down. Using your fist, press firmly down into the center of the dough. Fold the edges of the dough toward the center, pressing out all bubbles. Unless your recipe indicates that the dough should double in bulk a second time, turn it out of the bowl and shape as directed below. If a second rising is called for, simply turn the dough over after punching down, re-cover lightly, and allow to double in bulk again, test, punch down, and shape.

SHAPING THE LOAF

Turn the punched-down dough out of the bowl and set it on a lightly floured board or other work surface. Dust a rolling pin lightly with flour and with gentle but firm pressure, flatten the dough into a rectangle the approximate length of your pan and about ¾-inch thick.

Starting with the narrow end farthest away from you, roll the dough toward you into a loaf approximately as long as the pan. Pinch all seams together, turn the ends under and place the loaf, seam-side down, in a greased loaf pan. If your recipe makes 2 loaves, divide the dough in half after turning it out of the bowl by pressing down firmly with the side of your hand, then roll out each half as directed.

BAKING THE BREAD

Yeast bread recipes generally indicate that the shaped loaf must double in bulk in the pan before baking or at least rise for a specified time. Follow the directions in the recipe, then bake as directed. Your loaf or loaves are perfectly baked when the pan resounds with a hollow sound when lightly tapped with a finger-nail, but appearance counts, too. The top of each loaf should be smooth, shiny, and golden brown in color; the sides and bottom should also be nicely browned. A pale color calls for further baking: unless the recipe indicates otherwise, allow the bread to bake for another 10 to 15 minutes until it does brown. If you wish, you may brush the top with egg yolk before returning it to the oven for further baking.

Turn the bread out of the pan as directed in the recipe. Should your loaf or loaves prove stubborn when it's time to remove the bread from the pan, carefully loosen the edges with a sharp knife and/or give the bottom of the pan a sharp rap with your hand.

Unbaked bread dough freezes nicely. To prepare a loaf for freezing, proceed as directed in your recipe up to the point where the dough is ready to be shaped. Line your pan with aluminum foil, then roll up and shape the dough so that it fits loosely in the pan and has room to expand while freezing. Cover with plastic wrap and freeze at 0 degrees F. or below. Lift the solidly frozen bread and aluminum foil liner from the pan, wrap tightly with additional aluminum foil or plastic wrap and return to the freezer immediately.

To bake, set the frozen loaf in a well-greased pan 6 or 7 hours before baking time. Cover and allow to double in bulk in a warm, draft-free place for about 6½ hours, then bake as directed.

KUGELHOPF

(YIELD: 1 CROWN-SHAPED LOAF)

1¼ Cups almonds
½ Cup milk
1 Package dry active yeast
½ Cup warm water
8 Tablespoons (1 stick) butter, cut in pieces
⅓ Cup granulated sugar
2 1-by-½-inch strips lemon zest (thin outer skin of the lemon, with none of the bitter white underskin included)
4 Eggs, at room temperature
4 Cups all-purpose flour, sifted
1 Teaspoon salt
1 Cup currants

I   Finely chop C or grate K* S* ½ cup of the almonds, reserving the rest. Set chopped or grated almonds aside.

II   Scald the milk in a saucepan and cool to lukewarm. Sprinkle the yeast into the lukewarm water, allow to dissolve, then stir into the lukewarm milk.

III   Place butter, sugar, and lemon zest in container C or bowl K S.* Cream together by turning motor quickly on and off 10 times.

IV   Add eggs, 1 at a time, turning machine quickly on and off 4 times after each addition.

V   Add yeast mixture and process by turning machine quickly on and off 3 times.

VI   Cuisinart users: spoon half of this mixture into a bowl and set it aside. Combine sifted flour and salt and sift half of this into container or bowl. Turn machine quickly on and off 4 or 5 times, then add half of the reserved unchopped almonds and currants and turn machine quickly on and off 4 times more or until batter is well blended. Pour into another large bowl. Repeat the process with remaining ingredients. Mix both portions of batter

* KitchenAid and Starmix users: Grate all nuts at one time and mince lemon zest by hand. Add ¾ cup nuts and the grated zest when adding the currants. Line your buttered mold with remaining ½ cup nuts.

together. KitchenAid and Starmix users: sift flour and salt into bowl and beat until well blended. Stir in nuts and currants by hand.

VII   Cover with a linen towel and set in a warm, draft-free place for about 2 hours or until double in bulk.

VIII   Generously butter the bottom and sides of a Kugelhopf or other 10-cup tube mold and sprinkle with the reserved chopped almonds.

IX   Punch down the batter and arrange it in the mold. Cover the mold lightly and allow batter to rise in a warm, draft-free place until it fills the mold three-fourths full. Bake in a preheated 375 degree F. oven for 50 to 60 minutes or until a toothpick inserted in the top comes out clean. Turn mold upside down and place on a wire rack to cool for 15 minutes, then loosen bread with a knife or spatula, turn out of mold, and continue to cool.

WALNUT-HONEY BREAD

(YIELD: ENOUGH TO SERVE 6 TO 8)

1½	Cups pecans
1½	Cups walnuts
1¼	Cups honey
1	Cup milk
¼	Cup light-brown sugar
6	Tablespoons butter
2	Egg yolks
1	Teaspoon each salt and ground anise
¾	Teaspoon ground cinnamon
¼	Teaspoon ground nutmeg
2¼	Cups all-purpose flour

I   Coarsely chop C S or grind or grate K pecans and walnuts. Set aside.

II   Heat honey, milk, and sugar, stirring constantly until sugar dissolves. Pour into container C S or bowl K. Turn on machine and add butter, 1 tablespoon at a time, allowing each piece to melt before adding the next. Allow mixture to cool 10 minutes, and then beat in the egg yolks, one at a time.

III   Preheat oven to 325 degrees F.

IV Combine spices with flour and sift into liquid ingredients. Blend C K S until well mixed.

V Fold in reserved nutmeats and pour Into a greased and floured 9¼ × 5¼ × 2¾ loaf pan. Bake for 1¼ hours, or until center of loaf springs back when lightly pressed with the fingers.

VI Remove from oven and cool in pan for 15 minutes before turning out onto a wire rack. Serve at room temperature, cut into thin slices.

BLACK WALNUT–FRUIT BREAD

(YIELD: 1 LOAF)

½ Cup each *dried figs and dried apricots*
1 Cup *rolled oats*
3 *1-by-½-inch strips orange zest (thin outer skin with none of the bitter white underskin included)*
1 *Egg*
½ Cup *tightly packed brown sugar*
1 Cup *all-purpose flour, sifted*
1 *Teaspoon baking soda*
½ *Teaspoon salt*
1 Cup *buttermilk*
⅓ Cup *butter, melted*
½ Cup *black walnut halves (or plain walnuts will do nicely), coarsely chopped*
Lemon-Orange Glaze (see page 345)

I Cuisinart users: coarsely chop together the figs, apricots, oats, and orange zest, then set aside. KitchenAid and Starmix users: coarsely grind the dried fruit, oats, and zest together; set aside.

II Preheat oven to 350 degrees F.

III Place egg in container C or bowl K* S*. Turn machine quickly on and off 3 times. Add sugar and whirl for 5 or 6 seconds.

IV Combine the sifted flour, baking soda, and salt and sift together. Add half the dry ingredients to container or bowl, and turn machine quickly on and off 8 times; add ½ cup buttermilk and turn machine on and off 4 times more.

V Repeat Step IV, alternating dry ingredients and butter-milk, but turn machine on and off only *twice* after adding the remaining buttermilk. Add dried fruit mixture, nuts, and melted butter and process by turning machine quickly on and off 3 or 4 times more. Batter should be well mixed.

VI Line a buttered loaf pan with waxed paper and pour in the batter. Bake for 55 minutes, or until a toothpick inserted in the center comes out clean. Cool, then ice with the glaze, allowing part of it to drip down the sides of the bread.

* KitchenAid and Starmix users: add ingredients as directed, but mix well after each addition.

APRICOT AND NUT BREAD

(YIELD: 1 LOAF)

1   Cup honey
1   Cup milk
½   Cup granulated sugar
½   Cup dried apricots
½   Cup pitted dates
1   Cup walnuts
5   Tablespoons butter, cut in pieces
2   Egg yolks
2½   Cups all-purpose flour
1   Teaspoon each *salt, baking soda, ground anise, and ground cinnamon*

I Combine honey, milk, and sugar in a saucepan, and stir over medium flame until sugar is completely dissolved; re-move from heat and set aside to cool for 10 minutes.

II Meanwhile, cover apricots with hot water and soak for 5 minutes. Drain and coarsely chop C S or grind K apricots along with dates and nuts. Set mixture aside.

III Preheat oven to 325 degrees F.

IV Place butter in container C or bowl K S along with cooled honey-milk mixture. Add egg yolks and whirl for 4 or 5 seconds, or until well mixed.

V Sift together the flour, baking soda, and spices into the container. Turn machine C quickly on and off 3 times, stopping once to scrape down the sides. Add the chopped fruit-nut mixture and whirl 2 seconds more. KitchenAid and Starmix users: beat in dry ingredients until well mixed, then add fruit-nut mixture.

VI Scrape batter into a buttered and floured loaf pan and bake for 1¼ hours or until toothpick inserted in the center comes out clean. Cool in the pan for 15 minutes, then turn out on a rack. Serve thinly sliced with sweet butter or cream cheese.

BANANA BREAD

(YIELD: 1 LOAF)

> 1½ Tablespoons milk
> 1 Teaspoon lemon juice
> 3 Medium-size very ripe bananas, cut in 1-inch pieces
> 2 Eggs
> 1 Cup granulated sugar
> ½ Cup butter (1 stick), at room temperature, cut in pieces
> 2 Cups all-purpose flour
> 1½ Teaspoons baking powder
> ½ Teaspoon baking soda
> ¼ Teaspoon salt
> 1 Cup each *pitted dates and pecans or walnuts, coarsely chopped C S or ground K*
> ¾ Cup golden raisins

I Combine milk and lemon juice and set in warm oven for a few minutes to sour. Set aside.

II Preheat oven to 350 degrees F.

III When using the Cuisinart machine, place bananas, eggs, sugar, and butter in container. Whirl for 5 seconds, adding soured milk through spout. KitchenAid or Starmix users should beat these ingredients together until well mixed.

IV Combine flour, baking powder, baking soda, and salt and sift over batter. Add fruit and nuts.

V When using the Cuisinart machine, process by turning machine quickly on and off 6 to 8 times, stopping the motor once to scrape down container sides. KitchenAid and Starmix users, add one-third of the flour at a time, beating each time until well incorporated.

VI Spoon into well-buttered loaf pan and bake for 1 hour, or until a toothpick inserted in the center comes out dry. Loosen edges after removing from oven and turn out on a rack to cool. Serve warm or at room temperature.

DATE AND NUT BREAD

(YIELD: 1 LOAF)

1	Cup pitted dates
1	Cup tightly packed light brown sugar
4	Tablespoons butter, cut in pieces
3/4	Cup boiling water
1¾	Cups all-purpose flour
1	Egg
1	Tablespoon brandy
1	Teaspoon baking soda
½	Teaspoon salt
1	Cup walnut halves
3/4	Cup currants

Directions for all machines:

I Preheat oven to 350 degrees F.

Directions for Cuisinart users:

II Place dates, sugar, and butter in container. Turn on machine only long enough to pour in boiling water through the spout, then immediately turn off.

III   Add flour, egg, brandy, baking soda and salt. Process by turning machine quickly on and off 3 times.

IV   Add walnuts and currants and turn machine quickly on and off 2 or 3 more times or until well mixed.

Directions for KitchenAid and Starmix users:

II   Chop dates coarsely by hand; then place in a large metal bowl with sugar, butter, and boiling water.

III   Add flour, egg, brandy, baking soda, and salt and mix well.

IV   Grate or hand-chop walnuts and stir into batter with currants.

Directions for all machines:

V   Turn mixture into a buttered loaf pan and bake for 50 minutes or until a toothpick inserted in the center comes out clean. Remove from pan and cool on a rack.

OLD-FASHIONED CUSTARD CORNBREAD

(YIELD: ENOUGH TO SERVE 6 TO 8)

1½   *Cups milk*
2   *Tablespoons butter, melted*
1   *Egg*
½   *Cup all-purpose flour, sifted*
¾   *Cup yellow corn meal**
2½   *Tablespoons light brown sugar*
1   *Teaspoon baking powder*
½   *Teaspoon salt*

I   Preheat oven to 400 degrees F.

II   Place 1 cup of the milk, the melted butter, and egg in container C or bowl K S. Process by turning machine quickly on and off 2 or 3 times, or until mixture is well mixed.

---

* KitchenAid users: grind your own corn meal if you like.

III Combine the flour, corn meal, sugar, baking powder, and salt; sift together over the top of the milk-egg mixture. Process by turning machine quickly on and off 3 or 4 times or until mixture is well blended, stopping once to scrape down sides of container or bowl. Batter will be very thin.

IV Pour batter into a well-buttered 8-inch square baking dish. Carefully spoon remaining ½ cup milk over batter, allowing it to float on top. Bake for 20 minutes, then remove from oven and cut in squares. Serve hot.

CREAM BISCUITS

(YIELD: ABOUT 1½ TO 2 DOZEN)

2	Cups sifted all-purpose flour
½	Teaspoon salt
2	Teaspoons baking powder
4	Tablespoons butter, frozen
¾	Cup heavy cream

I Preheat oven to 450 degrees F. Sift together flour, salt, and baking powder.

II Cut frozen butter in ¼-inch slices. Place half the slices in the bottom of the container C. Spoon the flour mixture over the butter and push the remaining slices of butter down into the flour. Turn machine quickly on and off 2 or 3 times to cut the flour and butter together. (KitchenAid and Starmix users: follow directions for cutting butter into flour in Pie Pastry [see page 358], then beat in cream.)

III Start machine again and pour the cream through the container spout in a steady stream. Stop the motor as soon as cream has been added.

IV Scrape dough from container, knead it once or twice, and roll out ¼ inch thick on a lightly floured board.

V Cut in 2-inch rounds and bake 12 to 15 minutes on an oiled baking sheet or until golden brown.

CARROT WHOLE-WHEAT BREAD

(YIELD: 1 LOAF)

½   *Cup finely grated C K S carrots*
1   *Cup water*
½   *Cup corn meal*
¼   *Cup honey*
2   *Tablespoons* each *light brown sugar and molasses*
¼   *Cup vegetable oil or 4 tablespoons butter*
½   *Cup milk*
½   *Teaspoon ground cinnamon*
¼   *Teaspoon* each *salt and ground cloves*
     Grated zest of one orange (thin outer skin, with none
     of the bitter white underskin included)
1   *Package dry active yeast*
¼   *Cup lukewarm water, at room temperature*
¾   *Cup whole-wheat flour*
2 to 3   *Cups all-purpose flour*
½   *Cup golden raisins*

I   Simmer carrots in 1 cup water until tender, then drain, reserving ½ cup liquid.

II   Place carrots, ½ cup carrot liquid, corn meal, honey, sugar, molasses, oil, milk, spices, zest, and yeast in container C and let stand 10 minutes. Whirl 10 seconds. KitchenAid and Star-mix users: hand-mince zest and beat all ingredients until well mixed.

III   Add whole-wheat flour. Mix for 15 to 20 seconds, or until flour is well incorporated, stopping once or twice to scrape down sides.

IV   Transfer dough to a large bowl, cover with a dish towel and let rise in a warm, draft-free place for 30 minutes.

V   Stir in ½ cup all-purpose flour, then transfer mixture to container C or bowl K S. With the motor running, add as much remaining flour as necessary a little at a time until the dough forms a ball. Add the raisins and knead the dough following directions for your machine given on pages 286 and 287.

VI   Turn dough into a well-oiled bowl, turning once to grease the top. Cover and let rise in a warm, draft-free place until double in bulk (about 40 minutes).

VII Punch down dough and turn it over, then re-cover and let rise again for 45 minutes.

VIII Punch down again and turn out of bowl. Roll out into a long rectangle 8 inches wide. Beginning at a short end, roll up tightly to form an 8-inch loaf. Turn ends under and place the loaf, seam side down, in an oiled $9\frac{1}{4} \times 5\frac{1}{4} \times 2\frac{3}{4}$ inch loaf pan. Cover and let rise in a warm, draft-free place until double in bulk (about 40 to 50 minutes).

IX Preheat oven to 325 degrees F. Bake for 1 hour. Loosen sides of loaf with a sharp knife after taking from oven. Turn out and cool on a wire rack.

DOWN-UNDER CHEESE BUSTERS

(YIELD: 1 DOZEN)

$\frac{1}{2}$	Cups grated C K S Cheddar cheese
$\frac{1}{2}$	Cup (1 stick) butter, cut in pieces
2	Cups all-purpose flour, unsifted
6 to 7	Tablespoons water
	Pinch or two cayenne pepper

To prepare in the Cuisinart machine:

I Place butter in container and cover with the flour. Process by turning machine quickly on and off 5 or 6 times or until mixture resembles coarse meal. Add the cheese, then turn the machine on and off 5 or 6 times or until the cheese is well incorporated.

II Sprinkle 6 tablespoons water and the cayenne pepper over the flour and turn the machine quickly on and off 8 times or until the dough forms a ball. Whirl in the remaining water only if the dough will not hold together.

To Prepare in KitchenAid or Starmix machine:

I Work butter and flour together until mixture resembles coarse meal following directions given in Pie Pastry (page 358). Add cheese and knead into mixture.

II Sprinkle 6 tablespoons water and cayenne pepper over mixture. Then stir well with a fork until dough comes clean from sides of bowl, adding remaining tablespoon of water if necessary.

To Roll Out the Dough:

I Preheat oven to 450 degrees F.

II Roll out dough to ¼-inch thickness on a lightly floured board and cut in 3-inch rounds. Prick each round a dozen times with a fork. Place on a buttered baking sheet and bake for 15 minutes.

BREAD DOUGHNUTS

(YIELD: ABOUT 24)

2 to 3	Cups sifted all-purpose flour
1	Package dry active yeast
¼	Cup granulated sugar
1	Teaspoon salt
1	Cup milk, at room temperature
1	Egg, at room temperature
4	Tablespoons melted butter, at room temperature
	Vegetable oil for deep frying
	Granulated sugar
	Ground cinnamon

I Whirl C K S 1 cup of the flour, the yeast, sugar, and salt for 5 seconds.

II Add milk and beat 10 seconds or until well mixed. Let stand 5 minutes.

III With the motor running, add the egg, 2 tablespoons melted butter, and 1 cup flour in that order, then add remaining flour, 1 tablespoon at a time, until the dough forms a ball around the blades or dough hook. Beat in the remaining melted butter.

IV Knead the dough according to the directions for your machine, then place in a lightly oiled bowl, turning once to grease the top. Cover and set in a warm, draft-free place for 1 hour or until dough doubles in bulk.

VI Punch dough down; turn out on a clean pastry board and flatten with a rolling pin into a large rectangle ½ inch thick. Cut into circles using a doughnut cutter or into strips 1 inch wide and 4 to 5 inches long using a knife. Arrange on baking sheets and set in a warm, draft-free place for 1 hour or until double in bulk.

VII To fry doughnuts, pour oil to a depth of 1½ inches in a deep, heavy skillet. As soon as the temperature of the oil registers 370 degrees F., fry doughnuts, a few at a time, in hot oil until lightly browned on both sides, turning once. Strips of dough should be twisted before frying. Drain briefly on paper towels before sprinkling with sugar and cinnamon while still warm.

POPOVERS

(YIELD: 8 POPOVERS)

2   *Eggs*
1   *Cup milk*
1   *Cup all-purpose flour, sifted*
½   *Teaspoon salt*

I Preheat oven to 450 degrees F. Set a well-buttered popover pan or muffin tin inside to heat briefly.

II Meanwhile, place eggs and milk in container C S or bowl K. Whirl for 8 to 10 seconds. Combine flour and salt and sift together over egg mixture, then whirl for 10 seconds.

III Pour batter into hot popover pan, filling each cup half full; bake for 20 minutes, then reduce heat to 375 degrees F. and bake until the popovers turn brown and crisp. Serve hot.

CHEESE POPOVERS

Prepare popover batter as directed, but sift combined flour and salt together into a separate bowl. Mix in ¼ cup finely grated C K S Cheddar cheese, then add to egg and milk mixture in container or bowl.

YORKSHIRE PUDDING

Puffy, golden Yorkshire Pudding makes any straightforward meat meal much more interesting. In this case, it may be baked in beef drippings. The pudding may also be baked in butter and served as a sweet, with honey or jam.

(YIELD: ENOUGH TO SERVE 4 TO 6)

> 4 *Eggs*
> 1½ *Cups milk*
> 2 *Cups sifted all-purpose flour*
> 1 *Teaspoon salt*
> ½ *Cup heavy cream*
> 8 *Tablespoons butter or pan drippings from roast beef*

I All ingredients should go into container C S in the order mentioned.* Break eggs into container. Add 1 cup of the milk, then whirl for 8 to 10 seconds.

II Combine flour and salt and sift over egg-milk mixture. Whirl for 10 seconds or until mixture is smooth.

III Transfer egg batter to a bowl and with a fork beat in remaining milk and heavy cream. Cover with a towel or aluminum foil and refrigerate for 2 hours.

IV Preheat oven to 450 degrees F.

V Place the butter in a large shallow baking pan and set it in the oven to heat. Mix batter well with a fork, then pour into the sizzling butter. Bake for 15 minutes, or until pudding rises.

VI Reduce heat to 375 degrees F. and bake for 10 to 15 minutes, or until pudding puffs and turns crisp and brown. Cut into squares before serving hot.

* KitchenAid users: sift flour-salt mixture over eggs and beat to a smooth paste, then add milk and cream and beat again until lump-free. Proceed with recipe as directed.

MATZO MEAL

(YIELD: ABOUT 1 CUP)

3 *Matzos, broken in pieces*

I Place matzo pieces in container C S, then whirl until a coarse meal is formed.

II Store, tightly covered, in a cool, dry place.

CROUTONS

(YIELD: ABOUT 3 CUPS)

12 *Slices leftover bread, with crusts removed*
3 *Tablespoons* each *vegetable oil and butter*

I Cut the bread into cubes; sauté in the oil and butter, stirring frequently, until golden brown on all sides.

II Cool before serving with soups and salads.

GARLIC CRUSTS

(YIELD: ENOUGH TO SERVE 6)

3 *Tablespoons* each *vegetable oil and butter*
1 *Clove garlic, peeled and minced*
6 *Small whole slices leftover bread*

I Heat the oil and butter; add garlic and stir briefly, then add the bread and sauté to a golden brown on both sides, turning once.

II Remove from pan and allow crusts to cool slightly before serving.

TOAST POINTS

(YIELD: ENOUGH TO SERVE 6)

12 Slices white bread
Melted butter

I Toast bread, then trim crusts and cut each slice diagonally twice into 4 triangles.

II Just before serving, brush 1 side of each triangle with melted butter and bake in an oven preheated to 350 degrees F. for 10 to 15 minutes or until crisp.

DESSERTS

BLANC MANGE À LA FRANÇAISE · FRENCH MILK PUDDING

This classic French dessert was once an afternoon's work . . . but with the assistance of your food processor it now may be prepared in less than 10 minutes.

(YIELD: ENOUGH TO SERVE 6)

1	Cup blanched almonds
2	Cups water
¾	Cup milk
⅓	Cup heavy cream
⅔	Cup granulated sugar
1½	Tablespoons unflavored gelatin
¼	Cup cold water
2	Tablespoons Cointreau or kirsch

I Whirl almonds in container C Ⓚ Ⓢ for 60 seconds or until very fine.

II Turn on machine and add ½ cup of the water, 1 tablespoon at a time, through the spout.

III With the motor still running, add remaining water through the spout in a very thin, steady stream. Whirl mixture for an additional 60 seconds after last of water has been added.

IV Dampen a linen towel and drape over a deep bowl. Pour in half the almond mixture and drain off the liquid into the bowl; gather up ends of towel and twist tightly to extract every last bit of the almond milk. Repeat with remaining almond mixture.

V Combine almond milk, milk, cream, and sugar in a saucepan. Soften gelatin in the ¼ cup cold water and add to the mixture in the saucepan. Bring slowly to a boil, stirring constantly, until gelatin and sugar dissolve. Do not let the pudding boil.

VI Remove from heat and stir in the Cointreau or kirsch; cool the pudding and pour into an oiled mold. Refrigerate until set. To serve, unmold on a chilled dish and serve alone or surrounded with cooked, drained fruit.

Ⓚ KitchenAid users: a classic method for a classic dessert—grate the nuts and then pound, using a mortar and pestle. Or for less work, put your blender to work if you own one.

Ⓢ Starmix users: add 3 tablespoons of the water with the nuts and whirl until a very fine smooth paste is formed. Continue with Step III and so on.

MOUSSE AU CHOCOLAT · CHOCOLATE MOUSSE

This is perhaps the smoothest, most delicious mousse you will ever have the pleasure of serving (or eating). Since I do not recommend the use of uncooked egg whites (see end of charts), whipped cream is used here to give the mousse its "puff," and the results are delectable.

(YIELD: ENOUGH TO SERVE 6)

> 4 *1-Ounce squares semisweet chocolate*
> ¾ *Cup granulated sugar*
> ⅓ *Cup water*
> 4 *Egg yolks*
> 2 *Tablespoons cognac or strong coffee*
> 1 *Cup heavy cream*

I Melt the chocolate over hot water in the top of a double boiler.

II Meanwhile, boil the sugar and water together until clear and syrupy.

III Scrape the chocolate into the container,* turn on the machine, and while it is whirling, pour the hot syrup over the

* KitchenAid users: do this process by hand or use the flat blade and stainless steel bowl warmed by the hot water jacket.

chocolate, then drop in the egg yolks one at a time. Add the cognac. Turn off the machine. Cool the mixture to room temperature.

III Whip Ⓒ K S the heavy cream until stiff.

IV Fold the chocolate mixture thoroughly into the whipped cream. Spoon into individual serving dishes or a soufflé dish and chill for 2 hours for the smaller servings and 4 hours for the larger. Serve cold.

Ⓒ Cuisinart users: whip the cream by hand or electric beater.

MOUSSE AU PRALIN DE NOISETTES · HAZELNUT PRALINE MOUSSE

(YIELD: ENOUGH TO SERVE 6)

    2   *Tablespoons unflavored gelatin*
   ½   *Cup fresh orange juice*
    5   *Egg yolks*
    5   *Tablespoons granulated sugar*
   ½   *Cup heavy cream*
   ½   *Cup Hazelnut Praline Powder (see page 326)*
    2   *Tablespoons bourbon*

I Stir gelatin into orange juice and set aside to soften for 5 minutes. Stir over hot water until gelatin dissolves.

II Meanwhile, in the top of a double boiler over hot water, or using the hot water jacket K, beat together egg yolks and sugar until mixture thickens and turns pale yellow. Stir in the dissolved gelatin, then remove from heat and cool mixture to room temperature.

III Beat cream by machine K S or by hand C until stiff; fold into gelatin mixture along with praline powder and bourbon. Turn into a fancy glass serving dish and refrigerate until set. Garnish with pipings of whipped cream and sprinkle with praline powder.

COCONUT MOLD

A cooling tropical dessert, this recipe was sent to me by Pearl Orient, a Japanese friend.

(YIELD: ENOUGH TO SERVE 4 TO 6)

  1   *Cup Coconut Cream (see page 273)*
  ¾   *Cup milk*
  ¼   *Cup heavy cream*
  ⅔   *Cup granulated sugar*
  2   *Tablespoons (2 packages) unflavored gelatin*
  ¼   *Cup cold water*
  1   *Tablespoon rum*
      Maraschino cherries, halved

I   Prepare coconut cream as directed; combine with the milk, cream, and sugar in a saucepan. Stir the gelatin into the cold water and allow to soften, then stir into the hot coconut cream mixture.

II   Cook over low heat, stirring constantly, until the sugar and gelatin dissolve, but do not allow to boil.

III   Remove from the heat, stir in the rum and set aside to cool. Meanwhile, oil a decorative 4-cup mold and arrange halved maraschino cherries attractively, round side down, in the decorative depressions in the bottom of the pan. Pour in just enough coconut mixture to cover the cherries and set the mold in the freezer to firm slightly; add the remaining cream mixture, then refrigerate until completely set.

IV   To serve, unmold on a chilled serving plate.

STRAWBERRY BAVARIAN CREAM

This elegant dessert is also marvelous when frozen. Use fully ripe berries for peak flavor and rich pink color.

(YIELD: ENOUGH TO SERVE 6)

  3   *Pint boxes fully ripe strawberries, well washed*
      and hulled

    1 1/4   *Cups confectioners' sugar*
          Juice of 1 lemon
      2   *Tablespoons unflavored gelatin*
    1 1/2   *Cups cold water*
    1 1/2   *Cups heavy cream*

I   Pick out and set aside 6 of the most perfect berries. Purée C K S remaining berries with the sugar and lemon juice.

II   Soften gelatin in the cold water, then stir over hot water until dissolved.

III   Beat the gelatin into berries and chill the mixture (in the container if convenient or in a large bowl) until it begins to thicken and become syrupy.

IV   Beat cream until stiff by machine K S or by hand C and fold into partially firm strawberry mixture.

V   Rinse a fancy mold in cold water and spoon in the strawberry cream. Chill until firmly set.

VI   To unmold, moisten a tea towel with hot water and wrap around the mold. Set a serving plate on top, then quickly turn over so the frozen cream slides out. Garnish with reserved berries (either whole or quartered) arranged attractively around the cream.

APRICOT MOLD HÉLÈNE

(YIELD: ENOUGH TO SERVE 4 TO 6)

    2   *Cups milk*
   1/3   *Pound stale ladyfingers*
    6   *Eggs*
   1/3   *Cup granulated sugar*
       Canned or dried apricots

I   Heat milk and pour over ladyfingers; let stand 10 minutes, then place mixture in container C or bowl K S. Add eggs and sugar. Process by turning machine quickly on and off 2 or 3 times or until well mixed.

II Preheat oven to 350 degrees F. Lightly butter a fancy baking mold, dust with sugar and pour in the batter. Set mold in a pan of hot water and bake for 40 to 50 minutes or until pudding is set. To serve, unmold on a serving plate and surround with stewed dried apricot halves.

CREAM PUFFS

(YIELD: ABOUT 1 DOZEN LARGE, 2 DOZEN SMALL)

> 1 Recipe Pâte à Chou (see page 358)
> Whipped K S cream or Pastry Cream (see page 354)

I Preheat oven to 425 degrees F.

II Drop pâte à chou mixture by teaspoons for small puffs, or, if you're making large puffs, either by tablespoons or by forcing mixture through a pastry bag fitted with ¾-inch round tube, onto a buttered baking sheet. Allow enough room between puffs so they will not touch as they expand.

III Bake for 15 minutes, then reduce heat to 375 degrees F. and bake until puffs are a light golden brown, about 15 to 18 minutes. Take care not to overbrown—the sides of the puffs should feel rigid when they are done.

IV Remove from oven and allow to cool completely before filling with whipped cream or pastry cream. This makes a soft puff. If you prefer your puffs to be firmer, slit each as it comes from the oven so that steam can escape, then return to the turned-off oven (leaving oven door slightly ajar) to dry for 10 minutes. Remove and set aside to cool completely before filling.

ÉCLAIRS

(YIELD: ABOUT 1½ DOZEN)

> 1 Recipe Pâte à Chou (see page 358)
> Whipped K S cream or Pastry Cream (see page 354)
> Chocolate Frosting (see page 344)

I Preheat oven to 425 degrees F.

II Fill a pastry bag fitted with a ¾-inch round tube (or no nozzle at all) with the puff paste. Force the mixture through the bag to make strips about 1 inch wide and 4 inches long on a buttered baking sheet. Allow enough room between strips so that éclairs will not touch as they expand.

III Bake for 15 minutes, then reduce heat to 375 degrees F. and bake until éclairs turn a light golden brown, about 15 to 18 minutes.

IV Remove from oven and allow to cool completely before filling with whipped K S or pastry cream and icing with chocolate frosting.

PROFITEROLES

(YIELD: ABOUT 2 DOZEN)

> 1 Recipe Pâte à Chou (see page 358)
> Whipped K S cream or
> Pastry Cream (see page 354) or French
> vanilla ice cream

I Preheat oven to 425 degrees F.

II Drop walnut-size balls of pâte à chou mixture on a buttered baking sheet, allowing enough room between so that puffs will not touch as they expand. Paint tops with a glaze made by beating 1 egg with 1 teaspoon water.

III Bake for 15 minutes, then reduce heat to 375 degrees F. and bake until lightly browned, about 15 to 18 minutes. Take care not to overbrown—the sides of the puffs should feel rigid.

IV Remove from oven and allow to cool completely befor filling with whipped K S cream, pastry cream or firm ice cream and top with Chocolate Praline Sauce (see page 273).

GÂTEAU SAINT-HONORÉ

(YIELD: ENOUGH TO SERVE 8)

> 1   Recipe Pâte Sucrée (see page 363)
> 1   Recipe Pâte à Chou (see page 358)
> 1   Egg yolk
> 1   Teaspoon water
> 1   Recipe Caramel Syrup (see page 274)
> 1   Cup heavy cream
> 3   Tablespcons confectioners' sugar
> 1   Teaspoon vanilla extract
> 1   Recipe chilled Crème Saint-Honoré (see page 355)

I Prepare tart and chou pastries as directed. Roll out tart pastry into a circle 9 or 10 inches in diameter and about ¼ inch thick; prick top surface with the tines of a fork and set on a buttered baking sheet.

II Preheat oven to 425 degrees F. Fit a pastry bag with a ¾-inch round tube, then fill bag with chou pastry and pipe a "halo" or border 2 inches high around the outside rim of the tart pastry round. Mix together egg yolk and water; brush chou pastry surfaces with this glaze. Bake for 15 minutes, then reduce heat to 375 degrees F. and bake for 10 to 15 minutes longer or until the halo puffs up and turns golden brown.

III Shape the remaining chou pastry into small Cream Puffs (see page 310), brush with egg yolk glaze, and bake along with the halo-topped pastry circle; or return oven heat to 425 degrees F. after removing halo from oven, set glazed cream puffs on a buttered baking sheet, and bake for 15 minutes, then lower heat to 375 degrees F. and bake until puffs are golden brown and quite rigid, about 15 to 18 minutes longer.

IV Allow both halo and puffs to stand until cool. Meanwhile, prepare caramel syrup as directed. Dip bottoms of puffs one at a time in hot caramel syrup and arrange side by side in a circle on top of the halo. Spoon any leftover syrup over the tops of the puffs.

V Beat cream by machine K S or by hand C until it stands in soft peaks, add sugar and vanilla, and continue to beat until stiff. Fill each cream puff with whipped cream piped through a pastry tube. Spoon the Crème Saint-Honoré into the center of the halo and decorate with swirls of remaining whipped cream. Serve at once.

CROQUEMBOUCHE

(YIELD: ENOUGH TO SERVE 8)

> 1   Recipe Pâte Sucrée (see page 363)
> 1   Recipe Pâte à Chou (see page 358)
> 1   Recipe Crème Pâtissière (see page 354) or
>   whipped K S cream
> 1   Recipe Caramel Syrup (see page 274)

I   Prepare tart pastry as directed. Preheat oven to 425 degrees F. Roll out into a ¼-thick circle 8 or 9 inches in diameter; set on a buttered baking sheet and prick in several places with a fork. Bake for 10 to 15 minutes or until golden, then remove from the oven and set aside to cool completely.

II   Meanwhile, prepare chou mixture as directed and drop by teaspoons on a buttered baking sheet, allowing enough room between puffs so the sides do not touch as they expand. Bake at 425 degrees F. for 15 minutes, then lower the heat to 375 degrees F. and bake for an additional 15 to 18 minutes, or until the puffs turn golden brown and their sides feel rigid. Remove from the oven and allow to cool completely before filling with pastry cream or whipped cream piped through a pastry bag.

III   To assemble the croquembouche, prepare the caramel syrup as directed and set aside to keep hot. Place the pastry crust on a serving plate. Using a pair of tongs, gently dip the filled cream puffs one at a time into the hot syrup and arrange in a circle on the outer rim of the pastry crust. Continue to build successive circles of cream puffs, each circle smaller than the next, so that a pyramid shape or Christmas tree is formed.

PARIS-BREST

(YIELD: ENOUGH TO SERVE 6 TO 8)

> 1   *Recipe Pâte à Chou (see page 358)*
> 1/4 *Cup blanched almonds*
>   *Whipped K S cream or*
>   *Crème Pâtissière (see page 354)*
> 1/4 *Cup slivered, toasted almonds*
>   *Confectioners' sugar*

I Prepare puff shell paste as directed. Preheat oven to 425 degrees F.

II Outline an 8-inch circle on a well-buttered and floured baking sheet. Fill a pastry bag fitted with a 3/4-inch round tube (or no nozzle at all) with the chou mixture and force through into a ring about 1½ inches high following the line of the outlined circle.

III Coarsely chop C S or grate K blanched almonds and sprinkle over the top of the ring; bake for 15 minutes, then reduce heat to 375 degrees F. and bake about 20 to 25 minutes longer or until the ring is golden and quite rigid.

IV Cool completely after taking from the oven, split horizontally and spread the inside surface with the filling of your choice. Replace the top and dust lightly with the sugar and toasted almonds.

PAIN DE LA MECQUE · MECCA CAKE

(YIELD: ENOUGH TO SERVE 6 TO 8)

> 1   *Recipe Pâte à Chou (see page 358)*
>   *Granulated sugar*
>   *Whipped K S cream or*
>   *Crème Saint-Honoré (see page 355) or*
>   *preserved fruit*

I Prepare puff shell paste as directed. Preheat oven to 425 degrees F.

II Fill a pastry bag fitted with a ¾-inch round tube (or no nozzle at all) with the paste, then begin in the center of a well-buttered baking sheet and force the paste through into a large spiral round.

III Dust the top of the paste lightly with sugar and bake for 15 minutes; reduce heat to 375 degrees F. and bake until light golden brown, about 18 to 20 minutes.

IV Remove from oven and allow to cool completely before splitting horizontally. Spread the inside surface with the filling of your choice and set the top back on.

NAPOLEONS

(YIELD: ENOUGH TO SERVE 6)

> 1   *Recipe Pâte Feuilletée (see page 359)*
>   *Crème Pâtissière (see page 354)*
>   *Apricot preserves*
>   *Fondant Icing (see page 342)*
> 2   *1-Ounce squares semisweet chocolate, melted*

I Prepare, roll out, and turn puff pastry as directed.

II Preheat the oven to 425 degrees F. Roll the puff pastry into a 12-by-14-inch rectangle about ⅛ inch thick; cut into 3 strips about 4 inches wide and 14 inches long. Arrange on a buttered baking sheet, prick the surface at intervals with a fork, and bake only until golden brown. The pastry should not be highly puffed.

III Allow to cool after removing from the oven, then arrange in layers with pastry cream in between, leaving the top layer bare. Brush the top layer lightly with a thin coating of strained apricot preserves and ice with white fondant icing. Dribble thin ribbons of melted chocolate in a zigzag pattern over the icing. Use a sharp knife that has first been dipped in hot water to slice the layers into serving portions.

FRUIT TURNOVERS

Enclose any of a number of fresh fruits in a flaky envelope of paper-thin puff pastry and indulge in a delectable dessert.

(YIELD: ENOUGH TO SERVE 6)

4 Tart baking apples, peeled and cored, or
5 Medium freestone peaches, peeled and pitted, or
2 Ripe mangoes, peeled
1 Cup granulated sugar
1 1-Inch piece stick cinnamon
½ Teaspoon vanilla extract
2 Cups water
1 Recipe Pâte Feuilletée (see page 359)
1 Egg
1 Tablespoon milk
Confectioners' sugar

I Thickly slice C K S fruit. Stir the sugar, cinnamon stick, and vanilla extract into the water and poach the sliced fruit over low heat until it is tender but still has a bit of crunch, then set aside to cool in the syrup.

II Roll out the chilled puff pastry ¼ inch thick and cut into 4-inch squares. Use a slotted spoon to arrange some of the poached fruit, along with whatever syrup clings to it, on one side of the center of each square. Moisten the edges of the squares and fold over to form triangles; seal by pressing lightly with your fingers. Place the turnovers on a moistened baking sheet and refrigerate for 20 minutes.

III Preheat the oven to 425 degrees F. Mix together the egg and milk and lightly brush the tops of the turnovers; prick each turnover in several places with a sharp fork and bake for 30 to 35 minutes. Five minutes before taking from the oven, lightly dust the tops of the turnovers with confectioners' sugar to give them a nice glaze. Serve warm, topped with whipped K S cream if desired.

OTHER FRUIT TURNOVERS

Fruits like cherries, sliced C K S strawberries, raspberries, blueberries, or almost any other soft berry serve equally well as turnover fillings. Halve and pit cherries, then poach as directed above for sliced fruit. When using any berries, spoon small amounts to one side of the center of each pastry square, sprinkle with granulated sugar and a few drops of rum or sherry, then proceed as directed.

CORNETS FEUILLETÉS À LA CRÈME · LADY LOCKS
(YIELD: ABOUT 1½ TO 2 DOZEN)

> 1   Recipe Pâte Feuilletée (see page 359)
> 1   Recipe Crème Pâtissière (see page 354) or
>   whipped K S cream

I   Lightly flour a pastry board and roll out the chilled puff pastry to ⅛ inch thickness. Cut into strips about 1 inch wide and 8 inches long.

II   Preheat oven to 450 degrees F. Butter the lady locks (metal cone pastry forms available wherever gourmet utensils are sold); then, starting at the narrow end of the cone, wind a pastry strip around each, allowing the edges to overlap a bit. Fasten the ends securely.

III   Line a baking sheet with parchment paper and arrange the cones so their sides do not touch. Bake for 15 minutes or until the pastry cones puff and turn golden brown.

IV   Slip the cones off the metal forms after removing from the oven and allow to cool completely before filling with pastry cream or whipped cream piped from a pastry bag.

DESSERT OMELET VARIATIONS

Because omelets yield so readily to any number of fillings, they serve admirably for dessert as well as for main course entrées. You can create interesting sweet fillings and textures. For example:

I. Fill with sautéed apple or peach slices C K S, topped with a dollop of sour cream; sprinkle the omelet with sifted confectioners' sugar before serving.

II. Fill with cream cheese and orange marmalade, whirled C S together; top with an orange slice and sifted confectioners' sugar.

III. Or combine with ingredients of your own choosing, in the style of Apple Macaroon Omelet (see page 319).

CHOCOLATE PRALINE SOUFFLÉ OMELET
(YIELD: ENOUGH TO SERVE 2)

     2   1-Ounce squares dark sweetened chocolate
     2   Tablespoons water
     4   Egg yolks
    ½   Cup granulated sugar
    ¼   Cup Hazelnut Praline Powder (see page 326)
     6   Egg whites
         Granulated sugar
         Chocolate Praline Sauce (see page 273)

I Combine chocolate with 2 tablespoons water; melt over hot water, stirring constantly with a fork. Set aside to cool.

II Preheat oven to 325 degrees F. Place egg yolks and ½ cup granulated sugar in container C or bowl K S. Whirl for 10 seconds or until mixture is thick and pale yellow. Add cooled chocolate and praline powder; turn machine quickly on and off 6 times or just long enough to mix ingredients well.

III Beat egg whites by machine K S or by hand C until stiff but not dry. Fold gently into chocolate mixture until thoroughly incorporated.

IV Turn soufflé mixture into a well-buttered oval baking or gratin dish. Smooth the soufflé top with a spatula, then make a lengthwise furrow along the center and a few gashes along the sides. Sprinkle surface lightly with sugar and bake for 20 minutes; or until puffy and brown on top. Serve hot with sauce on the side.

APPLE MACAROON OMELET

(YIELD: ENOUGH TO SERVE 2)

> 1 *Medium apple, peeled, cored, and cut in quarters*
> 2 *Tablespoons butter*
> 2 *Tablespoons granulated sugar*
> 4 *Dry Macaroons (see page 337), broken in pieces*
> 4 *Eggs*
> 2 to 3 *Drops almond extract*
> *Confectioners' sugar*

I Thinly slice C K S apple. Heat 1 tablespoon of the butter, add apples, and sprinkle with 1 tablespoon of the sugar, then sauté until apple is barely soft. Keep warm.

II Meanwhile, whirl the macaroons C Ⓚ S for 3 to 4 seconds, then add the eggs and almond extract and remaining tablespoon sugar. Whirl for 6 to 8 seconds or until well mixed. Heat remaining butter in a separate skillet; pour in egg mixture and cook omelet as directed (see page 137).

III When omelet is set on bottom but still creamy on top, arrange sautéed apples down the center, then flip, fold, and slide from pan as directed. Top omelet with sifted confectioners' sugar before serving hot.

Ⓚ KitchenAid users: pulverize macaroons with a rolling pin and then proceed as directed.

DUTCH PANCAKE

(YIELD: ENOUGH TO SERVE 6)

> 1 *Cup milk*
> 2 *Cups sifted all-purpose flour*
> ½ *Teaspoon salt*
> 4 *Eggs*
> 1 *Cup light cream or half-and-half*
> 8 *Tablespoons butter (1 stick)*
> *Confectioners' sugar*
> 2 *Tablespoons lemon juice*

I Pour milk into container C S or bowl K. Combine sifted flour and salt and sift together over milk. Mix by turning machine on and off 3 or 4 times or until well mixed.

II Add eggs one at a time and whirl for 4 or 5 seconds after each addition. Add cream and beat until all ingredients are well incorporated.

III Cover batter and refrigerate for at least 2 hours to allow flour to absorb liquids.

IV Preheat oven to 450 degrees F. Place butter in a 10-inch glass pie plate. Set in oven only long enough to melt butter.

V Remix pancake batter by hand or in container C S or bowl K for 2 or 3 seconds to make sure it is smooth, then pour into the hot butter to a depth of only ½ inch.

VI Bake for 15 minutes or until pancake rises, then reduce heat to 375 degrees F. and bake for 10 or 15 minutes longer or until the pancake top puffs and turns crispy brown. Sprinkle lavishly with confectioners' sugar and lemon juice before cutting into wedges. Serve hot.

APPLE DELIGHT

(YIELD: ENOUGH TO SERVE 8)

2½   Cups rolled oats
2   Tablespoons all-purpose flour
2   Teaspoons baking powder
½   Teaspoon ground cinnamon
2   Eggs
⅔   Cup granulated sugar
½   Cup (1 stick) butter, melted
2   Medium apples, peeled and cored
¼   Cup walnuts
1   Tablespoon brown sugar

I Cuisinart users: place oats, flour, baking powder, cinnamon, eggs, sugar, and melted butter in container, then process by turning machine quickly on and off 2 or 3 times or until ingredients are well mixed. KitchenAid and Starmix users: mix ingredients by hand or use mixing beater in steel bowl.

II Preheat oven to 350 degrees F.

III Thinly slice C K S apples. Coarsely chop C S or grate K nuts.

IV Divide batter between two buttered and floured 9-inch cake pans. Arrange apple slices over each portion of batter and sprinkle with nuts and brown sugar.

V Bake for 20 minutes, then raise heat to 500 degrees F. and bake 5 minutes more. Remove from oven, loosen edges of cakes, and cool in the pans for 5 minutes, then loosen bottoms and slide cake onto serving dishes. Serve with French vanilla ice cream.

PONTICA

For breakfast, or brunch or late-night snack . . . Pontica is a honey of a dish.
(YIELD: ENOUGH TO SERVE 6)

> 1½ *Cups shelled pistachio nuts*
> 12 *Slices white bread*
> 3 *Eggs*
> 3 *Tablespoons milk*
> 1½ *Cups fine bread crumbs*
> 6 *Tablespoons butter*
>   *Honey*

I Finely chop C S or grate K nuts. Set aside.

II Trim crusts and cut bread into rounds. Beat C K S eggs and milk together. Dip bread pieces first in the egg mixture and then in bread crumbs, and fry in the butter until light brown on both sides, turning once.

III Remove from pan, cover each pontica with 1 tablespoon honey, and sprinkle with chopped nuts. Serve warm.

STEAMED DATE AND NUT PUDDING

(YIELD: ENOUGH TO SERVE 8 TO 10)

> ¾ Cup hot water
> ¼ Cup dark rum
> 1 Cup pitted dates
> ½ Cup each *vegetable shortening and granulated sugar*
> 2 Eggs
> ½ Cup unsulfured molasses
> 1 Teaspoon baking soda
> 2 Cups all-purpose flour
> 1 Teaspoon baking powder
> ½ Teaspoon each *salt, ground cinnamon, and nutmeg*
> ¼ Teaspoon each *ground cloves and ginger*
> ¾ Cup walnuts
> Hard Sauce (see page 273) or French vanilla ice cream

I Bring water and rum to a boil, then pour over dates and let stand for 30 minutes. Drain dates and reserve liquid.

II Cream together shortening and sugar in container C or bowl K* S*. Add eggs and molasses and whirl for 4 or 5 seconds, stopping once to scrape down sides of container.

III Dissolve the baking soda in the reserved liquid from the dates. Combine flour, baking powder, and spices and sift over creamed ingredients. Turn machine on and off quickly 6 or 7 times. Add date liquid and turn machine on and off 8 times or until mixture is well blended, stopping once or twice to scrape down sides of container.

IV Add walnuts and reserved dates,* whirl for 3 or 4 seconds, then turn mixture into a buttered 2-quart pudding mold. Cover the mold tightly with aluminum foil and set on a rack in a large kettle.

V Crush 1 or 2 pieces of aluminum foil and arrange around mold to keep it from tipping over. Add enough boiling water to the kettle to reach three-fourths of the way up the sides of the mold. Cover the kettle with a sheet of aluminum foil, secure

---

* KitchenAid and Starmix users: add ingredients in order given and mix well after each addition. Chop or grind nuts and dates in advance, then stir into the pudding mixture just before turning out into the mold.

the foil with a tight-fitting lid, and steam the mold for 1¾ hours over medium-low heat, adding more water as necessary to keep the level at its original depth.

VI To test for doneness, lift the mold from the boiling water and remove the foil cover. If the top of the pudding is firm and springy when pressed with your fingers, it is done. If the top is unformed and sticky, re-cover as before and continue to steam until the top tests done. Remove the pudding from the mold immediately and serve hot with hard sauce or French vanilla ice cream.

AVOCADO CREAM PARFAIT RIO DE JANEIRO

A sweet that is not overly sweet, a smooth ambrosial cream that doubles as dessert and as an accompaniment to afternoon tea.

(YIELD: ENOUGH TO SERVE 6)

- 3 Large ripe avocados, peeled and seeded
- 1 Cup granulated sugar
- ⅓ Cup heavy cream
- ¾ Tablespoon lime juice
- ¼ Teaspoon salt
  Sweetened whipped K S cream

I Purée C K S avocados. Add the sugar, ¼ cup at a time, while the motor is whirling. Blend in the heavy cream, lime juice, and salt in this same manner.

II Spoon mixture into 6 parfait glasses in alternate layers with sweetened whipped cream, ending with a layer of avocado cream. Chill well before serving cold, garnished with a dollop of sweetened whipped cream.

WATERMELON GRANITÉ

(YIELD: ENOUGH TO SERVE 6)

- 6 Cups cubed watermelon, seeded
- ¾ Cup granulated sugar
- 3 Tablespoons lemon juice

I Purée C S or beat K together all ingredients until sugar dissolves.

II Pour mixture into refrigerator tray; freeze until fairly firm but not solid. Return mixture to machine and whirl 5 seconds. Serve immediately, or if mixture has become slushy, refreeze until it just holds its shape.

CARROT KHEER

If you are searching for a really unusual sweet to please and intrigue guests or family, you might enjoy this unique East Indian treat.

(YIELD: ABOUT 20 PIECES)

2 *Medium carrots, scraped*
3 *Cups milk*
¾ *Cup granulated sugar*
6 *Tablespoons butter*
2 *Tablespoons raisins*
2 *Tablespoons* each *pecans and almonds*
2 *Teaspoons dried coconut*
1 *Teaspoon ground nutmeg*

I Finely grate C K S carrots.

II Bring milk to boil in a large heavy skillet. Add carrots, then continue to cook over medium heat, stirring frequently, until mixture thickens (about 45 minutes).

III Stir in sugar and continue to cook, stirring constantly, for 20 minutes.

IV Add butter, reduce heat to low, and continue stirring until most of the butter has been incorporated.

V Remove from heat and stir in raisins; then pour mixture into a shallow dish.

VI Finely chop C S or grate K S nuts and combine with coconut and nutmeg. Sprinkle nut mixture evenly over carrot mixture. Allow candy to cool before cutting into squares.

MARZIPAN

(YIELD: ABOUT 2¼ CUPS)

> ¾ Cup Unsweetened Almond Paste (see page 374)
> 4 Tablespoons sweet butter, cut in pieces
> 2 Tablespoons kirsch
> 2 Teaspoons corn syrup
> ¼ Teaspoon almond extract
>   Confectioners' sugar
>   Yellow and green food coloring

I Cream together C K S the almond paste and butter for 5 or 6 seconds or until light and fluffy. Add the kirsch, corn syrup, and almond extract and whirl until well mixed. Turn the mixture out of the container or bowl and divide into 3 portions.

II Return 1 portion to container or bowl; gradually add confectioners' sugar a little at a time, whirling after each addition, until mixture is firm and not at all sticky. Wrap in wax paper and store in a cool, dry place.

III Repeat Step II with each of the remaining portions separately, but, if you wish, add 3 or 4 drops of yellow food coloring to one portion and the same amount of green coloring to the other.

SUGAR-FROSTED DATES

(YIELD: 2 DOZEN)

> 24 Pitted dates
>   White, yellow, and green Marzipan (see above)
> ½ Cup granulated sugar
>   Almond or pecan halves (optional)

I Stuff each date with a piece of marzipan large enough to show between the halves, then roll the dates in the sugar. If desired, top marzipan pieces with almond or pecan halves.

II Cover and store in a cool, dry place.

SUGAR-FROSTED PRUNES

(YIELD: 2 DOZEN)

24 *Pitted dried prunes*
¾ *Cup kirsch*
White, yellow, and green Marzipan (see page 325)
½ *Cup granulated sugar*
Candied cherries

I Cover the prunes with the kirsch and allow to soak for 2 hours. Drain well (reserving the kirsch for fruit salad) and pat the fruit dry with paper towels.

II Carefully pull the prunes apart and stuff each with a good-sized piece of marzipan. Roll each prune in sugar and top with a bit of candied cherry.

III Cover and store in a cool, dry place.

VANILLA SUGAR

Here's an intriguing and difficult-to-find gourmet staple that your food processor makes easy to keep on hand. Tightly sealed, it will keep indefinitely.

(YIELD: ABOUT 2 CUPS)

2 *Vanilla beans, cut in ½-inch pieces*
2 *Cups fine granulated sugar*

I Whirl C S vanilla beans and sugar for 20 to 25 seconds or until beans are thoroughly blended with the powder.

II Store in tightly sealed jar. Sift before using.

HAZELNUT PRALINE POWDER

(YIELD: ABOUT 1 CUP)

¾ *Cup granulated sugar*
¼ *Cup water*
¼ *Teaspoon cream of tartar*
½ *Cup hazelnuts (filberts), coarsely chopped*

I Bring sugar, water, and cream of tartar to a boil in a heavy saucepan. Add hazelnuts and cook mixture without stirring until syrup turns a light caramel color.

II Lightly butter a shallow pan and pour in the syrup. Let stand until mixture cools and sets.

III Break praline into pieces and whirl in Cuisinart or Starmix until reduced to a fine powder. Store tightly covered in a cool, dry place.

CAKES & COOKIES

AUSTRIAN CHEESE CAKE

. . . the most beautiful cheesecake in the world.

(YIELD: ENOUGH TO SERVE 12 OR 16)

Ingredients for Bottom Crust:
     1   *Recipe Kuchen Crust (see page 364)*

Ingredients for Filling:
     1   *Vanilla bean*
   28   *Ounces cream cheese, cut in pieces*
     3   *Eggs*
    ¾   *Cup granulated sugar*
    ⅓   *Teaspoon salt*

Ingredients for Topping:
     1   *Cup dark raisins*
    ¼   *Cup water*
  1½   *Cups poppy seeds*
     1   *Cup granulated sugar*
    ½   *Cup milk*
    ½   *Teaspoon vanilla extract*
         Juice of 1 lemon
         Streusel Topping (see page 374)

To Bake Bottom Crust:

    I Preheat oven to 350 degrees F.

    II Use your fingers to press dough firmly over bottom of assembled 9-inch spring-form pan. Bake for 20 minutes; cool in pan. Do not remove crust.

Directions for Filling:

    I Split vanilla bean, scrape out seeds, and place these in container C or bowl K S with half the cream cheese, egg, sugar, and salt. Whirl until mixture is smooth and no pieces of cream cheese remain. Transfer to a large bowl and repeat process with remaining cream cheese and eggs. Add this to mixture in bowl. Mix well.

    II Pour cheese mixture over cooled crust. Return oven to 350 degrees F. and bake the cake for 1 hour, then remove and cool on a wire rack.

Directions for Topping:

    I Coarsely chop C S or grind K raisins. Place in a saucepan with the water and cook over medium heat until water evaporates.

    II Meanwhile, Starmix users, crush poppyseeds in container. Cuisinart and KitchenAid users, use a mortar and pestle (or a blender) to crush poppy seeds to a dark gray powder, then add to the raisins along with the sugar and milk. Simmer over low heat, stirring constantly, for 15 or 20 minutes or until mixture is very thick.

    III Remove poppy seed mixture from heat and cool. Mix in the vanilla extract and lemon juice and spread over the cooled cake. Do not remove cake from pan.

    IV Sprinkle Streusel Topping over poppy seed mixture, then slide cake under broiler until the top browns slightly. This topping burns easily so keep an eye on it. Serve cake cold or at room temperature.

ORANGE-FLAVORED CHEESE CAKE WITH CHOCOLATE ICING

(YIELD: ENOUGH TO SERVE 8 TO 10)

Ingredients for Filling:
- 1   Recipe Chocolate Cookie Crust (see page 370)
- 2   8-Ounce packages cream cheese, cut in pieces
- 1   2-Inch piece vanilla bean (or ½ teaspoon vanilla extract)
- ½   Cup granulated sugar
- ¼   Teaspoon each orange extract and grated zest (thin outer skin) of 1 orange
- 2   Eggs, separated

Ingredients for Topping:
- 1   4-Inch vanilla bean (or 1 teaspoon vanilla extract)
- 1   Cup sour cream
- 1   Tablespoon granulated sugar

Ingredients for Icing:
- 3   1-Ounce squares semisweet chocolate
- 2   Tablespoons each water and granulated sugar
- ¼   Teaspoon orange extract
- 2   Egg yolks
- 4   Tablespoons butter

I   Prepare Chocolate Cookie Crust as directed. Press over the bottom of assembled 9-inch spring-form pan. Bake for 5 minutes in an oven preheated to 300 degrees F., then cool.

II   Whirl cream cheese in container C or bowl K S until light and puffy. Split the vanilla bean, scrape out the soft inside, and add, along with the sugar, orange extract, and orange peel, to the cream cheese; whirl mixture for 8 seconds, or until well-mixed, stopping once or twice to scrape down sides of container or bowl.

III   Turn the machine on and add the egg yolks 1 at a time to container or bowl. Continue to whirl for 10 seconds or until well mixed after the final egg yolk has been incorporated. Turn cream cheese mixture out into another bowl.

IV   Preheat oven to 300 degrees F.

V Beat egg whites by machine K S or by hand C until stiff, and fold into cream cheese mixture. Turn the filling into the cooled crust and bake for 1 hour.

VI Remove cheese cake from oven and prepare the topping: split the 4-inch vanilla bean, scrape out the soft inside, and add to container C or bowl K S with the sour cream and sugar. Whirl for 6 or 7 seconds or until well mixed, then spread over top of hot cheese cake.

VII Return cheese cake to the oven and bake at 300 degrees F. for 10 minutes. Remove from oven and allow cake to cool thoroughly before removing from pan.

VIII To prepare icing, heat chocolate, water, sugar, and orange extract in the top of double boiler over boiling water, stirring occasionally, until chocolate melts.

IX Add egg yolks, 1 at a time, beating well after each addition, then cook over boiling water, stirring constantly, for 3 minutes.

X Remove mixture from heat and allow to cool for 5 minutes. Beat in butter, 1 tablespoon at a time, by hand or whirl in container or bowl. Spread frosting over cooled cheese cake, reserving a small amount. Stir 2 or 3 drops of water into the reserved frosting and dribble down the sides of the cake. Serve cheese cake slightly chilled.

HONEYED NUT TORTE

(YIELD: ENOUGH TO SERVE 12 TO 16)

Ingredients for Torte Layers:

2	*Cups walnuts*
6	*Zwieback, broken in pieces*
2	*Teaspoons baking powder*
1¼	*Teaspoons cinnamon*
¼	*Teaspoon each salt and powdered anise*
7	*Eggs, separated*
2	*Teaspoons vanilla extract*
1	*Cup granulated sugar*

Ingredients for Syrup:
- 3 Cups water
- 1 Cup honey
- 1 Cup granulated sugar

Ingredients for Topping:
- 2 8-Ounce packages cream cheese
- 4 Egg yolks
- ¾ Cup granulated sugar
- 3 Tablespoons rum

I Preheat oven to 325 degrees F.

II Cuisinart users: place nuts, zwieback, baking powder, and spices in container. Whirl for 8 seconds. Add egg yolks and vanilla to container C. Turn machine quickly on and off 6 times or until well mixed, stopping once to scrape down sides of container. KitchenAid and Starmix users: chop or grind nuts and zwieback separately and place in bowl with baking powder and spices. Beat in egg yolks until well mixed.

III Pour batter into separate bowl and set aside.

IV By machine K S or by hand C, beat egg whites until foamy, and continue beating while gradually adding the sugar. Beat until stiff, then fold into batter.

V Divide batter among 3 well-buttered cake pans and bake for 30 minutes. Cool a bit on cake racks after removing from the oven, then carefully loosen layers while still warm and place on separate racks or plates to cool further.

VI Meanwhile, boil together water, honey, and sugar for 30 minutes. Cool to room temperature.

VII Pour one-third of the syrup over each of the torte layers; refrigerate honey-soaked layers for at least 4 hours.

VIII To assemble the torte, place cream cheese, egg yolks, sugar, and rum in container C or bowl K S. Whirl until ingredients are well mixed and cream cheese is smooth. Place 1 torte layer on a serving plate. Cover with cheese topping, allowing some topping to drip over the edges. Ice the remaining torte layers in the same manner and stack one on top of the other. Decorate the top with walnut halves and chill torte for several hours or overnight. Serve cold.

NUT CAKE WITH LEMON-ORANGE GLAZE

(YIELD: ENOUGH TO SERVE 12)

> $\frac{1}{2}$ Cup blanched almonds
> $1\frac{1}{2}$ Cups walnuts
> $1\frac{1}{4}$ Cups pecans
> 2   Cups confectioners' sugar
> $2\frac{1}{2}$ Tablespoons cornstarch
> 9   Egg whites
>   Butter Cream Icing I or II (see page 343)
>   Lemon-Orange Glaze (see page 345)

I Preheat oven to 275 degrees F.

II Finely chop C S or grate K nuts. Set aside in large bowl with the sugar and cornstarch.

III Beat K S or hand-whip C egg whites until stiff but not dry. Fold in nut mixture.

IV Divide batter between 2 buttered and floured 9-inch cake pans. Bake for $1\frac{1}{2}$ to $1\frac{3}{4}$ hours, or until the cakes begin to shrink from the sides of the pans. Remove from the oven and cool for 5 minutes, then turn out on wire racks and cool to room temperature.

V Spread icing between layers and cover top with glaze.

PÂTE À GÉNOISE · LIGHT BUTTER CAKE

> 5   Eggs
> $\frac{2}{3}$ Cup granulated sugar
> $\frac{1}{2}$ Teaspoon each vanilla extract and/or grated lemon zest
> 1   Cup plus 2 tablespoons cake or all-purpose flour
> 8   Tablespoons (1 stick) melted butter

I Place the eggs, sugar, vanilla extract, and lemon zest in the metal bowl K and fill and attach the hot water jacket, or combine these ingredients in a bowl over fairly hot water. Using the wire whip K S, a portable electric beater or a rotary eggbeater, beat until the mixture turns light and airy and doubles its volume. This should take about 3 to 4 minutes with the KitchenAid, 5 minutes with an electric beater or 20 minutes by hand. The object is to beat enough air into the batter to produce a gossamer-light, delicately textured cake. Remove the bowl from its hot water bath and continue beating until the mixture cools.

II Preheat the oven to 350 degrees F. Using the slowest speed of your processor K, or by hand with a metal spatula, fold in the flour, 1/3 cup at a time, alternately with the melted butter. Each addition must be thoroughly incorporated before adding the next.

III Butter and flour the appropriate-size cake pan—2 8-inch cake pans for layers, a 10-inch square pan for a square cake or if you plan to make petits fours, or a jelly roll pan—and pour in the batter. Set the pan or pans on the second rack from the bottom of the oven and bake for 25 to 30 minutes, or until the top of the cake springs back when lightly pressed with the fingers. Remove from the pan after taking from the oven and allow to cool to room temperature on a wire rack.

PETITS FOURS

1 Recipe *Pâte à Génoise* (see above)
Butter Cream Icing I or II (see page 343), or jam or marmalade
Fondant Icing (see page 342)

I Prepare the génoise batter as directed. Pour into a buttered and floured 10- or 12-inch square baking pan to a depth of 3/4 inch. Bake as directed, then remove from the pan and cool on a wire rack.

II Cut into squares or any desired shape when cool, then split each little cake and fill with a thin layer of butter cream icing, jam, or marmalade. Chill for at least 2 hours.

III To ice the petits fours, dip into warm fondant that has been colored and flavored to taste.

STRAWBERRY SHORTCAKE

Fresh peaches and/or sautéed apple slices are also marvelous served with shortcake—but in these cases try substituting ice cream for the whipped cream.

       8   Cups thoroughly ripe strawberries
       1   Cup granulated sugar
           Lemon juice
       1   Cup heavy cream
           A drop or two of vanilla or almond extract
           Shortcake (see page 373)

   I Brush or rinse sand from strawberries. Slice 5 cups of the berries C K S, and mix with ¾ cup sugar and a bit of lemon juice. Refrigerate. Cut the remaining berries in half and refrigerate.

   II Whip cream by machine K S or by hand C until it begins to thicken, then sprinkle in the remaining sugar a bit at a time along with the flavoring, and beat until stiff.

   III To serve, spread the bottom shortcake layer with the sliced berries and half the whipped cream. Top with remaining cake layer and remaining whipped cream. Garnish with the halved berries and serve immediately.

BANANA PUMPKIN SPICE CAKE
(YIELD: ENOUGH TO SERVE 8)

       ½   Teaspoon lemon juice
       ¼   Cup warm milk
       ⅓   Cup vegetable shortening
       1   Cup granulated sugar
       ½   Cup Pumpkin Purée (see page 223)
       1   Very ripe banana, cut in 1-inch pieces
       2   Cups all-purpose flour
       2   Teaspoons baking powder
       ½   Teaspoon baking soda
       1   Teaspoon cinnamon
       ¼   Teaspoon each salt, allspice, and ground nutmeg
       1   Egg
       ¾   Cup pitted dates
     1½   Cups walnuts
       ¾   Cup peach jam
           Butter Cream Icing II (see page 343)

I Stir lemon juice into milk and let stand for 10 minutes to sour.

II Preheat oven to 350 degrees F.

III Place shortening and sugar in container C or bowl K S. Cream until well mixed (15 seconds for Cuisinart machine). Add the pumpkin and banana and beat in well (8 seconds for Cuisinart machine).

IV Sift together the flour, baking powder, baking soda, and spices.

V To mix the cake in your Cuisinart machine, add half the dry ingredients to container. Process by turning machine on and off 8 times. Scrape down container sides, add the egg and half the liquid ingredients, and turn machine quickly on and off 6 times. Alternately add remaining dry ingredients and liquid ingredients, turning machine quickly on and off and scraping down after each addition. Add the dates and 1 cup of the walnuts to container, and turn the machine quickly on and off 8 times. KitchenAid and Starmix users: chop S or grate K the nuts and hand-chop the dates separately. Add the dry and liquid ingredients as directed, but mix well after each addition. Mix nuts and dates into batter just before turning out into pan.

VI Pour batter into a well-buttered 9-inch tube pan and bake for 1 hour or until the cake tests done.

VII Cool in pan for 10 minutes, then remove and cool on a wire rack. Spread the peach jam over the cooled cake. Coarsely chop C S or grate K the remaining walnuts and press over the cake, or ice with Butter Cream Icing.

CARROT CAKE

(YIELD: ENOUGH TO SERVE 8)

3	Medium carrots, scraped
1	Cup blanched almonds
9	Eggs, separated
1⅔	Cups granulated sugar
⅛	Teaspoon ground cinnamon

I   Preheat oven to 275 degrees F.

II   Finely grate C K S carrots. Squeeze dry with paper towels and set aside. Finely chop C S or grate K almonds and set aside.

III   Place egg yolks and sugar in container C or bowl K S. Beat until mixture is thick and creamy, then blend in carrots, almonds, and cinnamon.

IV   Beat by machine K S or by hand C egg whites until stiff but not dry. Fold into carrot mixture.

V   Lightly butter a 9-by-13-inch baking dish. Pour in batter and bake for 1¼ to 1½ hours. Set pan on wire rack after taking from oven and cool before cutting into squares.

MACAROONS

(YIELD: ABOUT 1½ DOZEN)

> 1   *Cup Unsweetened Almond Paste (see page 374) or*
> *½ pound canned almond paste, cut in pieces*
> 1   *Cup granulated sugar*
> *Whites from 2 small eggs*
> ¼   *Teaspoon almond extract*
> *Generous pinch of salt*

I   Preheat oven to 325 degrees F. Line a baking sheet with brown paper cut to fit (a neatly trimmed paper bag will do nicely).

II   Place almond paste, sugar, 1 egg white, almond extract, and salt in container C or bowl K S. Whirl until smooth, stopping once to scrape down container or bowl sides. If mixture seems stiff, add as much of the remaining egg white, a bit at a time, as necessary to produce a soft but well-formed mixture, blending well after each addition.

III   Turn mixture into another bowl and beat with a wooden spoon.

IV Drop dough by spoonfuls, or squeeze from the fluted nozzle of a pastry bag, about 1½ inches apart on the paper-lined baking sheet. Bake for 30 minutes or until lightly browned. Cool after taking from the oven; then remove by dampening back of paper gradually until macaroons loosen easily.

WITWE KUSSE · WIDOW'S KISSES
(YIELD: ABOUT 2 DOZEN)

¾   *Cup blanched almonds*
¼   *Cup diced candied citron*
4   *Egg whites*
½   *Cup plus 1 tablespoon granulated sugar*

I Finely chop C S or grind K S almonds and set aside. Finely chop C S or hand-chop K the citron.

II Preheat oven to 300 degrees F.

III Set egg whites and sugar in the top of a double boiler over simmering water. Use a rotary beater to beat the mixture until it forms fairly firm peaks, then remove the pan from the hot water and stir in the almonds and citron.

IV Drop batter by teaspoons on a well-greased baking sheet. Bake for 25 to 30 minutes or until centers are set. These kisses should not be browned.

FUDGE BROWNIES
(YIELD: 16 SQUARES)

2   *1-Ounce squares unsweetened chocolate*
8   *Tablespoons butter, cut in pieces*
1   *Cup granulated sugar*
½   *Cup all-purpose flour*
2   *Eggs*
1   *Teaspoon vanilla extract*
1   *Cup walnuts or pecans, chopped or grated C K S*

I Melt chocolate over hot water; set aside to cool.

II Meanwhile, preheat oven to 350 degrees F. Place butter in container C or bowl K S. Whirl 20 seconds or until light and fluffy, then add sugar and whirl 10 seconds or until creamed.

III Add flour; process by turning machine quickly on and off 5 times or until well incorporated. Add 1 egg, turn motor quickly on and off twice, then add the second egg along with the vanilla and turn motor quickly on and off 6 or 7 times or until ingredients are well incorporated.

IV Add cooled chocolate and turn machine on and off 5 times. Add the nuts and turn machine on and off 3 more times or beat until batter is well mixed. Turn into a well-buttered 8-inch-by-8-inch pan and bake for 30 minutes. Cool to room temperature before cutting into squares. Serve plain or with ice cream and Chocolate Praline Sauce (see page 273).

GRANDMOTHER'S OATMEAL COOKIES
(YIELD: ABOUT 2 DOZEN)

2	*Ounces fresh coconut*
½	*Cup vegetable shortening*
1	*Cup tightly packed light brown sugar*
1	*Egg*
¾	*Cup all-purpose flour*
¼	*Teaspoon each baking soda, salt, and ground cinnamon*
⅛	*Teaspoon baking powder*
1¼	*Cups rolled oats*
¼	*Cup walnut halves broken in quarters*
¼	*Cup raisins*
¾	*Cup semisweet chocolate bits*

I Preheat oven to 350 degrees F.

II Coarsely chop C or grate K S coconut. Set aside.

III Cream together shortening and sugar in container C or bowl K S until smooth. Add egg and turn machine on and off 4 or 5 times or until ingredients are well incorporated.

IV Combine flour, baking soda, salt, cinnamon, and baking powder; sift together into container or bowl. Process by turning machine quickly on and off 8 times or until well blended.

V Stir coconut, oats, walnuts, raisins, and chocolate bits into dough by hand. Drop by spoonfuls on an ungreased baking sheet and bake for 10 to 12 minutes or until lightly browned.

CARROT COOKIES

(YIELD: ABOUT 2½ DOZEN)

2	Medium carrots, scraped
12	Tablespoons (1½ sticks) butter
1	Cup granulated sugar
1	Egg
	Zest (thin outer skin, with none of the bitter white underskin included) from ¼ medium orange, minced
2¼	Cups sifted all-purpose flour
2	Teaspoons baking powder
½	Teaspoon salt
⅛	Teaspoon each ground allspice and nutmeg
1	Cup pecans, chopped C S or grated K
1	Cup currants

I Preheat oven to 375 degrees F.

II Grate carrots C K S, then set aside to drain.

III Cream butter and sugar together in container C or bowl K S.

IV Squeeze carrots dry, then add to creamed mixture along with egg and orange zest.* Process C by turning machine quickly on and off 3 or 4 times or by beating K S until egg is incorporated.

V Combine flour, baking powder, salt, and spices and sift over carrot mixture. Process C by turning machine quickly on and off 2 times, or beat K S until well mixed.

* KitchenAid and Starmix users: hand-mince orange zest.

IV Add nuts and currants, then process C by turning quickly machine on and off 3 or 4 times, stopping once or twice to scrape down container sides and stir ingredients or by beating K S as usual.

VII Drop cookie dough by spoonfuls from a greased teaspoon onto a well-greased cookie sheet and bake for 10 to 12 minutes, or until lightly browned around the edges. Loosen after taking from the oven and set on a rack to cool.

SAND TARTS

YIELD: 2½ DOZEN)

> 1 *Recipe Sand Tart Dough (see page 369)*
> 1 *Egg white*
> *Granulated sugar*
> 30 *Walnut or pecan halves*

I Preheat oven to 350 degrees F. Soften the dough by working it lightly with your fingers. Divide the dough into thirds. The dough will be quite sticky, so generously flour your rolling pin and pastry board. Divide each piece of dough in half and roll out one portion at a time. Cut into rounds (or triangles or stars) with a 2½-inch cookie cutter.

II Brush cookie tops with egg white, sprinkle with sugar, and set a half nut in the center of each. Arrange on baking sheets and bake for 10 minutes. Loosen cookies after taking from oven and cool on a wire rack.

ALLUMETTES

These puffed, flaky treats are extremely delicate and unusually delicious.

(YIELD: ABOUT 3 DOZEN)

> 1 *Recipe Pâte Feuilletée (see page 359)*
> 1 *Egg white*
> *Confectioners' sugar*

I Prepare puff pastry as directed. Roll out the chilled pastry about ¼ inch thick and cut lengthwise into 4-inch strips.

II Preheat oven to 400 degrees F. Mix together the egg white and enough confectioners' sugar to make a smooth, thin paste; brush this mixture over the surface of each strip.

III Cut the strips into pieces about 1½ inches wide and arrange on a moistened baking sheet, making sure that the edges do not touch. Chill in the refrigerator for 10 minutes, then bake for 10 to 12 minutes or until puffed and delicately golden. Serve warm or at room temperature.

FONDANT ICING

(YIELD: 1½ CUPS)

> 2   *Cups granulated sugar*
> ¼   *Teaspoon cream of tartar*
> 1   *Cup boiling water*

I Combine the sugar and cream of tartar in a small saucepan; stir until well mixed and the cream of tartar is no longer visible.

II Add the boiling water, stir until the sugar dissolves, then boil the mixture without stirring until it forms a soft ball when a small amount is dropped in a glass of water, or until the syrup registers 234 degrees F. on a candy thermometer.

III Remove the mixture from the heat and wipe away any sugar crystals that have hardened on the inside of the pan. Let stand until cool enough to handle, then turn onto a marble or enamel surface. Quickly work the mixture with a metal spatula until the icing turns smooth and frosty white, then knead it briefly with your hands until soft and creamy.

IV Store in an airtight container in the refrigerator for 2 days before using to ice cakes or petits fours.

BUTTER CREAM ICING I

(YIELD: ENOUGH ICING FOR A 2-LAYER CAKE)

> 4 *Tablespoons butter, cut in pieces*
> 3½ *Cups confectioners' sugar*
> 4 *Tablespoons heavy cream*
> 1 *Teaspoon almond extract*

I Place butter in container C or bowl K S. Whirl until creamy.

II Sift sugar, measure 1 cup, and beat ½ cup at a time into the creamed butter until sugar Is well incorporated and smooth.

III Cuisinart users: turn on the machine and add the remaining ingredients through the spout in this order: 1 cup sugar, 2 tablespoons cream, the remaining sugar and the remaining cream together with the almond extract. Continue to whirl only until mixture is smooth.

KitchenAid and Starmix users: add ingredients in the order given above, but beat in well after each addition.

BUTTER CREAM ICING II

(YIELD: ENOUGH ICING FOR A 2-LAYER CAKE)

> 8 *Tablespoons (1 stick) butter, cut in pieces*
> 3½ *Cups confectioners' sugar*
> 3 *Egg yolks*
> ¼ *Teaspoon ground nutmeg*
> 1 *Tablespoon rum, brandy, or orange or lemon juice*

I Cuisinart users: place butter in container C, add sugar, and whirl for 10 seconds. KitchenAid or Starmix users: beat butter in bowl K S. Sift sugar and add ½ cup at a time, beating well after each addition.

II Turn on motor C K S and add egg yolks one at a time, making sure each is well incorporated before adding the next.

Add nutmeg and rum (or other flavoring) and continue to whirl until smooth and creamy.

III Chill well before spreading.

CREAM CHEESE CHOCOLATE FROSTING

(YIELD: 2 CUPS)

> 2 *1-Ounce squares unsweetened chocolate*
> ¼ *Cup cream cheese, cut in pieces*
> 1½ *Cups confectioners' sugar*
> *Pinch salt*
> *Heavy cream*

I Melt chocolate over hot water.

II Whirl cream cheese in container C or bowl K S until light and fluffy, then while the machine is running, add the sugar through the spout, a little at a time, until completely incorporated.

III Add melted chocolate, salt, and as much of the heavy cream as necessary to make a spreadable icing. Whirl until smooth.

FONDANT ICING VARIATIONS

If desired, you may vary the flavor of the fondant to suit your taste. When ready to use, place the fondant in the top of a double boiler and heat over 1 inch of simmering water for 2 minutes. The fondant should be warm but not hot. For each ½ cup of warm fondant, stir in any of the following:

- ½ teaspoon vanilla extract

- ½ teaspoon instant coffee dissolved in 1 tablespoon boiling water

- 1½ squares unsweetened chocolate, melted

> · 1 tablespoon Grand Marnier, anisette, kirsch, rum, or other liqueur, or enough to make the icing the proper consistency for spreading

Fondant icing may also be variously colored. Tint it to any light pastel shade by adding food coloring drop by drop until the icing achieves the color you prefer.

LEMON-ORANGE GLAZE

(YIELD: ENOUGH FOR 1 LOAF CAKE)

1¼ *Cups confectioners' sugar*
  1 *Tablespoon* each *orange and lemon juice*

I Place all ingredients in container C or bowl K S.

II Whirl until smooth.

PIES

FRUIT PIE WITH CHEESECAKE TOPPING

This is perhaps the richest of the super-rich dessert pies.

(YIELD: ENOUGH TO SERVE 12 TO 16)

Ingredients for Pie:

½	Recipe Pâte Sucrée (see page 363)
2	Cups raisins
2	Large fresh peaches, peeled, pitted, and cut into quarters
½	Cup granulated sugar
3	Tablespoons Grand Marnier
4	Tablespoons cornstarch
¼	Teaspoon each *salt and ground nutmeg*
1	Cup water
1	Teaspoon each *red wine vinegar and butter*

Ingredients for Toppings:

1	Egg
¼	Cup granulated sugar
½	Vanilla bean, split lengthwise
8	Ounces cream cheese, cut in pieces
	Pinch salt
	Streusel Topping (see page 374)

I Preheat oven to 350 degrees F.

II Prepare pâte as directed; use the back of a spoon to press dough evenly over the bottom of an assembled spring-form pan. Bake on the middle rack of the preheated oven for 30 minutes, then remove and cool in the pan on a wire rack.

Directions for Filling:

I To chop the fruit in the Cuisinart machine, place raisins in container and whirl for 3 or 4 seconds, then remove and set aside. Add peach quarters to container and quickly turn machine on and off 2 or 3 times or until peaches are coarsely chopped. KitchenAid and Starmix users: coarsely chop fruit by hand.

II Place fruit, sugar, and Grand Marnier in a saucepan. Mix together the cornstarch, salt, nutmeg, and water; add to the fruit mixture. Cook over medium heat, stirring constantly, until fruit sauce thickens and turns clear, then remove from heat and stir in vinegar and butter. Set aside to cool.

III To prepare the topping, place egg and sugar in container C or bowl K S. Whirl for 6 seconds; scrape down.

IV Scrape out seeds from vanilla bean and add to container or bowl along with cream cheese and salt. Whirl mixture for 10 seconds or until well mixed. Spread cooled fruit mixture over the cooled crust. Spoon cheese mixture over fruit. Bake pie in 350 degree oven for 40 minutes. Cool in the pan on a wire rack.

V Sprinkle Streusel Topping over the cooled pie; slide pie under broiler about 5 inches from flame only long enough to lightly brown. This topping burns easily so keep an eye on it. Serve pie at room temperature or chilled.

PECAN PIE

⅟₂ Recipe Pie Pastry (see page 357)
1 Cup pecans
2 Cups corn syrup
4 Tablespoons all-purpose flour
2½ Tablespoons granulated sugar
5 Eggs
¾ Teaspoon salt
1¼ Teaspoons vanilla extract
2 Tablespoons melted butter

I Roll out pie pastry and line pie plate, crimping the edges of the pastry.

II Preheat oven to 375 degrees F.

III Cuisinart users: place all ingredients except the nuts in the container and whirl for 5 or 6 seconds or until well mixed. Add nuts and whirl 3 seconds more or until nuts are coarsely chopped. Starmix and KitchenAid users: coarsely chop or grate nuts first, mix remaining filling ingredients in metal bowl, then mix the two together.

IV Pour filling into pie shell and place pie in oven. Immediately lower heat to 350 degrees F. and bake for 40 to 45 minutes or until center is set but not firm. Cool to room temperature, chill in refrigerator, and serve cold with whipped K S cream or French vanilla ice cream.

MACADAMIA NUT PIE

Substitute 1½ cups salted macadamia nuts for the pecans in the Pecan Pie recipe (see above), and flavor filling with 2 tablespoons light rum. Proceed as directed.

TOASTED ALMOND CREAM PIE

(YIELD: ENOUGH TO SERVE 8)

>   8   Egg yolks
>   1   Cup granulated sugar
>   2   Cups milk
>   1   Teaspoon vanilla extract
>   2   Tablespoons rum
>   3   Tablespoons unflavored gelatin
>   1/3 Cup water
>   1   Recipe Chocolate Cookie Crust (see page 370)
>   2   Tablespoons butter
>   1   Cup blanched almonds
>   2   Cups heavy cream

I Place egg yolks and sugar in container C or bowl K S and process by turning motor on and off 7 times or until well mixed.

II Add 1 cup of the milk; turn machine quickly on and off 4 times or until thoroughly incorporated. Repeat with the second cup of milk.

III Transfer to the top of a double boiler over hot water and cook, stirring constantly, until mixture begins to thicken.

IV Remove from the heat; stir in the vanilla extract and rum.

V Soften the gelatin in 1/3 cup water, stir into the hot custard, and stir over low heat until gelatin is melted. Refrigerate until custard begins to set.

VI Meanwhile, prepare, bake, and cool pie crust as directed. Melt the butter on a baking sheet and toast nuts in a hot oven, stirring frequently, until lightly browned. Coarsely chop C or grate K S all but 10 of these.

VII Whip cream by machine K S or hand C until stiff. Set 1/2 cup aside in refrigerator and fold remaining whipped cream and chopped almonds into the partially set custard. Pour mixture into the cooled pie shell and refrigerate until set. To serve, pipe the reserved whipped cream around the edges of the pie and garnish with the reserved whole toasted almonds. Serve cold.

PUMPKIN PIE

(YIELD: ONE 10-INCH PIE)

½	Recipe Pie Pastry (see page 357)
1½	Cups Pumpkin Purée (see page 223)
1	Cup tightly packed dark brown sugar
½	Cup tightly packed light brown sugar
5	Eggs
¾	Teaspoon each salt, ground cinnamon, and ginger
3	Cups milk

I   Roll out pastry dough and use to line a 10-inch pie plate. Flute pastry edges.

II   Preheat oven to 400 degrees F.

III   Place purée, sugars, eggs, and spices in container C or bowl K S. Whirl until smooth and well blended.

IV   Cuisinart users: turn mixture into large bowl and stir in milk by hand. Mix thoroughly. KitchenAid and Starmix users: add milk to stainless steel bowl and mix by machine.

V   Pour pumpkin mixture into pie shell and bake for 1½ hours, or until knife inserted in the center of the pie comes out clean.

APPLE PIE

(YIELD: ENOUGH TO SERVE 6 TO 8)

1	Recipe rich Pie Pastry (see page 357)
8	Large McIntosh apples, peeled and cored
1¼	Teaspoons ground cinnamon
1	Teaspoon ground nutmeg
⅛	Teaspoon ground cardamom
1	Cup granulated sugar
	Juice of 1 lemon
2	Tablespoons butter
1	Egg yolk
	Heavy cream
2	Tablespoons maple sugar or light brown sugar

I Prepare pie dough as directed, roll out in 2 circles, and use 1 to line a 9-inch pie plate. Preheat oven to 450 degrees F.

II Thickly slice C K S apples, combine spices and sugar, and toss apples gently with the mixture, then arrange the fruit evenly over the pastry-lined pie plate.

III Sprinkle apples with lemon juice, dot with butter, and cover with the remaining crust; crimp the edges attractively and slit the top in several places to allow steam to escape.

IV Bake for 15 minutes; reduce heat to 375 degrees F. and bake for 30 minutes more. Remove pie from the oven, brush with a mixture of egg yolk and a bit of heavy cream, then sprinkle with maple or brown sugar and bake 10 minutes longer. Serve warm or at room temperature.

UPSIDE-DOWN APPLE TART TATIN

(YIELD: ENOUGH TO SERVE 4)

½ Recipe rich Pie Pastry (see page 357)
4 Medium apples, peeled and cored
5 Tablespoons butter, softened
9 Tablespoons granulated sugar
Heavy cream

I Prepare, chill, and roll out pie dough. Set aside. Thinly slice C K S apples. Preheat oven to 400 degrees F.

II Spread the bottom and sides of a 7½-inch glass pie plate with 3 tablespoons of the softened butter. Sprinkle with 6 tablespoons sugar so that the butter is well covered. Arrange apples neatly in overlapping slices over the sugar.

III Dot the top of the apples with the remaining butter and sprinkle with the remaining sugar. Cut pastry into a neat circle slightly smaller than the pie plate and place over the apples. Do not fasten crust to edges of plate.

IV Bake for 45 to 55 minutes or until crust is golden brown and sugar is caramelized as seen through the bottom of the plate. To serve, hold a serving plate firmly over the top of the hot pie, then flip over so tart is turned out in one piece. Serve at once with whipped K S cream.

MY AUNT MARY'S SHOOFLY PIE

A time-consuming recipe easily made with the miracle machines. The best recipe I know of for this very special pie.

(YIELD: ENOUGH TO SERVE 6 TO 8)

1/2	Recipe Pie Pastry (see page 357)
1	Cup each molasses and water
1 3/4	Cups all-purpose flour
3/4	Cup light brown sugar
3/4	Teaspoon baking soda
12	Tablespoons (1 1/2 sticks) cold butter

I Prepare, chill, and roll out pastry, then place in 9-inch pie plate, crimping edges.

II Combine molasses and water in a small saucepan and simmer together for 1 minute. Set aside to cool. Preheat oven to 375 degrees F.

III Sift together flour, sugar, and baking soda; place in container C S or bowl K. Cut 10 tablespoons of the butter in pieces and tuck down in the flour. Process by turning machine quickly on and off until mixture resembles coarse meal.

IV Pour 1/3 molasses mixture into the pie shell, then top with 1/3 crumb mixture. Alternate layers in the same fashion with the remaining molasses and crumb mixtures, ending with the crumbs.

V Dot top of pie with remaining butter and bake for 50 minutes. Serve warm or at room temperature.

CHESS PIE

(YIELD: ENOUGH TO SERVE 6 TO 8)

½   Recipe Pie Pastry (see page 357)
2¼ Cups light brown sugar
2   Tablespoons each corn meal and all-purpose flour
3   2-Inch strips minced or grated lemon zest (thin outer skin with none of the bitter white underskin included)
    Generous pinch salt
6   Eggs
8   Tablespoons (1 stick) butter, melted
¼   Cup lemon juice
½   Cup milk

I   Prepare, chill, and roll out pastry. Place in 9-inch pie plate and crimp edges.

II   Preheat oven to 375 degrees F. Place sugar, corn meal, flour, lemon zest, and salt in container C or bowl K S. Add eggs and whirl until well mixed. Add remaining ingredients and whirl until mixture is well blended.

III   Pour into pie shell. Bake for 60 to 70 minutes or until center of filling no longer appears moist. Cool on a wire rack to room temperature or serve chilled.

FROZEN LIME PIE

(YIELD: ENOUGH TO SERVE 8)

5   Egg yolks
1   Cup sweetened condensed milk
¼   Cup plus 3 tablespoons granulated sugar
1   Cup fresh lime juice
1   Recipe Graham Cracker Pie Crust or Pecan Pie Crust (see pages 371 and 372)
1   Cup heavy cream

I Whirl egg yolks, condensed milk, ¼ cup of the sugar, and 1 cup lime juice in container C or bowl K S until well blended.

II Pour mixture into your ice cube tray and place in freezer until partially frozen.

III Meanwhile, prepare and bake your choice of crust as directed; cool to room temperature.

IV Whip partially frozen lime mixture by whirling it for 3 or 4 seconds C K S. Pour into crust and freeze thoroughly.

V To serve, whip cream by machine K S or by hand C until thick. Stir in the remaining 3 tablespoons sugar and continue to beat until fairly stiff. Spread over the frozen pie and serve immediately.

CRÈME PÂTISSIÈRE · PASTRY CREAM

(YIELD: ABOUT 2½ CUPS)

2	Cups milk
1	1-Inch piece vanilla bean
6	Egg yolks
¾	Cup granulated sugar
½	Cup all-purpose flour
	Pinch salt

I Scald milk with vanilla bean; remove mixture from heat and discard bean.

II Place egg yolks, sugar, and flour in container C or bowl K S. Whirl for 15 or 20 seconds or until mixture is pale and foamy, then add hot, flavored milk in a thin, steady stream while the motor is running.

III Turn mixture into a saucepan, add salt, and cook, stirring vigorously with a wire whisk, until the mixture reaches almost the boiling point, but do not allow to boil. Continue to cook, stirring constantly, for 2 or 3 minutes, then remove from heat and strain. Allow the cream to cool, stirring occasionally to prevent a crust from forming. The mixture should be thick enough to hold its shape in a pastry shell. If it is too thick, turn the cream into the container C and whirl until the proper consistency is reached, or place in bowl K S and beat until smooth and manageable but not runny.

IV   Keep chilled.

PASTRY CREAM VARIATIONS

Crème au Café: Dissolve 1 teaspoon instant coffee in 2 tablespoons boiling water and add to strained pastry cream before cooling.

Crème au Chocolat: Mix 2 1-ounce squares melted semisweet chocolate (or 2 ounces grated C K S chocolate) into scalded milk before adding to egg yolk mixture.

Crème au Moka: Prepare *crème au chocolat* as directed. Mix 1 teaspoon instant coffee with 2 tablespoons boiling water and add to pastry cream after straining.

CRÈME SAINT-HONORÉ
(YIELD: ABOUT 4 CUPS)

2½   Cups Crème Pâtissière (see page 354)
1   Tablespoon (1 envelope) unflavored gelatin
2   Tablespoons cold water, rum, or Cointreau
4   Egg whites*
3   Tablespoons confectioners' sugar

I   Prepare pastry cream as directed. Soften gelatin in the cold water, then stir into hot pastry cream until dissolved. Set

---

* If you prefer not to use uncooked egg whites, substitute 1½ cups heavy cream and beat until soft peaks form; then add sugar and beat until stiff before folding into cooled pastry cream.

mixture in a bowl over ice cubes until chilled but not set, stirring from time to time to chill evenly. KitchenAid people: use the cold water jacket for your steel bowl if you prefer.

II Beat by machine K S or by hand K egg whites until they stand in soft peaks; add sugar and continue to beat until stiff. Fold into cooled pastry cream.

III Keep chilled.

CRÈME DE MENTHE PIE FILLING

(YIELD: ENOUGH TO SERVE 8)

> 2   *Tablespoons unflavored gelatin*
> 2½ *Cups heavy cream*
> 8   *Egg yolks*
> ½   *Cup granulated sugar*
> ⅓   *Cup each green crème de menthe and white crème*
>   *de cacao*

I Soften gelatin in 1 cup of heavy cream in the top of a double boiler. Heat mixture, stirring occasionally, until gelatin dissolves. Remove from heat and cool slightly.

II Beat the egg yolks into the gelatin mixture, either by hand or by whirling in container C or bowl K S. Stir in the crème de menthe and crème de cacao, then refrigerate mixture until it begins to thicken.

III Whip by machine K S or by hand C the remaining heavy cream. Set ¼ cup aside in the refrigerator and fold the remainder into the slightly thickened gelatin mixture. Turn the crème de menthe mixture into the cooled crust of your choice (see pages 370 to 373) and refrigerate until firm. To serve, garnish pie with reserved whipped cream piped through the decorative nozzle of a pastry bag, and decorate with small, mint-flavored chocolates broken in half and set here and there in the piped cream.

PASTES, PASTRY, & DOUGHS

NOTE ON PREPARING DOUGHS

Since everyone has a different method of measuring flour, it may occasionally happen that a dough may seem too dry to hold together or too sticky to roll out. If your dough fails to form a ball around the blades or dough hook, add a bit more liquid and whirl until the desired result takes place. Should your dough feel sticky to the touch after you turn it out of container or bowl, knead in a little extra flour with your fingers until the dough reaches a firm but manageable consistency. Frequently, especially in warm weather, the dough may turn into a greasy mass. If this happens, lightly work in flour on a heavily floured board before chilling, and always chill well before using.

PIE PASTRY

(YIELD: ENOUGH PASTRY FOR 1 DOUBLE-CRUST PIE)

11 to 12	Tablespoons cold *butter (1½ sticks) and 3 table-spoons* cold *shortening (or, for a tart pastry that is less rich, 7 tablespoons* each *cold shortening and butter)*
2½	Cups all-purpose flour
1¼	Teaspoons salt
8	Tablespoons ice water

To Prepare in the Cuisinart Machine:

I   Arrange cold butter and/or shortening by tablespoons around bottom of container. Combine flour and salt and sift together over shortening.

II   Turn machine quickly on and off 3 or 4 times or until the mixture resembles coarse meal.

III   Add as much ice water as necessary, 2 tablespoons at a time,* until the dough forms a ball. Chill for at least 15 minutes before rolling out.

To Prepare in the KitchenAid or Starmix Machines:

I   Sift together the flour and salt into the metal bowl. Tuck pieces of shortening well down into the dry ingredients. Using the flat beater K or the dough hook S, turn the machine to its lowest speed and whirl only until the mixture resembles coarse meal.

II   Add as much ice water as necessary,* 2 tablespoons at a time and turning the machine on and off after each addition, until the dough is well moistened and cleans the sides of the bowl. Refrigerate for at least 15 minutes before rolling out.

To Roll Out the Dough:

I   Divide dough in half.

II   Roll out each half on a lightly floured pastry board, taking care not to overwork the dough. If a single pie crust is called for, refrigerate or freeze the unused portion until needed.

---

* Since pie dough overworks easily, you may prefer to add the ice water by hand. In this case, use a fork to stir in as much as necessary to make the dough come clean from the sides of the bowl and mass against the mixing blade.

PÂTE À CHOU · PUFF SHELL DOUGH

One of the most versatile staples of the gourmet kitchen is Chou pastry. Cream Puffs (see page 310), Eclairs (see page 310), Gâteau Saint-Honoré (see page 312)—to name a few —utilize this wondrous puff paste.

12	Tablespoons butter, cut in 1/2-inch pieces
2	Teaspoons granulated sugar
1/3	Teaspoon salt
2	Cups water
1 1/2	Cups all-purpose flour
6 or 7	Large eggs

I Place butter, sugar, and salt in a small saucepan. Add the water and bring slowly to a boil. As soon as the butter melts, remove the pan from the heat and beat in the flour all at once until smoothly blended. Return the mixture to low heat and beat briskly with a wooden spoon until ingredients are thoroughly blended and the mixture pulls away from the sides of the pan.

II Scrape mixture into container C or bowl K S. Cover and process for 5 seconds or until well mixed. Add eggs one at a time (through the spout C) making sure each egg is well incorporated before adding the next. The finished mixture should be smooth and shiny.

III Use immediately, or to keep mixture 1 or 2 days, spoon into bowl, press plastic wrap directly down over surface to prevent excess exposure to air, and refrigerate until needed.

PÂTE FEUILLETÉE · PUFF PASTRY

2 1/2	Cups unbleached all-purpose flour
1	Cup cake flour
2	Teaspoons salt
1	Pound (4 sticks) chilled sweet butter
1	Cup ice water (more or less)

I Measure out and combine flours in container C or bowl K S; whirl 6 seconds or until well blended.

II Measure and remove 1/2 cup of the combined flours and set aside. Add salt to flour mixture remaining in container or bowl, then whirl 2 seconds more.

III Cut 4 tablespoons of the chilled butter in small bits, working quickly so it has no time to soften. Add to container or bowl, tucking the pieces well down into flour mixture. Turn motor on and off several times or until the mixture resembles coarse meal. If you overmix, the butter may soften and turn the mixture to a paste.

IV Add ⅔ cup ice water, whirl for 3 or 4 seconds, then add as much of the remaining ice water as necessary, 1 tablespoon at a time, until the dough comes clean from the sides of container or bowl and forms a ball around the blades or dough hook.

V Turn out the dough and knead a bit with your hands until smooth and worked together. Refrigerate for 20 minutes.

VI Remove the remaining butter from the refrigerator and soften by beating it evenly with a rolling pin and pressing with the heel of your hand. As soon as the butter is pliable but still firm, work in the reserved ½ cup flour with a wide spatula or the heel of your hand, lifting and pushing until the mixture becomes a smooth, firm mass, then set aside.

VII Dust a pastry board lightly with flour and roll the refrigerated dough into a rectangle about 8 inches wide and 16 inches long, pushing with the heel of your hand as well as your rolling pin to shape it so that its length extends directly in front of you. Use your spatula or the heel of your hand to spread the butter-flour mixture over the upper two-thirds of the dough rectangle, leaving a ½-inch edge along the top and sides as well as the third nearest you unbuttered.

The dough is now ready to be folded and rolled out at least 4 and up to 6 times, depending on what you intend as its ultimate use. Each successive rolling out and folding is called a "turn." The object is to create a series of flaky, paper-thin alternating layers of dough, butter, and air, so that each layer puffs up as it bakes and raises the pastry to the highest level possible.

In each "turn" the dough should be rolled as thinly as possible. Since air that is needed to make the pastry puff will be lost if the dough tears, it is important to keep it firm by chilling it well between each of the turns and at any point during the rolling out and folding process that it becomes too soft or too sticky to handle.

VIII To make the first turn, bring up the unbuttered lower flap of dough so that it covers half the buttered dough, then fold down the top flap. This gives you 3 layers of dough and 2 of butter. Seal the narrow ends of the dough package by pressing lightly with your fingers, then cover with plastic wrap and refrigerate 1 hour.

IX To make the second turn, position the dough on your pastry board with the seam to your right. Use your rolling pin to beat the cold, hard dough gently but evenly along its length once or twice until its starts to feel pliable. Do not tear the dough in the process. With quick, sure strokes, roll out into another rectangle about 8 to 10 inches wide and 16 inches long. Bring the narrow ends together to meet in the center of the rectangle, then fold from left to right as you would fold a book. Wrap and refrigerate 30 minutes.

X Position dough on your board with the seam to the right. Beat evenly once or twice with your rolling pin to soften the butter a bit, then roll out, fold, and turn as directed in Step VIII. Cover and refrigerate 30 minutes.

XI To make the fourth turn, roll out, fold, and turn as directed in Step X. At this point, the dough may be refrigerated for 2 hours, then used to enclose and bake meats, or for fruit tarts. If the dough is to be used for Patty Shells (see page 362), Vol-au-Vent (see below) or in any recipe where extra puffiness is essential, continue for 2 additional turns, rolling out and folding as in Step X and refrigerating 30 minutes between each turn. When 6 turns in all are complete, wrap and refrigerate for 2 hours before using.

Puff pastry will keep overnight in the refrigerator between any of the turns if you wish. It also freezes nicely: double-wrap in plastic wrap and cover tightly with aluminum foil after making the fourth turn and freeze at 0 degrees F.

VOL-AU-VENT

(YIELD: ENOUGH TO SERVE 6)

1   Recipe *Pâte Feuilletée (see above)*
1   *Egg*
1   *Tablespoon water*

I Roll out the puff paste to ½-inch thickness. Using an 8-inch cake pan as a guide, cut the paste into 2 large circles with a sharp knife, then cut a 7-inch circle from *one* of these 8-inch circles and set aside.

II Brush the surface of a baking sheet lightly with water and set on the *uncut* 8-inch circle, top side down. Moisten 1 inch of its outer edge and arrange the inch-wide cut-out rim of the second circle over it, top side down, so that the edges meet evenly. For a nice decorative effect, score the outside of the double shell by making ¼-inch crisscross cuts at regular intervals.

III Set the 7-inch circle back inside its cutout rim and refrigerate the shell for 15 minutes.

IV Preheat the oven to 450 degrees F. Beat the egg with the water and lightly brush only the top surfaces of the shell. Bake until the shell puffs and turns golden, about 5 to 10 minutes, then lower the heat to 375 degrees F. and bake for 25 to 30 minutes.

V Remove the smaller top circle of the shell after taking from the oven and fill the ring with creamed chicken or seafood. Replace the top before serving hot.

PATTY SHELLS

Patty shells are smaller versions of Vol-au-Vent (see above) and are prepared in essentially the same manner. Roll out the puff paste as directed, but cut the paste into 12 2½-inch circles. Place 6 of these circles top side down on a moistened baking sheet, lightly brush the top surfaces with water and set the remaining circles top side down over them. Use a sharp knife or a smaller cookie cutter to cut a smaller circle in the top of each double shell. Score the outside of each shell if you like. Refrigerate the shells for 15 minutes.

Lightly brush the top surface of each shell and bake as directed for Vol-au-Vent, but allow the shells to bake only 20 minutes after the oven temperature is lowered. To serve, carefully lift off the cut-out top, fill with your choice of fillings, then replace the top and serve immediately.

The puff paste may also be cut into other shapes if

desired. Try interesting patty shell variations like diamond shapes, ovals, or squares, or use small cookie cutters, then fill and serve the patty shells as hors d'oeuvres.

CHEESE PUFF PASTRY

Light, flaky, melt-in-the-mouth puff pastry is quickly transformed into delicious hot hors d'oeuvres that may be baked without the addition (or fuss) of fillings. Simply sprinkle Pâte Feuilletée (see page 359) with finely chopped C or grated K S Parmesan cheese each time you roll it out, then fold and refrigerate as directed. To prepare the cheese puffs for baking, roll out the dough to ½-inch thickness, then cut into 1½-inch strips or small fancy shapes, using small pastry cutters. Arrange on a moistened baking sheet, making sure the edges do not touch, and refrigerate for 15 minutes. Bake in a 425 degrees F. oven for 15 minutes or until puffy and golden. Serve hot.

PÂTE SUCRÉE

You'll find this rich, sweet crust backing up many an impressive dessert.
(YIELD: ENOUGH FOR 1 9-INCH CRUST)

> 1 Cup all-purpose flour
> 4 Tablespoons granulated sugar
> Pinch of salt
> 5 Tablespoons cold butter, cut in pieces
> 1 Extra-large egg
> Ice water

I Combine flour, sugar, and salt in container C or bowl K S. Whirl once. Tuck butter pieces down in flour mixture, then turn on and off until mixture resembles coarse meal.

II Add egg.

III Turn out of container or bowl, press into a ball, and knead lightly three or four times. If dough will not hold together, sprinkle with a few drops of ice water and knead three or four times more.

IV Cover tightly with wax paper or plastic wrap, and chill for at least 2 hours before rolling out.

KUCHEN CRUST

Follow the recipe for Pâte Sucrée (see above) but increase butter to 7 tablespoons and use only the yolk of the egg. Use your fingers to press dough down over bottom of assembled spring-form pan.

PÂTE BRISÉE

(YIELD: ENOUGH FOR 1 8-INCH TART)

> 1 *Cup all-purpose flour*
> *Pinch salt*
> 6 *Tablespoons* cold *butter, cut in pieces*
> 2 *Tablespoons* cold *vegetable shortening, cut in pieces*
> 1 to 2 *Tablespoons ice water (more or less)*

I Measure out the flour and salt and place in container C or bowl K S. Tuck butter and shortening down into flour mixture. Whirl only until mixture resembles coarse meal.

II Add 1 tablespoon ice water, turn machine quickly on and off, then add as much ice water as necessary by teaspoon, processing after each addition by turning machine quickly on and off, until dough cleans the sides of container or bowl and forms a ball around the blades or dough hook. If you have misjudged the amount of ice water needed and the dough is somewhat sticky, work in a little extra flour as you knead.

III Turn out the dough, knead it 2 minutes with your hands until smooth and worked together, then cover with wax paper or plastic wrap and refrigerate for at least 2 hours before rolling out. Dough will keep well in the refrigerator for 1 to 2 days; for longer storage, seal tightly with aluminum foil and freeze at 0 degrees F.

PASTA DOUGH

(YIELD: ENOUGH PASTA TO SERVE 4 TO 6; TO
SERVE 8 TO 10, REPEAT RECIPE)

    3   Cups flour
 1 1/3 Teaspoons salt
    2   Eggs
  1/3   Cup water

I Combine flour and salt and sift together into container
C or bowl K S; turn machine quickly on and off twice.

II Turn on machine and add eggs, 1 at a time, until both
are well incorporated, then start the machine again and add enough
water in a thin, steady stream to make a soft, well-formed, but
not sticky dough. Cover dough and set aside for 30 minutes.

III Knead dough according to directions for your machine
until it is smooth and elastic, then turn out onto a lightly floured
pastry board.

IV Divide dough into 4 equal-size pieces; roll out, one
piece at a time, into very thin, even sheets of pasta. Sprinkle each
sheet lightly with flour and cut into desired pasta shape as directed
below.

FORMING PASTA

Fettucine or Tagliatelle Loosely roll up each sheet of dough, then
cut rolled dough into 1/4-inch strips. Set aside on dish towels so
that noodles do not touch each other and allow to dry for 30
minutes. Cook for 5 minutes in a large amount of salted water.

Trenette Roll out each sheet of dough to $\frac{1}{16}$ inch thickness,
then cut into long, very thin strips about $\frac{1}{16}$ inch wide. Allow to
dry for 30 minutes, then cook as directed for fettucine or
tagliatelle.

Cannelloni Roll out pasta dough to slightly less than 1/8 inch
thickness, cut into 3-by-3 1/2-inch rectangles and spread on dish
towels until dry, about 30 to 40 minutes. Cook 6 at one time in a
large amount of boiling salted water, then gently remove with

a slotted spoon and slip immediately into cold water. Drain and spread on damp towels before filling and rolling up.

Lasagne   Roll out dough to ⅛ inch thickness and cut into strips 2 inches wide and 8 to 12 inches long. Dry, boil, and drain as with cannelloni noodles.

Should you happen to have your own pasta-making machine, simply divide dough into 4 to 8 pieces, shape each piece into a long narrow roll and flatten with a rolling pin to a width slightly smaller than the width of your machine. Put each strip through the machine's rolling side three times, moving the rollers closer together with each subsequent rolling. Then adjust your machine's cutting mechanism to desired width and cut dough into strips. Allow to dry, then cook or store as with hand-cut noodles.

WON TON DOUGH

(YIELD: ABOUT 2 DOZEN)

>   2 *Cups all-purpose flour*
>   1 *Teaspoon salt*
>   3 *Eggs*
>   *Lukewarm water*
>   2 *Pounds lean pork, cut in 1-inch cubes*
>   2 *Tablespoons soy sauce*
>   *Freshly ground black pepper*

I   Whirl together flour and salt in container C or bowl K S. Add 1 egg and whirl 3 seconds.

II   Add 1 tablespoon water, then turn the machine quickly on and off. Repeat this process until the dough is well formed and the proper consistency for kneading.

III   Knead dough according to directions for your machine until smooth and elastic. Cover with a towel and set aside for 20 minutes.

Won Tons

I   Finely chop C S or grind K pork. Sauté the meat until it turns gray. Remove from heat. Beat remaining eggs together and add to meat along with soy sauce and pepper.

II Roll out dough to a 6-by-24-inch rectangle. Cut in 2-inch squares, place 1 spoonful pork mixture in center of each square, bring each corner up over filling and gently press together, sealing with a few drops of water. Cook as directed for Won Ton Soup, page 126.

SPAETZLE

(YIELD: ENOUGH TO SERVE 6)

> 2¼ Cups all-purpose flour
> ⅔ Teaspoon salt
> Generous pinch ground nutmeg
> ⅔ Cup milk
> ⅓ Cup water
> 8 Cups water
> 2 Teaspoons salt
> ⅓ Cup butter
> ⅔ Cup bread crumbs

I Combine flour, salt, and nutmeg and sift together into container C or bowl K S. Mix together milk and ⅓ cup water. Turn on machine and pour in liquid in a slow, steady stream until a *soft* dough forms.

II Bring 8 cups water and 2 teaspoons salt to a boil in a large saucepan. Rub the dough through a large-holed flat grater (with smooth edges up) and let the bits fall into the boiling water as they form thin elongated dumplings (or if you have a spaetzle machine, by all means use it). Gently stir the dumplings to keep them from sticking together. Boil for 8 minutes. Drain dumplings well in a colander, then plunge them, colander and all, into cold water. Drain well again.

III Melt half the butter in a large skillet and sauté the spaetzle for several minutes or until they have absorbed the butter. Serve immediately on a hot platter sprinkled with bread crumbs sautéed to a golden brown in the remaining butter.

PIZZA DOUGH

(YIELD: ENOUGH TO MAKE 6 6-INCH PIZZAS OR 12 3-INCH PIZZAS)

4	Cups all-purpose flour
2½	Teaspoons granulated sugar
¾	Teaspoon salt
½	Package (1½ teaspoons) dry active yeast
¼	Cup lukewarm water
⅔	Cup milk, at room temperature
3	Tablespoons vegetable oil

To Prepare in the Cuisinart Machine:

I   Whirl flour, sugar, and salt together in the container. Dissolve yeast in lukewarm water, then add to container along with milk. Process by turning motor quickly on and off 8 times.

II   Add oil and whirl mixture 15 to 20 seconds or until dough forms a ball. (Add a bit of additional milk if dough will not form a ball or a bit of flour if dough seems sticky).

III   Break the dough into 8 pieces. Return to container, pressing dough down against the blades. Whirl until dough once again forms a ball.

IV   Repeat this process 4 to 5 times.

To Prepare in the KitchenAid or Starmix Machine:

I   Sift together flour, sugar, and salt into steel bowl. Dissolve yeast in lukewarm water, then beat into dry ingredients along with oil and milk until dough begins to form around the dough hook.

II   Knead according to directions for your machine until dough is smooth and elastic. Turn out of bowl.

To Roll Out the Dough:

I   Divide dough into 6 equal pieces, or, when making small pizzas, into 12 pieces of equal size. Shape each piece into a ball and set in a warm, draft-free place for 2 hours or until double in bulk.

Roll out each ball to a thin, flat circle, top with your favorite filling, and bake in an oven preheated to 450 degrees F. for 10–15 minutes. Serve hot.

PARMESAN CHEESE DOUGH

> 1 Cup each *all-purpose flour and very finely chopped C
> or grated K S Parmesan cheese*
> 7 Tablespoons *sour cream*
> 4 Tablespoons *butter, cut in ½-inch pieces*
> *Paprika*

I Combine flour and cheese in container C or bowl K S; whirl until well mixed. Add sour cream, then process by turning machine quickly on and off 8 times.

II Add butter and whirl C Ⓚ Ⓢ until a ball of dough forms against the blades. Scoop out dough, break into pieces, and push down against blade. Whirl again until dough ball forms. Turn mixture out and chill for at least 30 minutes before baking as directed in Parmesan Cheese Twists (see page 83).

Ⓚ Ⓢ KitchenAid and Starmix users: knead the dough according to directions for your machine until dough is smooth and elastic.

SAND TART DOUGH

> ½ Pound *butter (2 sticks), cut in pieces*
> 1½ Cups *granulated sugar*
> 1 Egg, *at room temperature*
> 2 Cups *all-purpose flour*

I Cream together the butter and sugar in container C or bowl K S. Add the egg and whirl until well incorporated.

II Add flour, ½ cup at a time, turning machine on and off 4 or 5 times after each addition. After all the flour has been incorporated, whirl for 9 seconds longer or until well mixed, stopping once or twice to scrape down sides and stir dough up from the bottom. Turn the dough out onto waxed paper and refrigerate overnight or for several days until needed.

MACAROON CRUMB CRUST

(YIELD: ENOUGH FOR 1 SINGLE PIE CRUST)

> 2 *1-Ounce squares semisweet chocolate*
> 2 *Tablespoons heavy cream*
> 1 *Cup filberts (hazelnuts)*
> 6 Dry *macaroons*
> 5 *Drops almond or mint flavoring or 2 teaspoons brandy*

To Prepare in the Cuisinart Machine:

   I   Melt chocolate in the top half of a double boiler and stir in the cream.

   II   Meanwhile, whirl the nuts in the container for 4 seconds, stopping once to scrape down.

   III   Add the macaroons, hot chocolate mixture, and flavoring, then whirl for 2 or 3 seconds more or until ingredients are thoroughly mixed.

To Prepare in the KitchenAid or Starmix Machine:

   I   Melt chocolate over hot water, then stir in cream. Grate K S nuts. Crush dry macaroons in a blender or with a rolling pin.

   II   Mix all ingredients together.

To Shape the Crust:

   I   Press macaroon mixture firmly and evenly against sides and bottom of pie plate.

   II   Chill thoroughly before filling.

CHOCOLATE COOKIE CRUST

(YIELD: ENOUGH FOR 1 SINGLE PIE CRUST)

> 5 *Tablespoons cold butter, cut in pieces*
> 15 to 18 *Thin chocolate wafer cookies (enough to make 1¼ cups), broken in pieces*
> 1 *Tablespoon granulated sugar*
> ⅛ *Teaspoon cinnamon*

To Prepare in the Cuisinart Machine:

I   Place butter in bottom of container.

II   Add remaining ingredients, then whirl for 3 or 4 seconds, stopping once or twice to scrape down container sides.

To Prepare in the KitchenAid or Starmix Machine:

I   Bring butter to room temperature.

II   Put cookies through grinder K S or crush into fine crumbs in a blender or with a rolling pin.

III   Combine all ingredients and mix thoroughly.

To Shape the Crust:

I   Preheat oven to 300 degrees F.

II   Press mixture firmly and evenly against sides and bottom of a 9-inch pie plate. Bake for 5 minutes.

GRAHAM CRACKER PIE CRUST

(YIELD: ENOUGH FOR 1 SINGLE PIE CRUST)

18 to 20	Single graham crackers
4 to 8	Walnuts, pecans, or blanched almonds (optional)
1/4	Cup granulated sugar
4	Tablespoons cold butter, cut in pieces

I   Preheat oven to 375 degrees F.

II   Finely chop graham crackers and nuts C S or grind K. Mix well in container C or transfer to steel bowl and mix K S.

III   Add sugar and butter, then whirl 2 or 3 seconds more or until well mixed.

IV   Turn buttered crumbs out into 10-inch pie plate. Set a 9-inch pie plate over and press down firmly with both hands to insure an even distribution of crumbs on the sides and bottom.

V   Remove smaller pie plate and bake in the preheated oven for 5 or 6 minutes, or until the crust is golden but not brown. Cool and fill as you like.

PECAN PIE CRUST

(YIELD: ENOUGH FOR 1 SINGLE PIE CRUST)

1   *1-Ounce square unsweetened chocolate, cut in half*
6   *Tablespoons cold butter, cut in pieces*
1/2   *Cup pecans*
3/4   *Cup all-purpose flour*
5   *Tablespoons light brown sugar*
1/2   *Teaspoon salt*
1   *Tablespoon rum or cold water*
1   *Teaspoon vanilla extract*

To Prepare in the Cuisinart Machine:

I   Whirl chocolate in container for 30 seconds or until finely chopped.

II   Add butter and pecans. Combine flour, sugar, and salt and sift together into container. Turn machine quickly on and off 5 or 6 times. Add rum or water and vanilla, then turn on and off again 6 or 7 times or until thoroughly blended, stopping once to scrape down container sides.

To Prepare in the KitchenAid or Starmix Machine:

I   Grate K S chocolate and keep chilled. Chop S or grate K the pecans and place in steel bowl. Add butter and chocolate and process until well mixed.

II   Sift together the flour, sugar, and salt. Beat the dry ingredients into the butter, pecans, and chocolate until thoroughly blended. Sprinkle with the rum or water and vanilla, and beat again until the mixture holds together.

To Shape the Crust:

I   Preheat oven to 350 degrees F.

II   Roll mixture out between 2 sheets of waxed paper and fit into 9-inch pie plate.

III   Bake until lightly browned, then remove from the oven and cool before filling.

ZWIEBACK CRUMB CRUST
(YIELD: ENOUGH FOR 1 SINGLE PIE CRUST)

> 1   *Cup walnuts*
> ¾   *Cup candied ginger*
> 1   *Box (6 ounces) zwieback*
> 1   *Cup granulated sugar*
> ¼   *Teaspoon each ground ginger and cinnamon*
> ⅔   *Cup melted butter*

To Prepare in the Cuisinart Machine:

I   Whirl nuts and candied ginger in container for 4 seconds.

II   Break zwieback in pieces, and add to container along with sugar and spices.

III   Whirl for 3 seconds, then pour in butter through spout. Turn machine off as soon as butter has been added.

To Prepare in the KitchenAid or Starmix Machine:

I   Finely grind K S nuts, candied ginger, and zwieback.

II   Mix together all ingredients.

To Shape the Crust:

I   Preheat oven to 325 degrees F.

II   Press zwieback mixture firmly and evenly against sides and bottom of pie plate.

III   Bake for 10 minutes.

SHORTCAKE

Serve this crunchy shortcake at breakfast with butter and jam or as a vehicle for strawberries (see Strawberry Shortcake, page 335).

> 2⅓   *Cups all-purpose flour*
> ⅓   *Cup granulated sugar*
> 1½   *Teaspoons baking powder*
> ½   *Teaspoon salt*
> 7   *Tablespoons butter, cut in pieces*
> ⅓   *Cup milk*
> 2   *Eggs*

I Preheat oven to 375 degrees.

II Sift dry ingredients into container C or bowl K S. Add the butter and turn the motor on and off 8 times or until mixture resembles coarse meal. Beat milk and eggs together in a cup, pour over flour mixture, and turn machine quickly on and off 8 times or until well mixed.

III Lightly butter a 10-inch heavy skillet or Dutch oven, sprinkle lightly with flour, and shake out excess. Flour your hands thoroughly and pat the dough to fit the bottom of the pan. Bake 35 minutes or until nicely browned. Remove cake from pan and cool for 5 minutes on a wire rack. Use a large sharp knife to split the cake into 2 layers, then butter inside surfaces.

UNSWEETENED ALMOND PASTE

(YIELD: 1 CUP)

> 1¼   Cups blanched almonds
> 1½ to 2   Tablespoons water

I Place almonds in container C S. Whirl for 60 seconds.

II With the motor still going, pour 1½ tablespoons water through the spout, and whirl until mixture forms a ball in the machine, adding remaining water if necessary.

III Cover tightly, store in refrigerator, and use for preparing Marzipan (see page 325) or Macaroons (see page 337).

STREUSEL TOPPING

(YIELD: ENOUGH TOPPING FOR 1 16-INCH CAKE)

> ½   Cup walnuts
> ½   Cup all-purpose flour
> ½   Cup light-brown sugar
> 8   Tablespoons (1 stick) cold butter, cut in pieces

I Place nuts, flour, and sugar in container C S or bowl K*.

II Tuck butter well down into mixture, then whirl until the nuts are finely chopped and the mixture resembles coarse meal.

* KitchenAid users: finely chop nuts separately; proceed as directed.

HEALTH FOODS

SPANISH-PEANUT BUTTER

The best peanut butter ever—very special.

(YIELD: ABOUT 1 CUP)

       2 Cups very fresh Spanish peanuts, with skins on
     1/4 Teaspoon salt
       2 Tablespoons chopped C S Spanish peanuts (optional)

   I Place 2 cups peanuts and salt in container C S. Whirl for 2 minutes, 10 seconds, stopping as necessary to scrape down container sides.

   II If a chunk-style peanut butter is preferred, stir in 2 tablespoons chopped peanuts after turning into storage jar. Keep chilled.

MOLDED MOCK SALMON MOUSSE

There are times when you wish to serve some special "something" that contains no meat or fish—when a friend who is a vegetarian comes to lunch, for example. On these occasions this tasty salad could save the day. The flavor is surprisingly close to its real-fish counterpart.

(YIELD: ENOUGH TO SERVE 6)

3/4 Cup raw cashew nuts
8 Medium carrots, scraped and cut in 1-inch pieces
3 Tablespoons plain yogurt
1 1/2 Tablespoons Spanish-Peanut Butter (see above)
3/4 Teaspoon fresh dill leaves, with all tough stems removed
1/4 Teaspoon salt
1 Tablespoon unflavored gelatin
1/3 Cup plus 2 tablespoons water
3/4 Teaspoon lemon juice
Thinly sliced C K S lettuce

I Coarsely chop C Ⓚ S nuts and set aside. Whirl carrots, 2 handfuls at a time, for 3 or 4 seconds, removing each batch before adding the next.

II Return nuts and carrots to container C S. Add yogurt, peanut butter, dill leaves, salt, and 2 tablespoons water. Whirl for 5 or 6 seconds, or until well blended, stopping as necessary to scrape down container sides.

III Soften gelatin in 1/3 cup water, add lemon juice, and heat over very low flame until gelatin dissolves.

IV Combine gelatin and carrot mixtures. Rinse a fish mold or other fancy mold with cold water, pour in the carrot-gelatin mixture, and refrigerate until set.

V To serve, wrap a hot towel around outside of mold, then turn out onto a bed of shredded lettuce.

Ⓚ KitchenAid users: run the nuts, carrots, and dill together through the fine blade of your grinder. Repeat the process, then mix all ingredients well. The flavor will still be first-rate even though the texture will not be quite so fine as that of a real salmon mousse.

NATURAL CEREAL

(YIELD: ABOUT 6 CUPS)

1 Cup coconut, cut in ½-inch pieces
1 Cup raw cashew nuts
12 Dried apricots, cut in half
3 Cups old-fashioned hull-less rolled oats
1 Cup wheat germ
1 Cup sunflower seeds
12 Dates, pitted and hand-chopped
1 Cup currants or ⅔ cup raisins

I Preheat oven to 350 degrees F.

II Coarsely chop C S or grind K S the coconut, cashews and apricots.

III Combine the coconut-nut mixture, oats, wheat germ, and sunflower seeds. Spread thinly over a baking sheet and bake for 5 minutes, then reduce heat to 300 degrees F. and bake for 15 minutes longer, stirring every few minutes. The cereal will smell toasty and turn light brown as it begins to dry out.

IV Cool the toasted ingredients after taking from oven.

V Mix together all ingredients. Refrigerate in airtight jars until needed.

INSTANT BREAKFAST BARS

(YIELD: ABOUT 2 DOZEN)

1 2-Ounce piece fresh coconut
3 Cups Natural Cereal (see above)
¼ Cup Tiger's Milk powder (carob flavor)
1½ Teaspoons cinnamon
3 Egg whites

I Preheat oven to 350 degrees F.

II Chop C S or grate K coconut.

III Add cereal, Tiger's Milk, and cinnamon and mix well.

IV Beat C S or by hand K the egg whites until stiff but not dry. Fold into dry ingredients and drop by spoonfuls on a buttered baking sheet. Bake for 10 minutes. Transfer to a rack to cool.

NUT-STUFFED FRESH MUSHROOMS
(YIELD: ENOUGH TO SERVE 6)

12 *Large fresh mushrooms*
1 *Piece goat's cheese (2 inches × 2 inches × 3 inches), cut in 1-inch pieces*
½ *Cup raw cashew nuts*
3 *Scallions, with 3 inches green top, cut in ½-inch pieces*
3 *Tablespoons heavy cream*
⅛ *Teaspoon each ground nutmeg and chili powder*
¼ *Cup wheat germ*

I Remove stems from mushrooms and set caps aside. Cut stems in ½-inch pieces.

II Place cheese and nuts in container C ⓚ S. Whirl for 3 or 4 seconds, stopping once to scrape down container sides. Add scallions and mushroom stems and whirl for 2 or 3 seconds more.

III Add cream and spices, then whirl only long enough to blend ingredients.

IV Stuff mixture into mushroom caps and top with a generous sprinkle of wheat germ. Chill and serve cold or arrange in a baking dish, pour in a little milk, and bake at 350 degrees F. for 30 minutes.

ⓚ KitchenAid users: grate cheese and nuts, then chop vegetables and mix ingredients by hand.

NUT PUDDING

(YIELD: ENOUGH TO SERVE 6)

⅓   Cup raw cashew nuts
1½   Slices stale brown bread, cut in quarters
3   1-inch strips minced orange zest (thin outer skin of orange, with none of the bitter white underskin included)
1   Piece goat's cheese (1 inch × 1 inch × 3 inches)
2¼   Cups milk
1   Tablespoon butter
3   Eggs
4½   Tablespoons granulated sugar
  Generous pinch salt
½   Teaspoon cinnamon
1   Tablespoon honey

I   Place nuts, bread, and orange zest in container C S. Whirl for 5 or 6 seconds, stopping once to scrape down container sides. KitchenAid users: grate or grind nuts and bread. Set aside with orange zest.

II   Grate C K S cheese. Mix with the nuts and crumbs and use the mixture to line the bottom of a deep baking dish.

III   Preheat oven to 350 degrees F.

IV   Heat milk and butter to scalding. Beat together eggs, sugar, and salt C K S and gradually add hot milk mixture.

V   Spoon egg-milk mixture over nut-crumb mixture and sprinkle with cinnamon. Place baking dish in a pan with hot water and bake for 40 minutes or until custard is set. Serve warm, topping each portion with ½ teaspoon honey.

STRAWBERRY-APPLE SHERBET

(YIELD: ENOUGH TO SERVE 6)

2   Cups plain yogurt
2   Cups fresh, ripe strawberries, hulled and cut in quarters
1   Medium apple, peeled, cored, and cut in eighths
¼   Cup honey

I Freeze yogurt in a refrigerator tray.

II Purée strawberries, apple, and honey in container C S or by using special attachment K.

III Add frozen yogurt in cubes or pieces and whirl with strawberry purée until thoroughly blended.* Return mixture to refrigerator tray and freeze.

* KitchenAid users: mix and mash with a fork.

THREE-FRUIT SHERBET
(YIELD: ENOUGH TO SERVE 6)

> 1 Cup whole cranberries
> 2 Large Delicious apples, peeled, cored, and cut into eighths
> ½ Cup orange juice
> 7 Tablespoons honey
> ¼ Cup plain yogurt

I Finely chop C S or grind K cranberries and apples.

II Add orange juice, honey, and yogurt to berries and apples.

III Pour into freezer tray and freeze until mushy. Then whirl in container or stir with a fork and refreeze.

FROZEN APPLE-HORSERADISH CREAM
(YIELD: ENOUGH TO SERVE 6)

> 1   2½-Inch piece fresh horseradish root, scraped
> 3   Medium apples, cored
> 1½ Cups plain yogurt
> 1½ Tablespoons honey
>   Salt

I Finely grate C K S horseradish and apples.

II Combine with yogurt and honey in container C* S or bowl K. Add salt to taste and whirl only long enough to blend.

III Pour mixture into an ice cube tray and freeze until mushy, then whirl for a second or two in Cuisinart container or beat with a fork. Refreeze until hard.

IV Soften cream slightly before serving over cold meat or fish.

* Cuisinart users: use your plastic blade.

BABY FOODS

PREPARING BABY FOODS IN YOUR FOOD PROCESSOR

Is there a baby in your house? Here's another area where your food processor can come in handy. Preparing baby foods from ingredients you choose and cook yourself is easy and convenient when you put your Cuisinart or Starmix processor to work. The KitchenAid machine has a colander and sieve attachment, but this functions most efficiently only when soft cooked fruits and vegetables such as applesauce or prunes are being prepared. Your best bet when you are cooking the other foods in this section is to put your blender to work when puréeing is called for.

Before feeding home-cooked foods or introducing new ones, talk it over with your pediatrician. Point out the many benefits:

• The food you give your infant or toddler will be the freshest available.

• Home-prepared baby foods have more pure meat, eggs, vegetables, and fruits per portion than their commercial counterparts.

• Best of all, home-cooked baby foods can be made without the additives and fillers customary in commercially prepared baby foods. For while you may be used to salt with your food, your baby does not crave or need it, although commercial baby foods do contain this seasoning.

When preparing any of the recipes listed in this section, always process to the consistency suitable for your baby—that is, to the texture baby likes best and can easily swallow. Thin the foods, if necessary, with an additional 2 to 4 tablespoons broth, formula, milk, fruit juice, or water. And remember, while proper processing should produce a perfectly smooth purée, you may, if you like, doubly insure a velvety texture by rubbing foods through a fine strainer.

Baby purées are easy to keep on hand if you freeze them in conveniently sized portions. Simply prepare any purée (except those containing eggs or tapioca) as directed, using large amounts, then pour into ice cube trays (the kind with individual cubes) and freeze at 0 degrees F. Pop the cubes out of the trays while frozen, then place them together in a plastic bag, and store in the freezer up to a week.

BASIC VEGETABLE MIXTURE

(YIELD: ABOUT ¾ CUP)

> 1   *Large carrot, scraped and cut in ½-inch pieces*
> 1   *Rib celery, with all strings removed, cut in ½-inch pieces*
> ¾   *Cup water*

I   Finely chop carrots and celery C S or grind K.

II   Transfer chopped vegetables to a small saucepan, add ¾ cup water, then cover and simmer 15 to 20 minutes, or until tender. (For *Junior Food*, uncover vegetables during last 5 minutes of cooking to allow excess moisture to cook away.)

III   Remove from heat and allow to cool. Return to container. For *Junior Food*, whirl vegetable mixture 5 seconds. For *Infant Food*, whirl an additional 5 seconds or until puréed to the consistency your baby likes best.

BASIC VEGETABLE MIXTURE WITH POTATO

    1   *Large carrot, scraped and cut in ½-inch pieces*
    1   *Rib celery, with all strings removed, cut in ½-inch pieces*
    1   *Small potato, peeled and cut in quarters*
    1   *Cup water*

    I   Finely chop carrots, celery, and potato pieces in container C S or grind K.

    II   Set chopped vegetables in a small saucepan, add 1 cup water, then cover and simmer 15 to 20 minutes, or until tender. (For *Junior Food*, uncover vegetables during last 5 minutes of cooking to allow excess moisture to cook away.)

    III   Remove from heat and allow vegetables to cool slightly. Return to container. For *Junior Food*, whirl vegetable mixture for 5 seconds. For *Infant Food*, whirl an additional 5 seconds or until puréed to suitable consistency.

BASIC NOODLES AND MEAT

(YIELD: ABOUT 1½ CUPS)

    ½   *Cup noodles*
    2   *Cups water*
    ½   *Cup cooked chicken, turkey, beef, lamb, etc.*
1 to 3   *Tablespoons chicken broth*

    I   Cook noodles in water according to package directions, then rinse and drain well.

    II   Finely chop noodles and chicken with 1 tablespoon broth in container C S or grind K. Whirl 10 seconds for *Junior Food*, stopping once to scrape down container sides. For *Infant Food*, add 2 more tablespoons broth (more if desired) and whirl an additional 30 seconds, or until mixture reaches a consistency suitable for baby.

BASIC TAPIOCA

(YIELD: ABOUT ¾ CUP)

1½ Tablespoons minute tapioca
2   Teaspoons granulated sugar
1   Egg yolk
1   Cup formula or milk

I Mix together tapioca, sugar, and egg yolk in small saucepan. Add formula, or milk and cook over medium heat, stirring constantly, for 10 minutes.

II Pour mixture into container C S or blender and whirl for 10 seconds, stopping once to scrape down container sides.

BASIC OATMEAL

For the sake of convenience, freeze this in ice cube trays and use as needed.

(YIELD: ABOUT 1¾ CUPS)

⅔ Cup old-fashioned oats
    Water

I Cook oatmeal according to package directions, omitting salt.

II Place cooked oatmeal in container C S or blender. Whirl 8 seconds for *Junior Food*. For *Infant Food*, whirl an additional 40 seconds longer.

III Pour mixture into your ice cube tray and freeze, then transfer frozen cubes to *double-thick plastic* bag, twist tightly closed, and seal with a wire twist. Store at 0 degrees F. or below and use as needed.

IV To prepare 1 serving of baby oatmeal for *Infants*, place 2 frozen cubes of oatmeal and 2 tablespoons formula, milk, or water in a small saucepan over low heat until mixture reaches proper temperature for baby. For *Juniors*, thaw together 3 or 4 frozen cubes of oatmeal and 2 tablespoons milk or water.

MEAT FOR BABY

(YIELD: ABOUT ½ CUP)

⅔ Cup cooked chicken, turkey, beef, lamb, etc., cut in
    1-inch pieces
2 to 4 Tablespoons chicken broth

I Whirl meat in container C S or blender for 4 seconds, stopping once to scrape down container sides. Meat should be minced enough to serve as *Junior Food.*

II To make *Junior* meat more moist and tasty, add 1 tablespoon broth and whirl for 7 seconds more, stopping once to scrape down container sides.

III To prepare a much smoother mixture for infants, add 2 to 4 additional tablespoons broth and whirl for 30 seconds more, or until meat reaches the preferred consistency.

EGG YOLKS FOR BABY

These are far smoother and more delicious than the commercial variety.

(YIELD: ⅓ CUP)

4 Hard-cooked egg yolks (from medium-size eggs)
2 Tablespoons chicken broth, formula, milk, or
    other liquid

I Whirl C S egg yolks and 2 teaspoons broth for 4 seconds for *Junior Food.*

II To make egg yolks suitable for *Infant Food*, add 2 tablespoons broth (more, if desired) and process for an additional 3 seconds. Stop once to scrape down container sides.

MEAT AND VEGETABLE SOUP

(YIELD: ABOUT ⅔ CUP)

$\frac{1}{4}$ *Cup Basic Vegetable Mixture (see page 384)*
$\frac{1}{4}$ *Cup cooked meat, cut in ½-inch pieces*
$\frac{1}{4}$ *Cup chicken broth*

I   Place all ingredients in container C S or blender.

II   Whirl 15 seconds for *Junior Food*, stopping once to scrape down container sides. Whirl an additional 30 seconds for *Infant Food*, or until mixture reaches the consistency suitable for baby.

MEAT AND VEGETABLE DINNER

(YIELD: ABOUT ½ CUP)

$\frac{1}{4}$ *Cup Basic Vegetable Mixture (see page 384)*
$\frac{1}{4}$ *Cup cooked meat, cut in ½-inch pieces*
2   *Tablespoons chicken broth*

I   Place all ingredients in container C S or blender.

II   Whirl 15 seconds for *Junior Food*, stopping once to scrape down container sides. Whirl an additional 30 seconds for *Infant Food*, or until mixture reaches a consistency suitable for baby.

CARROTS AND SQUASH (OR COMBINATIONS OF OTHER SOFT VEGETABLES)

(YIELD: ABOUT 1 CUP)

1   *Medium carrot, scraped and cut in 1-inch pieces*
$\frac{1}{4}$ *Winter squash, peeled, seeded and cut in 1-inch pieces*
$\frac{2}{3}$ *Cup water*

I Drain vegetables. Place carrot and squash in container C S or blender. Whirl for 6 or 7 seconds, stopping once to scrape down container sides.

II Place vegetables in saucepan, add ⅔ cup water and cook over medium heat for 20 to 30 minutes or until tender.

III Return vegetables to container C S and whirl for 7 seconds for *Junior Food*. For *Infant Food*, add 2 tablespoons water or chicken broth and whirl about 35 seconds more, or until nicely puréed.

JUNIOR BEETS

(YIELD: ABOUT ½ CUP)

> 2 *Medium beets, cooked, peeled, and cut in ½-inch*
> *pieces*
> 2 *Tablespoons water*

I Add beets and 2 tablespoons water to container C S or blender. Whirl for 20 seconds, stopping once to scrape down container sides.

JUNIOR AND PUREED UNCOOKED PRUNES

(YIELD: ABOUT ¾ CUP)

> 10 *Prunes*
> *Water*

I Soak prunes in water to cover overnight, or according to package directions. Drain prunes, reserving liquid.

II Place prunes and 1 tablespoon reserved liquid in container C S or blender. Whirl 15 seconds, stopping once to scrape down container sides, to produce a consistency suitable for *Junior Food*. For very young or particular babies, add 3 tablespoons reserved liquid and process an additional 1½ minutes, then strain before serving.

COOKED PRUNES

(YIELD: ABOUT ¾ CUP)

      10   *Prunes*
            Water

I Place prunes in saucepan, add water to cover, and cook for 30 minutes, or until tender. Drain prunes, reserving liquid.

II Place prunes and 2 tablespoons reserved liquid in container C S or blender. Whirl for 15 seconds, stopping once to scrape down container sides, to produce a consistency suitable for *Junior Food*. For very young or particular babies, add 2 to 4 more tablespoons reserved liquid and process for an additional 1½ minutes or until mixture reaches desired consistency, then strain before serving.

BANANAS

(YIELD: ABOUT ½ CUP)

      1   *Ripe banana, peeled and cut in 1-inch pieces*
         Milk or formula

I Whirl banana in container C S or blender for 9 seconds, stopping once to scrape down sides, for *Junior Food*.

II For *Infant Food*, add 2 tablespoons milk or formula and whirl an additional 10 seconds or until mixture is puréed and perfectly smooth.

UNCOOKED APPLESAUCE

If fresh apple is included in baby's diet, this makes a good way to get started.

(YIELD: ABOUT ¾ CUP)

      2   *Large apples, peeled, cored, and cut in eighths*
    ½   *Cup water (optional)*

I For *Junior Food*, whirl apples in container C S or blender for 15 seconds, stopping twice to scrape down container sides.

II For *Infant Food*, whirl apples an additional 30 seconds, or until fruit reaches desired consistency. A few particles will remain on the container bottom, so scoop applesauce off the top or strain through a fine sieve.

III If you decide to cook this applesauce, simply place in a saucepan, add ½ cup water and cook for 10 minutes or until tender.

COOKED APPLESAUCE

(YIELD: ABOUT ¾ CUP)

    2   *Large apples, peeled, cored, and cut in eighths*
  ½   *Cup water*

I Cook apples in ½ cup water for 10 minutes or until tender.

II Place apples and cooking liquid in container C S or blender. For *Junior Food*, whirl 4 seconds. For *Infant Food*, whirl an additional 10 seconds or until puréed to a consistency suitable for baby.

PEARS, PEACHES, AND OTHER SOFT FRUITS

(YIELD: ABOUT ¾ CUP)

    2   *Large ripe pears, peaches, etc., peeled, cored, and*
         cut in eighths
  ½   *Cup water*

I Cook fruits in ½ cup water for 10 minutes or until tender.

II Place fruit and cooking liquid in container C S or blender. Whirl 4 seconds for *Junior Food*, stopping once to scrape down container sides. For *Infant Food*, whirl an additional 10 seconds or until puréed to the consistency suitable for baby.

OATMEAL AND FRUIT

Combine Basic Oatmeal (see page 386) with a variety of puréed fruits (see pages 389 to 391) simply by mixing them together in equal amounts and adding 1 or 2 tablespoons formula, milk, or water.

TAPIOCA AND FRUIT

Many delicious desserts can be prepared for baby merely by combining equal portions of Basic Tapioca (see page 386) and puréed fruits (see pages 389 to 391).

INDEX

ABOUT THE AUTHOR

YVONNE YOUNG TARR is a veteran cookbook writer. Her best-selling books include *The Ten Minute Gourmet Cookbook*, *The New York Times Bread and Soup Cookbook*, *The Farmhouse Cookbook*, *The Up-with-Wholesome, Down-with-Store-Bought Book of Recipes and Household Formulas*, and *The Tomato Book*.

She is married to sculptor William Tarr. They have two children, Jonathon and Nicolas.